LEGEND

ALSO BY ERIC BLEHM

FEARLESS

THE ONLY THING WORTH DYING FOR

THE LAST SEASON

LEGEND

ERIC BLEHM

A HARROWING STORY FROM THE VIETNAM WAR OF
ONE GREEN BERET'S HEROIC MISSION TO RESCUE A
SPECIAL FORCES TEAM CAUGHT BEHIND ENEMY LINES

CROWN PUBLISHERS
NEW YORK

All rights reserved.
Published in the United States by Crown Publishers,
an imprint of the Crown Publishing Group,
a division of Penguin Random House LLC, New York.
www.crownpublishing.com

CROWN is a registered trademark and the Crown colophon
is a trademark of Penguin Random House LLC.

Library of Congress Cataloging-in-Publication Data is
available upon request.

ISBN 978-0-8041-3951-9
eBook ISBN 978-0-8041-3952-6

Printed in the United States of America

Map on page xiv by Joe LeMonnier
Maps on pages 134–135, 154–155, and 196–197 by Chris Adams,
Rocketman Creative
Jacket and page iii photograph by Florian Stern/Gallery Stock

10 9 8 7 6 5 4 3 2 1

First Edition

This story is dedicated to all those
who served in the Military Assistance Command Vietnam,
Studies and Observations Group (MACV-SOG),
and the pilots, crews, and maintenance personnel of the
assault helicopter companies who supported their missions
during the war in Vietnam.

THE ANTIDOTE FOR FIFTY ENEMIES
IS ONE FRIEND.

—ARISTOTLE

CONTENTS

KEY MILITARY PERSONNEL FOR THE MAY 2 MISSION

Military Assistance Command Vietnam, Studies and Observations Group (MACV-SOG)

PROJECT SIGMA, DETACHMENT B-56

Lieutenant Colonel Ralph Drake, *Commander*

First Lieutenant Fred Jones, *Launch Officer*

Captain Robin Tornow, *U.S. Air Force Forward Air Controller (FAC)*

PROJECT SIGMA, DETACHMENT B-56 RECON TEAM

Sergeant First Class Leroy Wright, *Team Leader*

Staff Sergeant Lloyd Mousseau, *Assistant Team Leader*

Specialist 4 Brian O'Connor, *Radioman*

Tuan, *CIDG Interpreter*

Bao, *CIDG Point Man*

Chien, *CIDG Grenadier*

CIDG Rifleman

CIDG Rifleman

CIDG Rifleman

CIDG Rifleman

CIDG Ammo Bearer

CIDG Ammo Bearer

214TH COMBAT AVIATION BATTALION (CAB), 12TH COMBAT AVIATION GROUP, 1ST AVIATION BRIGADE

240th Assault Helicopter Company

Major Jesse James, *Commander*

Command and Control (C&C)

Major Jesse James, *AC*

First Lieutenant Alan Yurman (leader of 2nd Platoon), *CP*

Unknown, *CC*

Unknown, *DG*

First Lieutenant Fred Jones, *Detachment B-56 Mission Launch Officer*

Special Forces Major (name unknown), *Detachment B-56 Observer*

Greyhound One* (primary/lead)

Warrant Officer Larry McKibben, *AC*

Warrant Officer William Fernan, *CP*

Specialist 4 Dan Christensen, *CC*

Specialist 4 Nelson Fournier, *DG*

Staff Sergeant Roy Benavidez, *BM*

Greyhound Two (primary/wingman)

Warrant Officer Jerry Ewing, *AC*

First Lieutenant Bob Portman, *CP*

Specialist 5 Paul Tagliaferri, *CC*

Unknown, *DG*

---

*All helicopter numbers have been changed for clarity.

Greyhound Three (reserve/lead)
Warrant Officer Roger Waggie, *AC*
Warrant Officer David Hoffman, *CP*
Specialist 4 Michael Craig, *CC*
Unknown, *DG*
Unknown, *BM*

Greyhound Three (second crew)
Warrant Officer Roger Waggie, *AC*
Warrant Officer David Hoffman, *CP*
Warrant Officer William Darling, *CC*
Chief Warrant Officer 2 Thomas Smith, *DG*
Staff Sergeant Ron Sammons, *BM*

Greyhound Four (reserve/wingman)
Warrant Officer William Armstrong, *AC*
Warrant Officer James Fussell, *CP*
Specialist 4 Gary Land, *CC*
Specialist 4 Robert Wessel, *DG*
Specialist 5 James Calvey, *BM*

3RD PLATOON MAD DOG GUNSHIPS
AC = aircraft commander/pilot, right seat/rockets
CP = copilot, left seat/miniguns
CC = crew chief/left-door gunner
DG = right-door gunner

Mad Dog One (first fire team/lead)
Chief Warrant Officer 2 William Curry, *AC*
Chief Warrant Officer 1 David Brown, *CP*
Sergeant First Class Pete Jones, *CC*
"Swisher," *DG*

Mad Dog Two (first fire team/wingman)
Chief Warrant Officer 2 Michael Grant, *AC*
Chief Warrant Officer 1 Ron Radke, *CP*
Specialist 4 Steven Hastings, *CC*
Specialist 4 Donald Fowler, *DG*

Mad Dog Three (second fire team/lead)
Chief Warrant Officer 2 Louis Wilson, *AC*
Warrant Officer Jesse Naul, *CP*
Specialist 5 Paul LaChance, *CC*
Specialist 4 Jeff Colman, *DG*

Mad Dog Four (second fire team/wingman)
Chief Warrant Officer 2 Gary Whitaker, *AC*
Warrant Officer Cook, *CP*
Specialist 5 Pete Gailis, *CC*
Specialist 4 Danny Clark, *DG*

Mad Dog Five (emergency backup gunship,
flown from Bearcat for extraction)
Chief Warrant Officer 2 Don Brenner, *AC*
First Lieutenant Rick Adams, *CP*
Specialist 4 John White, *CC*
Unknown, *DG*

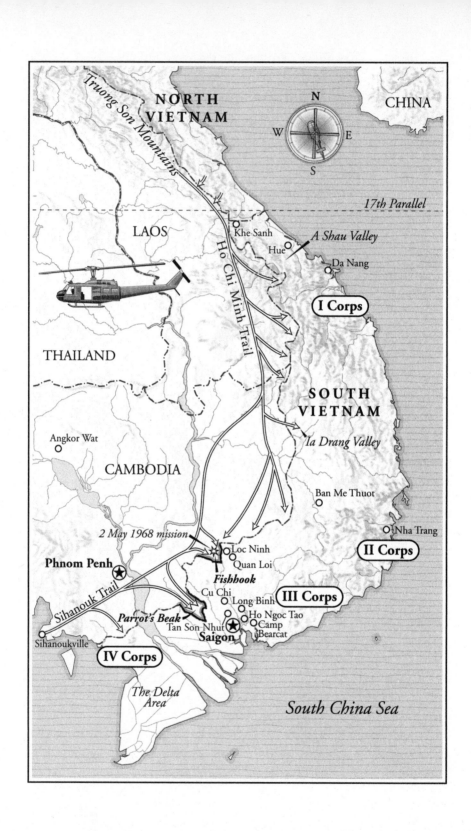

PROLOGUE

THIS STORY BEGINS in a U.S. government–issued body bag.

The date was May 2, 1968; the location, Loc Ninh Special Forces camp near the Cambodian border in South Vietnam. Inside the zippered tomb lay a stocky, five-foot-six-inch U.S. Army Green Beret staff sergeant named Roy Benavidez. Earlier that day he had jumped from a hovering helicopter, then ran through withering enemy gunfire to reach what remained of an American-led twelve-man Special Forces team surrounded by hundreds of North Vietnamese Army soldiers.

A few strides into his heroic dash, a bullet passed through his leg and knocked him off his feet. Determined to reach his comrades, he rose and continued his sprint, zigzagging through enemy fire for almost seventy-five yards before he went down again, this time from the explosion of a near-miss rocket-propelled grenade. Ignoring both the bullet and shrapnel wounds, he crawled the remaining few yards into the beleaguered team's perimeter, took control, provided medical aid, and positioned the remaining men to fight back the endless waves of attacking NVA while he called in dangerously close air support.

For the next several hours, Benavidez saved the lives of eight men during fierce, at times hand-to-hand combat before allowing himself to be the last man pulled into a helicopter that had finally made it to the ground amidst the relentless onslaught. There he collapsed motionless, atop a pile of wounded and dying men. His body—a torn-up canvas of bullet holes, shrapnel wounds, bayonet lacerations, punctures, burns, and bruises—painted a bloody portrait of his valor that day.

FOR NEARLY a decade his story, and the story of the May 2 battle, remained untold. That was until Fred Barbee, a newspaper publisher from Benavidez's hometown of El Campo, Texas, got wind of it and ran a cover story in the *El Campo Leader-News* on February 22, 1978. The intent of his article was twofold: to honor Benavidez by recounting his heroics and to berate the Senior Army Decorations Board for its staunch refusal to bestow upon Benavidez what Barbee believed was a long-overdue and unfairly denied Congressional Medal of Honor.

Barbee wanted to know what the holdup was. His tireless research elicited few answers from the Decorations Board, whose anonymous members, he quickly learned, answered to no one—not congressional representatives, not colonels (two of whom had lobbied for Sergeant Benavidez), and certainly not a small-town newspaper publisher.

But Barbee wouldn't let it go. He was perplexed when the board cited "no new evidence" as its most recent reason for denying the medal, when in fact there was plenty of new evidence. Topping the list was an updated statement written by Benavidez's commanding officer, citing previously unknown facts that corroborated the sergeant's legendary actions. There was also testimony from the helicopter pilots and aircrews who witnessed the battle from the air or listened in on the radio as events transpired. According to the board, although these accounts were compelling, there was no eyewitness testimony from anybody *on the ground*. This criterion seemed impossible to meet; almost nobody on the ground May 2 had survived either that day or the war. The few who had were off the grid, having either become expatriates or burned their uniforms and melted into an American populace that more often than not had shamed them for their service in Vietnam.

"What, then, happened on that awful day . . . in the Republic of Vietnam?" Barbee questioned in his article. "Or, perhaps this particular action on May 2, 1968, actually took place outside the boundaries of Vietnam, perhaps in an area where U.S. forces were not supposed to be, perhaps that is the reason for the continuing runaround. . . ."

THE ASSOCIATED Press picked up Barbee's article, and it circulated into some of the American news sections of international papers. By July of 1980, it had traveled halfway around the world to the South Pacific, finding its way into the hands of a retired Green Beret and Vietnam veteran who was living in Fiji with his wife and two young children.

Brian O'Connor immediately recognized the date in the article, May 2, 1968; the hours-long battle was his worst, most horrific memory from what was known as "the secret war." He remembered being under a pile of bodies on a helicopter, slippery with blood and suffocating. Now, as he read the story, O'Connor was appalled to learn that Benavidez had never received the Medal of Honor. He knew he would have to revisit and recount his memory of the battle—in detail. He owed it to the man who had, against all odds, saved his life.

Determined to set the record straight, O'Connor dated a sheet of paper July 24, 1980, and addressed it to the Army Decorations Board:

"This statement," O'Connor wrote, "on the events that happened on 2 May 1968 is given as evidence to assist the decision made on awarding the Congressional Medal of Honor to Master Sergeant Roy Benavidez. Because of the classified nature of the mission, some important details will be left out which should not in any way affect the outcome of the award."

Page after page, the darkness flowed from his pen as O'Connor re-lived the nightmarish day. From the insertion of his twelve-man team deep behind enemy lines to the desperate hours when they were sur-rounded and vastly outnumbered by what many estimated was a battal-ion or more of well-armed North Vietnamese Army soldiers. He pieced together the torn and sometimes blurry snapshots from his memory, re-counting the deaths of his teammates one by one, as well as the several helicopter rescue attempts beaten back by a determined enemy that was on the verge of overrunning their position:

> The interpreter, who now had his arm hanging on to the shoulder by a hunk of muscle and skin, tugged at me to say the ATL [assistant team leader] wanted me. Firing and rolling on my side, I saw the ATL on his emergency radio and I nod-ded my head and the ATL hollered to me "ammo—ammo—grenades." Stripping the two dead CIDG [Civilian Irregular Defense Group, the South Vietnamese Special Forces] of their ammo and grenades, I moved a meter or two, where I threw the clips and grenades to a CIDG, who in turn threw them to the ATL. During the minute or two of calm, the interpreter and I patched our wounds, injected morphine syrettes, tied off his arm with a tourniquet, and ran an IV of serum of albumin in my arm for blood loss . . . while the one remaining CIDG observed for enemy movement. I looked over to the ATL, and they were doing about the same thing. . . . We had another few seconds of silence and the ATL shouted, "they're coming in." I figured a final assault to overrun us and we prepared for the

worst. . . . I caught a burst of auto fire in the abdomen and the radio was shot out. I was put out of commission and just laid behind [a] body firing at the NVA in the open field until the ammo ran out. . . .

I was ready to die.

1

STREET KID FROM CUERO

"Ayeeeee!" the boy soldier shouted as he charged forward and jumped into the void. His battle cry was muffled when he landed in the mountain of seeds—bits of cotton still attached—that were piled high on the floor of the huge tin warehouse near his neighborhood in Cuero, Texas.

It was the fall of 1942, and sneaking into the local cotton warehouse and jumping from its loft into the remains of the recent harvest was a favorite pastime for seven-year-old Raul "Roy" Perez Benavidez. His inspiration was the local theater, where he'd watched newsreels of American paratroopers in World War II jumping one after another from an airplane thousands of feet above the ground. While the airborne soldiers drifted down beneath their silk parachutes, the narrator told of the adventurous lives of the "Battalions in the sky! Specially trained for fighting in the jungle—the kind of wilderness in which the Japs have got to be whupped in the South Pacific!" And then Franklin Delano Roosevelt, the president of the United States, filled the screen. He sat at his desk and spoke to the forces fighting for freedom overseas—and to movie house audiences that included young Roy Benavidez in Cuero, Texas, who had paid the same nine cents for admission as the kids in the good seats but was upstairs in the segregated balcony, where clearly posted signs directed him and the rest of the "Mexicans and Negroes" to sit.

But when the lights went off and the screen lit up, Roy forgot about his lot in life—the personal battles, the fears, and how he'd earned those nine cents—and reveled in every minute of the fantasy. He imagined he was right there alongside the troops he was watching on screen, M1 rifle in hand, assaulting an enemy position on a distant shore.

"You young Americans today," FDR said, staring into Roy's eyes, "are conducting yourselves in a manner that is worthy of the highest, proudest traditions of our nation. No pilgrims who landed on the uncharted New England coast, no pioneers who forced their way through the trackless wilderness showed greater fortitude, or greater determination, than you are showing now!"

ROY WAS three years old when he moved into Cuero with his mother, Teresa, and two-year-old brother, Rogelio, "Roger," during the second week of November 1938. Just a few days earlier his father, Salvador Benavidez—a sharecropper and a vaquero (cowboy) on the nearby Wallace Ranch—succumbed to tuberculosis. Roy had been born on that ranch, brought into the world by a midwife in his parents' bed. It was the same bed he had watched his father's body lifted from and placed into a wooden box built by a neighbor. He would always remember the pounding of the hammer as the casket was nailed shut, then slid into the back of a pickup truck and put in the ground at the ranch's tiny cemetery, beneath a wooden cross.

In Cuero, Teresa soon found work tending the household of a well-to-do doctor. A year later she married Pablo Chavez, who worked at the local cotton mill. After another year, Roy and Roger were joined by their baby sister, Lupe, who received all of their stepfather's attention and most of their mother's. His stepfather wasn't cruel, just inattentive, offering little guidance to or affection for the two boys. They did, however, have plenty of freedom.

Situated on a branch of the Chisholm Trail, Cuero had been a frontier town where cowboys once congregated while driving their cattle from the southern plains to markets in the north. There were more automobiles than horses on the streets Roy explored, but the spirit of the Western town remained. Six-year-old Roy would observe a steady stream of men coming in and out of the "houses" strategically placed near the swinging doors of saloons located, it seemed, on every corner. He wanted to see what was going on inside but was always shooed away by the women wearing bright-red lipstick.

With its population of 4,700, Cuero was a thriving hub of business for the ranching, farming, rodeo, and agricultural industries. Roy was just another of the anonymous Mexican street kids who, charged with contributing to their family coffers, provided well-to-do farmers, ranchers, and businessmen labor for odd jobs: a dime shine for their shoes, a five-cent taco for their bellies, and the occasional philanthropic entertainment. Such shows would begin when a man wearing a pressed suit or fancy cowboy boots would gather some friends, then toss a handful of coins onto a street corner where the children were looking for work or selling their wares.

The men would laugh as the kids kicked up a dust storm scrambling for the coins. At first it was a game to Roy, like grabbing candy from a piñata—until, somewhere along the line, he realized the coins weren't free. They cost him his dignity.

The movies were the reason Roy continued to dive for the money, only now he did it angry. It had gone from being a game to a battle in which he hit and shoved the other kids first and grabbed for the coins second. "If you take them out," he told a relative, "there's less hands to grab the money, and you get to see a movie. If you hit really hard, maybe you get an ice cream, too."

He'd walk away as quickly as he could from the scramble, slapping the dirt off his clothes as if he could brush away the disgrace. The money in his pocket didn't outweigh the contempt and anger building in his heart. He began to fight with the kids on the street for fun and sport, and because he was good at it. Nothing made him happier than wrestling a kid bigger than him to the ground and making him cry uncle—or, better yet, just making him cry.

Roy WOULD remember his sixth year as the year he turned into "a tough, mean little kid . . . a general nuisance for anybody who got in my way." That was also the year his mother began coughing, just as his father had. There was blood in her handkerchief, and lots of people came to their little house, including the nuns who taught at his school and the priest from his church. They'd light candles and say prayers, and one day in early fall a nun gave him a dime to go to a movie.

Sitting in the balcony, Roy tried to forget the conversations he'd overheard between the visitors and his stepfather, who had made it clear that he would not be shouldering the burden of raising "Teresa's boys." In the darkness Roy tried to keep his mind off his uncertain future. Would he and Roger be sent to an orphanage or a labor camp? Would they be separated to live with strangers? All of his trying not to worry reminded him of what he most wanted to forget—that his mother was dying.

After the movie let out, Roy recruited some friends to sneak into the cotton warehouse and play war. He climbed the ladder to the loft and strived to be brave like the paratroops as he leaped into the unknown.

★

IN HER final weeks, Teresa sent word to Nicholas Benavidez, her late husband's brother, that his nephews would soon be orphans.

She died in the fall and was buried in the Cuero city cemetery following a service at Our Lady of Guadalupe Church. The funeral was a fog of anxiety and sadness for seven-year-old Roy, until a tall stranger introduced himself to the boys as their uncle.

He told the grieving brothers they would be coming to live with him and his family in El Campo, a small city eighty-five miles to the southeast. The boys packed their few belongings—including a small black-and-white photograph of their mother and father—and said brief good-byes to their half sister and stepfather, then headed to the bus depot, where Uncle Nicholas bought three tickets. Roy had never been on a bus before. He put his arm around his brother, gave him a squeeze, and, just like that, the road ahead brightened a little.

As they sat together in the back of the bus, Nicholas described the boys' new family: his wife, "your aunt Alexandria," and their eight children, "your new brothers and sisters." Grandfather Salvador, "your father's father," also lived with them, he said, then added, "He will tell you many stories." By the time they pulled into the El Campo bus depot, things were looking up. Roy couldn't imagine how a day that had started out so terribly could get any better. Then, noticing his nephew's worn-out shoes, a hole on one sole patched with a piece of cardboard, Nicholas told Roy, "Tomorrow we'll buy you a new pair of shoes."

WELL AFTER dark, Roy and Roger timidly entered their new home. An older man with a warm smile shook their hands and told them he was their grandfather. Then Nicholas introduced Alexandria and their children, ranging in age from seven to seventeen: Maria, Miguel, Eugenio, Nicholas, Elida, Evita, Joaquin, and Frank.

Grandfather Salvador said, "You must always remember that you are a Benavidez. You must always bring honor to our name."

"We are not rich," Nicholas continued. "We all work, and we share what we have. You will work alongside us."

"They go to school and study hard," said Salvador. "So must you. There are opportunities in this country for people who get an education."

The quick-fire assertions by their uncle and grandfather after they'd barely gotten inside the door constituted Roy and Roger's swift introduction to the rigid order expected in the Benavidez household.

"*Tienes hambre,* Rogelio?" Aunt Alexandria cut in. Roger nodded yes. "They are hungry," she said to her husband, ushering the boys into the kitchen for plates of tacos. Then she showed them to the attic bedroom, where the seven boys would be sharing four beds.

The following day, Alexandria added two envelopes to the eight she kept for each child's contribution to the family food, clothing, and school supplies fund, and Roy was assigned his first job: to shine shoes and cowboy boots at the bus depot after school and on weekends after church. With each shine—a nickel for shoes and up to a quarter for cowboy boots—his envelope thickened, as did his bond with his family members.

ROY ATTENDED public school with his siblings in El Campo that school year, until April 1943. That was the month when the Benavidez kids collected their final report cards, cleaned out their desks, and headed for the sugar beet fields of northern Colorado. All ten of them were pressed tightly together in the bed of the family truck, which pulled a trailer loaded with wooden boxes and milk crates Alexandria had packed with household essentials: bedding, cooking utensils, pots, dishes, a small red radio, and the family Bible.

This was old hat for the adults and older siblings, but for Roy and the other young children, it was high adventure. At a gas station stop late on their first day of driving, Nicholas told Roy he had a very important job for him: to relieve Eugenio, Gene, who had been keeping an eye on the trailer. If the ball hitch started rattling or the trailer swerved oddly, he was to knock on the window of the cab.

"You cannot fall asleep," Nicholas said, and Roy positioned himself for what he considered a great honor—his uncle trusted him!

Soon the drone of the road began to lull the Benavidez children to sleep. One by one they dropped off, sprawled like a litter of puppies as they slept the miles away. Gene was the last to fall asleep and, an hour later, the first to awaken, with a jolt. He glanced to the rear.

There was the trailer, still following them with the hypnotic sway of its dance on the road. And there was Roy, sitting upright, his head swaying back and forth in rhythm with the trailer and his eyes wide open, battling the weight of his eyelids. He had one hand under his chin, keeping his head up; with his free hand he was pinching himself on the arm to the point of bruising—determined to stay awake during his appointed vigil.

THEY DROVE for several days, camping at night, before reaching the fields near Timnath, Colorado. The migrant camp was a collection of one-room shacks built from scrap wood, with tin roofs, wood stoves, and no indoor plumbing or hot water.

The family slept and worked shoulder to shoulder, from sunrise to sunset. On their hands and knees, they weeded around and thinned the sugar beet plants with short-handled hoes—backbreaking work that was often reserved for the young. But Nicholas had a strong back, and if his family was on their knees, he was beside them. Nobody complained, so neither did Roy. It took weeks to thin what seemed to be oceans of fields.

The days were long, and he looked forward to the nights, when the children would play around the camp, its grid of dirt roads lit by the glow of kerosene lanterns and the fire rings that were the social gathering spots and where Grandfather Salvador told the stories that taught Roy about his heritage. Benavidez was a name that Salvador described as respected in the community—a hardworking, cultured family of God-fearing vaqueros and sharecroppers who first sank roots in Texas in the early 1800s and fought for their independence from Mexico as Texans and Americans—no different from the Europeans who had fought for independence from England. "You have Benavidez cousins who are fighting for America right now," he said to the children.

Roy grew to understand the distinction between his family and the hundreds of thousands of Mexican laborers they competed against for jobs and wages during World War II. Because men were needed in the military, there was a labor shortage, so in 1942 Congress enacted the Bracero Program (*brazos* is the Spanish word for arms), which encouraged Mexican migrants to cross the border and work legally in U.S. agriculture and industry.

"The name Benavidez is Mexican," Salvador said, "but we are Americans."

He also shared—often at the request of the kids—the stories of his days as a vaquero, when he would drive stock from pastures in the high mountains of Colorado or ride miles and miles of fence, stopping for repairs. A favorite of Roy's was the time his grandfather rescued a fellow vaquero whose horse had gone off the ledge on a narrow path, leaving the man hanging precariously to the slope.

Salvador would reenact how he'd gotten on his knees and leaned over the precipice. Unable to reach the man, he lay flat and used his belt as a rope to pull the cowboy to safety.

There was a moral in many of Salvador's stories, and this one was simple. "If someone needs help," he told the children, "you help them."

★

AT NIGHT Roy lay on his bedroll listening to Hank Williams and other country-western singers on the red radio. This same radio would broadcast—during nine-year-old Roy's third "tour" in the Colorado beet fields—that victory in Europe had been proclaimed on May 7, 1945.

While there was a peaceful quiet in the hedgerows of Europe the next morning, it was business as usual for Roy when his uncle jostled him awake in the dark to attack the remaining beet rows. Standard rows were a quarter to a half mile long; sixteen half-mile rows equaled an acre, and an acre brought the family around five dollars—a day's work, depending on how hard the ground was. When the morning school bell rang for his classmates back in El Campo, Roy had already been digging in the dirt for two hours.

Once the beet plants were thinned, the family would pick up work—harvesting onions or some other crop in the area—for the few weeks until the beets could be harvested. The youngsters' job was to gather the beets that were plowed from the ground and cut their leafy tops off; older children and women then loaded the beets into crates that were lifted into trucks by the men and hauled away. Roy marveled at the crates stacked like building blocks on the trucks; he knew the sweat that went into the filling of each and every one—the acreage required, the blisters, and the sheer boredom. Vaguely, he understood that every crate filled meant more money to sustain his family until the next harvest.

With the beet fields cleared, the Benavidez family moved south to the West Texas cotton fields, where the days were longer, the sun was hotter, and the rows of cotton seemed to stretch to a horizon Roy would never reach. When he finally did, he'd turn around and head back, picking cotton and pricking his fingers, over and over again. They dragged behind them dingy white sacks that fattened as they were filled. Emptied, they reminded Roy of the parachutes in the newsreels he'd watched.

On July 16, 1945, far beyond the horizon of Roy's imagination in a little country called Vietnam, seven operatives from the U.S. Office of Strategic Services (OSS) parachuted into a jungle encampment near Tan Trao, northwest of the city of Hanoi.

OSS Special Operations Team 13, code-named Deer Team, was cut from the same cloth as the daring three-man OSS Jedburgh teams that had parachuted into German-occupied France, Belgium, and Holland to train and work alongside the French Resistance and other anti-Nazi movements during the months prior to the Allied invasion on D-day. Their top-secret mission in the jungles of Vietnam was to provide weaponry, including M1 rifles, Thompson submachine guns, mortars, grenades, and bazookas, to approximately one hundred Vietminh guerrillas. The Americans would train the guerrillas, and in exchange the Vietminh would assist the Americans in gathering intelligence, carrying out sabotage, and ultimately fighting the Japanese who occupied their country and much of Indochina.

Vietnam, as well as neighboring Laos and Cambodia, was a colony of France, an ally of America, as well as the stated enemy of the Vietminh fighting for their independence. The second-in-command of this four-year-old national independence movement went by the name of Mr. Van but would soon—after proper weapons and guerrilla tactics training by the Americans—rise to prominence as General Vo Nguyen Giap. Giap's boss, the leader of this fledgling band of guerrillas and the man with whom the Americans worked directly, was Ho Chi Minh.

In the battlefields of a young boy's imagination that same summer, Roy kept on picking, passing the time with a stick in his belt for his gun, a cotton sack for his parachute, his adopted siblings in adjacent rows for his allies. While Roy's daydreams of being a paratrooper at war kept him going, Nicholas motivated the kids with a gumball that waited at the end of a row, a swim in the farmer's pond after a truck was filled, or an ice cream on Sunday if a field was cleared by Saturday night. He'd always point to Frank, the eldest, who could pull a thousand pounds of cotton in a day, as an example of what was possible. "No matter what you do," Nicholas said, "always try to be the very best."

If you were trying hard, and Uncle Nicholas noticed, he would acknowledge you with a nod, such as he'd given Roy for watching the trailer on that first long drive, or a pat on the back for good marks on a test at school. But for something exceptional, like pulling a thousand pounds of cotton in a day, you might get the highest praise of all from Uncle Nicholas: "I'm proud of you."

A MONTH after Roy's tenth birthday, on a September night in 1945 that was too hot to sleep, the little red radio announced to the Benavidez family that Japan had surrendered. World War II was over.

The multitude of soldiers, sailors, Marines, and airmen who had been stationed in Europe were welcomed home with parades. The *Dallas Morning News* ran a cover story of a celebration in San Antonio—one of hundreds that took place in cities across the nation—with the headline "300,000 Extend Wild Welcome to Heroes Returning from War."

For the previous three seasons, Nicholas had seized any opportune moment—passing a "Buy War Bonds!" poster in town or seeing a man in uniform—to point out that the food crops they'd harvested and the cotton they'd picked helped feed and clothe the troops. The most decorated soldier of the war, he informed his kids, was Audie Murphy, a young Texan from a sharecropper family, who had picked cotton before joining the army.

Roy returned to El Campo that October and started school like every other fall, with a brand-new jacket on his back and new shoes on his feet. In a small way, he felt he'd done his part to defeat the evil Axis powers, though he wished, as only boys who haven't seen battle do, that he'd actually gone to war.

A FEW weeks into his school year, Roy began pining for the fun they'd had in the fields. He was proud of his tough, callused hands but was embarrassed when he was unable to answer questions most of his classmates knew the answers to. Leaving school two months early and starting two months late meant he was always behind.

He was placed in groups of almost exclusively Hispanics, who, like him, were struggling to catch up with their grade level. The teachers might have thought they were helping by separating the class based on ability, but this practice promoted unjust stereotypes. The taunts Roy weathered over the years about the color of his skin or the food his family ate—"pepper belly" and "taco bender"—were bad enough, but nothing angered him more than "dumb Mexican."

He would take note of which kid said it, and at recess he'd exact his revenge. It didn't matter how big the kid was: the work in the fields had made his body strong and anger powered his fists. If it was a girl, he might kick dirt on her instead. Then the girl's brother or boyfriend would step in, usually with his own racially slanted taunt, and Roy would end up in the principal's office trying to justify the fact that he'd decked another kid because the kid wouldn't stop calling him or others disparaging names.

"Names are one thing," the principal would tell him. "Fists are another." But to Roy, the names hurt worse, and stung far longer, than a punch in the face. They made him meaner and madder, to the point that he would go after anybody who even looked at him wrong. In his words, he fought mostly "with white kids who had new shoes, or had money to buy whatever they wanted."

★

THE LIFE of Roy Benavidez could have gone in any of a number of directions but for the wise counsel of his uncle, who later joked that he'd clocked more hours in the principal's office with Roy than he had at either of his two jobs—the barbershop where he gave haircuts and the garage where he turned wrenches.

"He wasn't a rabble-rouser," Roy later told a friend. "He was a peacemaker." Nicholas did all he could to extinguish the flames of anger, bitterness, and resentment burning inside Roy. He never condoned the racism—never said it was right that Roy was not allowed to dine in or use the front door of the restaurant where he washed dishes, or sit at the counter and order a soda at the malt shop, or choose a good seat in the movie theater—but neither did Nicholas believe a fight would make the world change any quicker.

He explained to Roy that there was honor in restraint, that a response to a racial slur did not have to be physical. He could take it in stride and "fight" to better his station in life, living within the law and getting an education. Nicholas also pointed out that racism was an individual choice: there were Anglos who dished out slurs, and there were others who respected the Hispanic community and treated them as equals, just the way the Benavidez family considered the white cotton pickers they sometimes worked alongside. "*Cada persona tiene su historia*," Nicholas would say. "Every person has a story."

"Someday," he told Roy, "someone will open a door to you, and you must be there saying, 'Let me in.' My future and yours will be in a different world than Grandfather Salvador's. We will not give up our heritage, but we won't let it hold us back either. We will be judged by the way we act and by the respect we earn in the community."

As a bilingual barber and mechanic, Uncle Nicholas was an open ear for conversations from all walks of El Campo life, and when asked his opinion he always gave it straight. One afternoon two men—one Anglo and one Hispanic—got into a fender bender on the street outside the barbershop, where the sheriff was having a haircut. Without any witnesses, the sheriff had a difficult time getting to the bottom of the accident as the drivers yelled at each other in English and Spanish. Nicholas stepped in, heard both sides, translated the Spanish, and conferred with the sheriff, who then rendered the accident to be without fault.

And so, Nicholas "became known for resolving problems between the communities," Roy said. "He didn't do it with his hat in his hand and his eyes on the ground asking for favors, and he didn't do it with threats. If our folks were wrong, he'd say so and stick to it. If the Anglo side was wrong, he'd talk sense until their ears fell off or they agreed, just as he sometimes preached to us."

Soon after, a long-closed door at the Wharton County Sheriff's Office swung open and Nicholas was invited in. He was offered a part-time job as a deputy—the first Hispanic deputy in the history of the county.

It was 1947. Roy was twelve when he and Gene accompanied Nicholas to pick up his new badge and sign some documents. At the station a deputy told Nicholas that he would have the right to arrest Hispanics and blacks, but not whites. If a situation warranted such an arrest, Nicholas would have to bring in another deputy.

"No," Nicholas said. "If I wear this badge, then I will have the authority to arrest any person who breaks the law."

The deputy shook his head. "That's not going to fly, Nicholas."

"Then," said Nicholas, "I cannot accept the job."

"I'm going to have to speak with the sheriff," the deputy said.

Nicholas was called back to the station the following day. He came home with a badge—and the authority to arrest anybody who broke the law, regardless of the color of their skin.

Roy LEARNED just how serious his uncle was about fairness within the law when Deputy Benavidez was called upon to break up a brawl a few months into his new job, during a time when gangs were forming in El Campo and knives were starting to replace fists. After a firm talking-to, Nicholas sent the group of offenders, mostly teenage boys, on their way, except Roy and his younger brother, Roger, who had been doing their best to hide their faces in the crowd. Nicholas spotted them immediately, took them to the station, and locked them up for the evening.

His brief stint in the pokey did little to dissuade Roy, who continued to run with a group of older teens. He was arrested for burglary and, according to his military records, was "to be sent to Gatesville State School for Boys," a notorious labor camp in Texas that implemented hard labor to reform juvenile offenders.

On his way out the door from El Campo Middle School to the sugar beet fields the spring of his fourteenth year, Roy informed his teacher he wouldn't be returning in the fall. She tried to dissuade him, telling him he had potential and urging him not to throw his future away. But Roy never returned. After the harvest, when his siblings went back to school, he led the life of a school dropout, working odd jobs and giving more than half of his pay to his uncle and aunt. He still slept most nights in the attic with his brothers and ate at the family table.

One night his uncle caught him banging his way up the stairs, drunk after a night of too much beer. While Roy threw up, Nicholas launched into a lecture, pounding home the moral for what seemed like the thousandth time.

"Bad habits and bad company will ruin you, Roy," Uncle Nicholas said. *"Dime con quien andas, y te dije quien eres."* ("Tell me with whom you walk and I will tell you who you are.")

2

"LOOK SHARP, BE SHARP, GO ARMY!"

AROUND THE TIME Roy dropped out of school, Nicholas attempted to channel Roy's anger and quick-to-fists temperament into something positive—boxing—and for a time Roy excelled, making it to the state championship at the Will Rogers Coliseum in Fort Worth. There he was soundly beaten in his first match. The boy who won, living up to the code of sportsmanship taught by Golden Gloves, offered Roy a handshake in the locker room afterward, telling him, "You gave me a good fight." In response, Roy wrestled the kid into a bathroom stall and shoved his head in a toilet.

When he turned around, Roy saw a look of surprise and disappointment in the eyes of the other fighters, the coaches, and Roger, all of whom had witnessed his rage. Their stares tore into his conscience. Though this was the end of Roy's Golden Gloves days, it also represented a turning point in his life. For the first time, Roy felt regret instead of satisfaction from a fight he had initiated. He was ashamed of himself. He apologized to the boy, his coach, his uncle, his grandfather, his aunt, and his siblings, many of whom were still fighting in Golden Gloves. He even confessed his sin at church.

Whatever it was that had clicked, Roy finally understood what it meant to dishonor the Benavidez name, and he wanted to fix it. He wasn't sure how, but he was going to someday make it right. The way he saw it, he had two options for now: go back to school and get an education or continue working and contributing to the family's living expenses.

Embarrassed by his academic struggles, Roy later admitted that pride was what kept him from going back to school. He got a job pumping gas at a service station that was walking distance from the Benavidez house. He frequented the local Firestone tire shop, picking up parts for the gas station and skimming through car magazines, dreaming of building his own hot rod someday, once he could afford to move out of the attic.

Eventually, Art Haddock, who ran the counter and did the bookkeeping for Firestone, offered Roy a job making deliveries, changing tires, and cleaning up. Mr. Haddock, as Roy called him, was also a preacher at a Methodist church and a part-time mortician and funeral director. He understood better than most how precious life is, and he took a personal interest in seeing that Roy didn't throw his away.

Mr. Haddock always kept a Bible close by and referred to it often, as though it was the shop's employee handbook. If Roy cursed while trying to loosen a lug nut on a tire, Mr. Haddock would call him over and find a pertinent verse about taking the Lord's name in vain. If Roy left a job unfinished, Mr. Haddock would thumb through and find an apostle with an appropriate lesson. From Genesis to Matthew to Paul, he delivered the Gospel, preaching to Roy as he preached to his own children.

Over the course of two years of changing flats and selling tires, Roy opened up to Mr. Haddock, sharing with him much of his past—the

heartaches, the hardships, the racism, the fighting, the regrets, and the
shame he'd brought to the Benavidez name. Roy presented them as ob-
stacles that had held him back, but Mr. Haddock explained that each
obstacle had taken him down a unique path, that there was a reason for
each and every one of them. "God makes no mistakes," he told Roy.

One day, a representative from the Texas National Guard came
into the shop and asked if they would hang a recruiting flier in the
window, a flier with a photograph of one of Roy's childhood heroes,
Captain Audie Murphy. After the Korean War began in June 1950,
Murphy—in spite of his fame as the most decorated soldier in World
War II, his bestselling autobiography, *To Hell and Back,* and his celeb-
rity as a movie star—had shown his support for the war by joining the
National Guard, both to serve in the field and to have his photograph
used on recruitment posters. His unit, the 36th Infantry Division, was
not called into combat during the war, but Murphy was a skilled and
effective leader who trained and drilled new recruits.

Roy, seventeen at the time, spoke to a recruiter, then to Nicholas
and Mr. Haddock. They all, especially the recruiter, thought the Guard
seemed like a good idea—a chance to test the waters of the military.
Roy signed up.

Aside from his family, the Texas National Guard was the first real
team that Roy had ever been part of. He wore the uniform with pride,
spending a fair amount of time in front of the mirror admiring how he
looked. From his first days in the Guard's basic training, when many
complained about the hard work, he considered the military life fun
and interesting. "Better than changing tires," he told Mr. Haddock
when he returned from basic training. To Roy, the physical side of it
was nowhere near as exhausting or monotonous as working in the fields.
Overall, it was a pretty good deal. Three meals a day, a roof over his
head, hot showers, his own bed, and some extra money in his pocket
each month.

After two years of part-time service (two weeks each summer, plus one weekend a month) in the Guard, juggled with his job at the Firestone shop, Roy had risen to the rank of corporal. He could envision sergeant stripes on the horizon—but not in the Guard. "Look Sharp, Be Sharp, Go Army!" was the Army's recruiting slogan at the time, and that was Roy's plan: to join the real Army. He was going to become a paratrooper, see the world, and make his family proud. He would bring honor to the Benavidez name.

ON MAY 17, 1955, Roy took his Guard papers to the main recruiting depot on Austin Street in Houston, Texas. He strutted his 130 pounds of machismo past the Marine and Air Force recruiters and stood before a sergeant sitting at the U.S. Army desk.

"Sir," he said, "I want to go Airborne."

What happened next became legend among Roy's pals at his hangout in later years, the Drop Zone, a café and bar next door to the San Antonio Special Forces Association clubhouse near Fort Sam Houston. According to one retired paratrooper, "The sergeant looked over at Roy and said, 'I don't think you're big enough for the Airborne.'" Accounts of what happened next vary, but the gist remains the same. "Roy got right up in the sergeant's face and said, 'I can cut you down to my size quick enough.'"

Roy hadn't even a split second to regret his hot temper before the Marine recruiter appeared at his side. "Son, I think the Marines could use a young man like you," he said. But an Army captain quickly stepped in and sat Roy down in front of the now chuckling sergeant. "Get lost," he said to the Marine. Then, shaking Roy's hand, the captain said, "You're Army all the way, son. We need tough guys like you."

Roy explained to the grinning sergeant that he'd served three years in the Texas National Guard, that he had already made the rank of corporal, and that he'd been told by another recruiter that he could go directly to advanced individual training (AIT)—a fast track to a chance at Airborne. The sergeant nodded the whole time, right up to the moment Roy signed on the dotted line and committed to three years in the United States Army, solemnly swearing "to defend the United States against all enemies, foreign and domestic. . . . So help me God." A few days later Roy discovered that the recruiting sergeant had ignored his papers from his years in the Guard and that he would instead be a raw recruit, starting from the ground up.

And so, nineteen-year-old Private Benavidez headed back to basic training—with gifts from both of the father figures in his life. Mr. Haddock put his hand on Roy's shoulder and said, "The Lord bless thee and keep thee: The Lord make His face to shine upon thee, and be gracious unto thee: The Lord lift up his countenance upon thee, and give thee peace." Mr. Haddock then gave Roy something in parting no man had ever given him before. "He put his arms around me and gave me a hug. My first *abrazo,* from one man to another, came from an Anglo." Nicholas sent him off with five words, and his voice cracked a little when he said them: "I'm very proud of you." Roy turned quickly to hide his own emotions and tearing eyes. It wasn't the words alone that brought the tears; it was looking into his uncle's eyes and knowing how deeply the words were felt.

AFTER EIGHT weeks of basic training at Fort Ord, California, Roy traveled to Fort Carson, Colorado, for another eight weeks of AIT.

The last time he'd been in Colorado was on his hands and knees thinning sugar beets with a short-handled hoe. Now, just four years later, Roy stood tall and proud, rifle in hand, a squad leader, chosen by a platoon sergeant who built him up after realizing that Roy would not be beaten down. He instilled confidence in Roy, both in the field and in the classroom. "I ate it up," Roy said. "I discovered what a kick it was to sit in the front of the class and have the first answer rather than to hide in back and hope the teacher didn't call on me."

He left AIT with orders for overseas duty; he was going to Korea. The war was over, but he would help secure the demilitarized zone between North and South Korea. He returned to Texas for a two-week leave before embarking, stopping first in Cuero for a short visit with his half sister, Lupe. During that brief stay he came to the conclusion that despite being born in Cuero, El Campo was home, and that's where he headed next.

He was thrilled when Salvador invited him to sit down with the younger cousins and nephews, who now gathered around *him* to listen to *his* stories as a soldier. There were no tales of battle yet, except for one incident when Roy and a buddy ran into a pair of skunks while crossing a field during night training maneuvers. That battle, Roy said, shaking his head, was clearly won by the skunks. His sergeant ordered them to burn their uniforms. The children held their noses and giggled when he told them how, because of the smell, he was forced to march naked far behind the others.

Roy didn't mention to anybody, especially to Nicholas, that he had yet to control his fists, that he had gotten into a couple of scraps, even though they were now few and weeks between. And when he stood before his higher-ups—most of whom were combat veterans from Korea or World War II, the old-school, "brown shoe" Army—he got the feeling, from the light punishment they always administered, that they felt whoever he'd socked had it coming.

Roy's aunt Alexandria had told him that his blood was both Mexican, from his father, and Yaqui Indian, from his mother; Roy had studied the tribe and was intensely proud of his lineage. Because the Yaqui were fierce warriors, he felt that his "quick fists" temperament came from those genes. He described the tribe as "the toughest, meanest, and most ornery group of Indians that ever lived. Back when Cortés was conquering most of Mexico, he wisely chose to avoid the northern deserts, where the 'wild men' had . . . killed and eaten whole armies of Aztec and Toltec who had been trying to conquer them for hundreds of years."

IN 1956, Private First Class Benavidez was promoted to Corporal Benavidez and reported for duty at a base in Berlin, West Germany. He was a good soldier; not a model soldier, but a good one. He still tended to act and then think—"Ready, fire!"—without taking the time to aim. That impulsiveness was his glitch in life. It had gotten him sent to the principal, in hot water with Nicholas, in trouble with the law. And he might have been wearing those Airborne wings on his chest by now had he not been busted down in rank a few times. But he was learning.

In 1957 Berlin, the Wall between East and West still stood, and American soldiers stationed there were told their actions represented the United States of America and to keep that in mind when they were off base. A few weeks shy of the end of his sixteen-month duty assignment in West Germany, Roy and some friends went out for a Saturday night on the town. Outside a club, Roy overheard a heated argument in English between two men in civilian clothes; he recognized them as a couple of new second lieutenants from his unit. One was sloppy drunk and refusing to get into a cab. Roy walked up to the other young officer, introduced himself, and asked if he needed a hand.

"Sure," the man said, but when Roy reached over to help get the more inebriated officer into the backseat of the cab, the latter pushed Roy away and told his buddy to get "this little Mexican noncom" off of him, punctuating his outburst with more racial slurs.

One of Roy's friends said, "Deck him!" and Roy balled his fist, pulled back, and sent the lieutenant reeling into the backseat with a solid punch to the face. His buddy hopped in beside him, and the cab took off for the base.

Roy regretted instantly what he'd done. Back at base, he stressed over the potential repercussions all night. He had struck an officer, in public, with witnesses. That was a criminal offense.

He held his breath between prayers all the way till Monday, when he was summoned to the office of a captain to whom the second lieutenant Roy had knocked senseless reported. The captain, who wore a West Point class ring, was reading a file. Behind him was a plaque on the wall that read, "I do not lie, cheat or steal nor tolerate those that do," the honor code of West Point. Beneath were three words: "Duty, Honor, Country," the West Point motto.

"Corporal," he finally said, "you know why you're here. I understand there was a little trouble in town Saturday night. I've read your file, and you've been a pretty good soldier up until now. I'm going to ask you something. Think before you answer me. Corporal, did you or didn't you strike an officer Saturday night?"

He leaned back, crossed his arms, and waited.

Roy's superior, a sergeant, looked on while Roy tried to figure out whether this captain had just offered him a second chance. Maybe he knew the second lieutenant was a hothead drunk. Maybe he thought he'd deserved it. Or maybe he was going to base the extent of his punishment on Roy's answer. It was his word against two lieutenants. He could lie.

"Yes, Sir," Roy said. "I hit that officer."

The sergeant looked at Roy in disbelief, and the captain didn't say a word. After what seemed an eternity, he sent them into the hall, where Roy's sergeant laid into him for being the stupidest corporal who'd ever walked the face of the earth. While his sergeant continued to berate him for looking a gift horse in the mouth, the door to the captain's office swung open.

"Sergeant," the captain said, "return the PFC to his duties."

The sergeant's jaw dropped, and Roy let out a sigh of relief. The captain had demoted him from corporal to private first class. He'd only lost a stripe.

Before Roy returned to the States, the captain called him back into his office to ask why he had risked so much by confessing. Roy told the captain that he had been inspired by the West Point plaque behind his desk, which bore the same message he'd been hearing his whole life, just worded differently. He told the captain he wanted a career in the military, and he didn't want that career to be based on a lie.

Many things in Roy's life suddenly made sense to him. All those lectures, the morals, the Bible verses, everything he'd been spoon-fed for years in both Spanish and English by Grandfather Salvador, Uncle Nicholas, Aunt Alexandria, and Mr. Haddock translated perfectly into Duty, Honor, Country—*Deber, Honor, País*. The realization was a gift for Roy, a *regalo* that the West Point plaque had wrapped up in three words and put a bow on.

He made a personal vow that day. Even though he was a noncommissioned officer, he was going to adopt West Point's code—an officer's code—as his own. From there on out, he would do his very best to take a deep breath before pulling the trigger.

ROY RETURNED to El Campo for a thirty-day leave with one goal: to ask for a woman's hand in marriage. Her name was Hilaria "Lala" Coy, and he'd been writing to her throughout his deployment to Germany.

The great thing was that Lala, with her father's blessing, had been writing him back; this was because Roy had followed the proper courting protocol, having first asked Lala's father if he could correspond with his daughter. During his leave, Roy requested permission to call upon Lala, met her in the company of her family, and then his family, and then dated her with a chaperone. Ultimately, he was allowed to sit alone with her on her porch.

By the end of Roy's leave, Lala knew every chapter of his journey to serve his country—from his early years on the streets of Cuero to the fields of Colorado and South Texas to the times they'd noticed each other during community events, church, and the weekends when families came together for picnics and baseball games in the park. She teased him about one game in particular.

It had been the early 1950s, when the men and boys played while the women and girls watched. During one inning, Roy was so busy smiling and staring at Lala in the bleachers from his position in the outfield that he didn't see a pop fly when it plopped down in the grass beside him. His team yelled and screamed at him to pick up the ball, but nothing broke his trance.

They were engaged on December 30, 1958, just before Roy shipped out to military police (MP) school at Fort Benning, Georgia. Fort Benning was eight hundred miles away from El Campo, not a terribly long journey on a weekend pass when you're in love and driving a 1955 Chevrolet hardtop.

Lala and Roy were married in a 6:30 a.m. mass at St. Robert Bellarmine Church in El Campo on June 7, 1959. He wore a tuxedo; she wore a long lace gown and carried an orange-blossom bouquet. With eighteen attendants and 150 guests, both families were well represented in the all-day event, which included a reception in the parish hall, a barbecue at noon, and a four-tiered wedding cake. They received traditional blessings from Lala's parents at their home and from Nicholas and Alexandria at theirs. Their nuptials were complete when Lala and Roy made their secret *promesas*—promises for their lives as husband and wife—before a Catholic shrine.

★

THE NEWLYWEDS moved to Fort Gordon, Georgia, where Roy completed MP school and was selected to stay on after graduation and serve as the driver and personal guard for the post commander, General H. M. Hobson. At the same time, he put in two formal requests for jump school. Both were denied. He wondered if the times he'd been busted down in rank early in his career were the reason for the denials. The paratroopers were the elite in the Army, and the elite move up, not down.

"Patience and prayer," Lala told him.

One afternoon General Hobson announced to his staff that the commander of the 101st Airborne Division, General William C. Westmoreland, would be visiting the base to address the officers. He assigned Roy to be Westmoreland's driver.

While some generals were all business and treated their drivers like nothing more than drivers, Roy found Westmoreland to be friendly and approachable. The general even asked him a few polite questions, such as where he was from—and then the one question Roy had been praying for.

"Sergeant, have you ever thought about going Airborne?"

Being the chauffeur for a general is a cushy job in the Army, one that an unmotivated soldier could happily ride all the way to retirement. Roy later wondered if the general made a game out of asking that question of all his drivers, for entertainment value.

Roy could barely contain himself; he'd been trying to figure out a way to broach the topic before the general left the base. "Yes, Sir," he said. "Ever since I was a kid, even before I joined the Army. I've applied but haven't gotten accepted. I just want a chance, Sir."

"You must want to go pretty bad," the general replied.

"Yes, Sir. I'm up for reenlistment in a few weeks; I'll give it another try."

Twenty-four hours later, Roy drove Westmoreland to a waiting plane at Bush Field, Fort Gordon's airstrip, opened his door, and saluted as the general walked toward the aircraft.

"Good luck, Sergeant," Westmoreland said, then looked down and walked away in silence.

When Roy's reenlistment papers showed up two months later, they included an authorized invitation to attend jump school, compliments of Westmoreland himself.

JUST LIKE all the times he jumped from the loft of the cotton warehouse in Cuero, Roy never hesitated when he leaped from a low deck, then a higher deck, then a tower, and ultimately out of an airplane. Floating through the sky beneath the silk of a parachute washed him of his past. He was Airborne now, the paratrooper who had once lived only in his dreams. There was no horizon; he could see forever.

Roy returned to Fort Gordon at the end of 1959 with jump wings on his chest and a skip in his step. He and Lala packed their belongings, said good-bye to Georgia, and headed to North Carolina, where he was assigned to the 82nd Airborne Division at Fort Bragg.

As they traveled—sometimes while stopped at a café eating a burger and a shake, sometimes when they were cruising on the open road—they'd talk about their future and the family they prayed to become. The question was not whether they would have children, but how many they'd be blessed with.

"Getting an education is the most important thing in your life," he planned to tell them, just as Salvador had told him. Their studies would be their job, their contribution to the family, their way of honoring the Benavidez name. Their school year would not be interrupted by the harvest. They would graduate from high school, and then they would go to college. They would have degrees to hang on their walls. This was the dream he and Lala shared as a young couple looking toward tomorrow. Their success would be the measure of his success. The key to it all, Roy knew, was the plan he had mapped out in the Army.

In early 1965, they bought their first home, a mobile one. A lot of young Army couples were doing the same. With a trailer, no matter what base they ended up on, they could open the door and they were home. They celebrated their sixth wedding anniversary parked at the Bonnie Doone Trailer Park, not far from the main gates of Fort Bragg. There was an Airborne patch inside the window next to the door, a potted plant on each side of the front step, and on a wall a framed certificate, the equivalent of a high school diploma, which Roy had earned while taking the necessary courses, in addition to the heavy load of career courses for his military occupational specialty (MOS) as an Airborne infantryman.

Fall was in the air when Roy checked the air and tread on the trailer's tires, prepping it for the road. For the fifth time since they had married, they were moving. By the end of October the trailer was parked in the empty lot next to Lala's parents' home back in El Campo, and Roy was gone—but not off training or attending some short-term school. Lala's husband, Sergeant Roy Benavidez, the father of the baby growing inside her, had gone to war.

THE OFFICIAL date of the beginning of America's involvement in the Vietnam conflict would be argued for decades to come, including whether or not the weapons and training the OSS provided to Ho Chi Minh's Vietminh guerrillas during July and August of 1945 qualified as "involvement." Furthermore, did that brief period when the United States and the Vietminh were allied against the Japanese give Ho Chi Minh the credibility that would catapult his movement into the unified "One Struggle" of the Vietnamese people for independence? Under

Ho's (or as his people referred to him, Uncle Ho) communist leadership, the Vietminh battled the French in the First Indochina War for almost nine years, until May 7, 1954, when the battle at Dien Bien Phu forced the French into a peace conference the following day.

The conference in Geneva, Switzerland, sought to bring a lasting peace to Indochina. Its attendees hashed out a cease-fire, a promised future election, and a plethora of other diplomatic solutions, only a few of which would stick for more than a couple of years. The first was the decision that Vietnam would be split at the 17th parallel, with President Ho Chi Minh temporarily leading the communist north and a French-colonial-minded president, Ngo Dinh Diem, temporarily leading the capitalist south. The election that would reunify the country was set to take place in two years. But Diem, anticipating that the popular Ho would prevail in the slated national election, postponed it, and then canceled it completely.

Vietnam remained split, with Diem ruling the south autocratically (to the chagrin of the U.S government that had backed him for eight years) until he was assassinated on November 2, 1963, during a military coup led by a senior general of the Army of the Republic of Vietnam (ARVN), Duong Van Minh. The coup was encouraged, if not orchestrated by agents of the Central Intelligence Agency (the successor to the OSS), under the administration of President John F. Kennedy.

On November 22, 1963, Kennedy himself was assassinated in Dallas, Texas, and the anticommunism torch was passed to his vice president, Lyndon Baines Johnson. LBJ solemnly addressed Congress five days later, mourning the loss of "the greatest leader of our time." "And now the ideas and the ideals which he so nobly represented must and will be translated into effective action. Under John Kennedy's leadership, this nation has demonstrated that it has the courage to seek peace, and it has the fortitude to risk war. We have proved that we are a good and reliable friend to those who seek peace and freedom. We have shown that we can also be a formidable foe to those who reject the path of peace and those who seek to impose upon us or our allies the yoke of tyranny. This nation will keep its commitments from South Vietnam to West Berlin."

The U.S. commitment to General Duong Van Minh as president of South Vietnam lasted only a couple of months. He was overthrown by another general in the second of a string of seven military coups in less than a year and a half. During this period, a communist movement—the National Liberation Front of South Vietnam, or Vietcong (VC), and what everybody suspected was really the puppet of Ho Chi Minh and the North Vietnamese Army (NVA)—made great strides in what had been a growing insurgency. Number one on the Vietcong's charter had been to "overthrow the camouflaged colonial regime of the American imperialists and the dictatorial power of Ngo Dinh Diem, servant of the Americans, and institute a government of national democratic union." By the time a lasting leader, General Nguyen Van Thieu, became president of South Vietnam in June of 1965, the Vietcong were firmly entrenched, with guerrillas sneaking over the demarcation line of the 17th parallel to recruit locals and conduct acts of terrorism against the people of South Vietnam, kill American advisers, and engage the South Vietnamese Army in the small-scale but effective attacks of warfare.

The attacks were widely publicized, creating reams of evidence that justified the deployment of more and more American military advisers to aid the South Vietnamese Army in its fight against the communists; what had been hundreds of advisers soon became a few thousand.

The United States had fought communism overtly on the Korean Peninsula and covertly in its bastions worldwide. Now Uncle Sam was keeping a wary eye on Uncle Ho, anticipating an all-out invasion across the line of demarcation. Three U.S. presidents—Harry S. Truman, Dwight D. Eisenhower, and John F. Kennedy—had vowed to repel communist aggression in Indochina; the U.S. government, led by the fourth U.S. president to fervently oppose communism, Lyndon Johnson, sought and received congressional approval to increase American troops by the tens of thousands, to stop it at the 17th parallel.

Both the United States and North Vietnam accused the other of committing acts of terrorism and crimes against humanity. The reasoning and the politics, the truths and the lies, and the justifications and the history that would be written would be hotly debated forevermore.

ONE THING about Vietnam was certain, at least for Lala Benavidez: the quiet fear and sense of pride she felt when Roy was called to fight, called to do his duty, called to go to "A New Kind of War," as *Time* magazine described it on October 22, 1964. It was the same month Roy learned he would deploy as a military adviser to the South Vietnamese 25th Infantry "Tigers." He was going to fight the red tide of communism before it crossed the oceans and crashed onto the shores of America. He'd be battling "the lethal little men in black pajamas" who, just three months earlier, had "roamed the length and breadth of South Viet Nam marauding, maiming, and killing with impunity," as *Time* reported. "No highway was safe by night, and few by day; the trains had long since stopped running. From their tunneled redoubts, the communist Vietcong held 65% of South Viet Nam's land and 55% of its people in thrall."

The Vietcong—aka VC, Victor Charlie, or just Charlie—were the new bad guys on the block, the insurgent instruments of the communist plague vying to take over Indochina, one country at a time. If South Vietnam fell, U.S. officials felt, so, too, would the rest of Southeast Asia, like dominoes, gaining momentum as they toppled one after the other all the way to the American heartland. So went the political justification for U.S. involvement. The Vietcong, in Roy's mind, were no different from the Nazis and the Japanese in World War II.

By October 1, 1964, America had committed 125,000 troops to advise and fight beside the South Vietnamese Army. Sergeant Benavidez was part of what *Time* called "one of the swiftest, biggest military buildups in the history of warfare. . . . Day and night, screaming jets and prowling helicopters seek out the enemy from their swampy strongholds in southernmost Camau all the way north to the mountain gates of China."

Three short weeks after the American surge in troops, *Time* reported, "The Vietcong's once-cocky hunters have become the cowering hunted as the cutting edge of U.S. firepower slashes into the thickets of communist strength. If the U.S. has not yet guaranteed certain victory in South Vietnam, it has nonetheless undeniably averted certain defeat. As one top-ranking U.S. officer put it: 'We've stemmed the tide.'"

In 1965, the majority of Americans stood behind those serving in Vietnam. They were answering the call of duty and honoring the ideals of their late commander in chief, JFK. The president had made a promise to the world in his inaugural address four years earlier that Americans would "pay any price, bear any burden, meet any hardship, support any friend, oppose any foe to assure the survival and the success of liberty."

President Johnson echoed JFK's sentiment in a press conference in July 1965. "We did not choose to be the guardians at the gate, but there is no one else. Nor would surrender in Viet-Nam bring peace, because we learned from Hitler at Munich that success only feeds the appetite of aggression. The battle would be renewed in one country and then another country, bringing with it perhaps even larger and crueler conflict, as we have learned from the lessons of history. . . . As long as there are men who hate and destroy, we must have the courage to resist or we will see it all, all that we have built, all that we hope to build, all of our dreams for freedom—all, all will be swept away with the flood of conquest.

"So, too, this shall not happen. We will stand in Viet-Nam!"

ROY DIDN'T ship to Vietnam with the Marines, nor did he parachute in as a paratrooper; he flew into the war on a chartered commercial airliner. Once there, he taught the South Vietnamese how to counter the insurgency, while he simultaneously was learning how to survive the nuances of a jungle war. Most of what he'd learned in training was based upon conventional war, where the front was generally in front of you and the rear was behind. But the Vietcong—Charlie—didn't fight that way; it wasn't the "able, baker, Charlie, dog, easy" war Audie Murphy had fought in the 1940s. Everything, right down to the U.S. military's phonetic alphabet, had changed. This was the "alpha, bravo, Charlie, delta, echo" war. Charlie. Wouldn't you know it? "Charlie" for both wars. Charlie was everywhere . . .

Roy had been trained to keep a wary eye on the locals, who appeared as innocent, smiling villagers by day, but were potentially AK-47-wielding, rocket-toting Vietcong guerrillas by night. Still, he couldn't help respecting the Vietnamese people when he'd see families working long hours side by side in the fields, the young children barefoot and half naked, tending their crops.

He heard his fellow soldiers' reactions to the Vietnamese. Some called them savages, backwards, gooks—proclaiming them all to be suspected killers and closet commies. More empathetic GIs felt for the villagers, whose simple way of life had been shattered by the war. They saw the children forced to do manual labor instead of going to school, shook their heads, and said, "That's sad." And Roy would respond, "Reminds me of my childhood," which always elicited a laugh.

Roy looked to the advisers who were in-country before him as mentors. One, an Aussie he knew only as Dickie, had come to Vietnam after fighting the communists in Malaysia. While on patrol and reconnaissance missions, he taught Roy to move with the rhythm of the jungle's natural sounds—never rush. If bamboo was creaking, he stepped when it creaked. He walked toe to heel, not heel to toe, testing the ground, easing his weight. He didn't step and look, he looked and then stepped; and since foreign advisers were prized targets for VC snipers, he blended in, not only with his surroundings, but also among the troops he led. "Don't slap at mosquitoes—only 'round eyes' do that," Dickie told Roy.

The first and last rule of reconnaissance, according to Dickie, was "Be alert; stay alive." Always have an option. Where's your cover? Self-preservation meant team preservation; team preservation meant self-preservation. In a village, on a road, along a jungle pathway, always be alert; don't trust anybody or anything.

Much of Roy's job involved building the infrastructure that would house the hundreds of thousands of future American troops. He patrolled the countryside one day and provided security for task forces building wells, schools, and roads the next. He helped build camps for refugees fleeing the communists who had forced them into service against what the north deemed a corrupt and unstable South Vietnamese government. The south, in return, accused the northern insurgents of terrorism, which was actually a key strategy of recruitment. If a young man refused to join the Vietcong, he would be made an example—losing a finger, a hand, or his head, which would be displayed prominently on a stake.

Despite its terrorist tactics, the north claimed it was trying to unite the north and the south, while the Americans were hypocrites, stepping into a country whose people would, if given the choice, choose communism and unification over forced and corrupt democracy.

The situation was, in a word, complicated.

Roy, ALONG with every American whose boots hit the ground in Vietnam, was given a sturdy card with a brief introduction and "Nine Simple Rules":

The Vietnamese have paid a heavy price in suffering for their long fight against the communists. We military men are in Vietnam now because their government has asked us to help its soldiers and people in winning their struggle. The Vietcong will attempt to turn the Vietnamese people against you. You can defeat them at every turn by the strength, understanding, and generosity you display with the people. Here are nine simple rules:

1. Remember we are guests here: We make no demands and seek no special treatment.
2. Join with the people! Understand their life, use phrases from their language and honor their customs and laws.
3. Treat women with politeness and respect.
4. Make personal friends among the soldiers and common people.
5. Always give the Vietnamese the right of way.
6. Be alert to security and ready to react with your military skill.
7. Don't attract attention by loud, rude or unusual behavior.
8. Avoid separating yourself from the people by a display of wealth or privilege.
9. Above all else you are members of the US Military Forces on a difficult mission, responsible for all your official and personal actions. Reflect honor upon yourself and the United States of America.

Roy later described the Nine Rules as "not only 'simple,' but 'simplistic.' I might have been a kid again, being told by Aunt Alexandria how to behave at a birthday party."

The most important rule he learned was from Dickie, and that was "Don't trust anybody or anything." This is what Roy kept in the forefront of his mind when he geared up for a patrol in early 1966 and headed down a jungle path.

"Democracy, communism, 'domino theory'—all those things made sense someplace," Roy would recount. "Maybe they made sense in conference rooms ten thousand miles from Vietnam, but they meant nothing there. What we had to work with were a bunch of farmers in one uniform with U.S. weapons on one side and a bunch of farmers in another uniform with Russian weapons on the other side. Our guys didn't want to shoot them; their guys weren't too crazy about the idea either. Killing the 'round eyes' was the only thing they could both agree on. My fellow soldiers and I had been hearing the truth about the situation from the other advisers. We were also starting to see a slow trickle of body bags and wounded. I don't really believe that even our training personnel had any real idea about what we were walking into."

3

THE DARKEST WHITE

Roy woke up in a fog. He didn't know who he was, where he was, or how he'd gotten there. All he could understand was that everything around him was white. The people wore white. The floor was white. The bed he was lying in, the walls, the ceiling. Everything was white.

A big blank spot had taken the place of his memories and reason. He had no awareness that he had been floating for several days in a white purgatory that was the Beach Pavilion at the Brooke Army Medical Center at Fort Sam Houston, San Antonio, Texas.

There were clues in the fog—circles and squares that occasionally took shape and started to make sense. But then they'd evaporate, and he'd slip back into the nothingness that was his past and present. If he could have read, the clipboard in a slot at the end of the bed he was lying in would have reminded him who he was: Sergeant Benavidez, Roy, P.; that he was in the Army; that the year was 1966 and the month was January. That he was thirty years old.

There were other clues in the room that might have answered some of his questions. The guy in the bed next to him had a bandaged stump where his leg used to be. The guy on the other side had no legs at all. Across the aisle, another guy had bandaged stumps in place of his hands, with burn bandages extending up his arms. Roy, by all appearances, was in one piece. No visible wounds commemorated the fact that his childhood dream had come true, that he'd gone to war and seen battle.

LATE IN January 1966, the first weekend after Roy was medevaced from Vietnam, a green-eyed woman with dark hair sat with him at the Fort Sam Houston hospital—a 150-mile drive from El Campo. "It's Lala," she told him as she held his hand. The doctors had suggested that family members talk to Roy about his past, so Lala would bring along his cousin Leo or his older brother Gene or his uncle Nicholas, and they would sit beside his bed and talk to him, and talk, and talk. Roy opened his eyes for the first time during these early visits, but he didn't respond.

He had no recollection of Lala, nor was he aware that the bump on her belly was their first child, conceived just before he'd deployed. The doctors told Lala candidly that the concussion from the suspected land mine Roy had stepped on jolted his brain so violently that they didn't expect him to regain his senses. Even if he did, they were all but certain he would never walk again. However, they considered him lucky. The theory was that the mine—or a large flat piece of it—had jettisoned from the earth and impacted his rear with hundreds or thousands of pounds of pressure. The damage—a twisted spine and fractured bone and cartilage—was visible only in X-rays. But amid the damaged remains of Roy's spine, the spinal cord itself appeared intact, and for this Lala was grateful. Never once did she leave the hospital without lighting a candle in the chapel and praying for her husband to return to her.

The fog was a blessing for Roy. It protected him, for a time, from the visions that would haunt him for the rest of his life. The "fog machine," as he described it, was likely traumatic brain injury, and the memories that appeared to him were as unpredictable as a Vietcong ambush.

One morning, the fog lifted for a moment, and Roy saw them, as clearly as he had seen them that day in Vietnam: three Vietnamese children nailed to the wall of a barrack that he and his platoon had helped build for the refugees fleeing their villages in the mountain highlands.

Two boys and a girl had been crucified, long nails through their hands and feet. They were hanging at chest height—target level—their smooth, innocent, small bodies ravaged by bullets. The wall around them was pristine: the VC were good shots. Several bullets had been aimed at one of the boys' heads. Little remained of his face.

Two women screamed and wailed on their knees before them, reaching out to touch what must have been their children. An older man, no doubt a father or a grandfather, had his hand cupped under the little girl's foot, catching the blood that dripped slowly from her toe.

Roy had been crying and screaming off and on for days, perhaps processing his memories from his combat tour. But on one day he found himself in a room seated in a chair at a table. He actually understood that he was seated in a chair. A chair with wheels—a wheelchair!

Spread out before him was an assortment of round and square pegs beside a plate with round openings and square openings. A puzzle toy for children.

He held the pieces in his hand and thought, *This is crazy. There's only one way to do it. The round pegs go into the round holes, the square pegs into the square ones.* He'd sat at this table many times, he was told by the medical staff, and had always drawn a blank. Today he inserted all the pegs into their rightful places.

The following day, the green-eyed woman visited Roy again. "Lala," he breathed.

As if a switch had been flipped, Roy knew who and where he was. How he'd gotten to where he was, however, remained a blank. Sometime later, Roy described his frustration: "My life was a movie in which the projectionist had completely omitted a reel in the middle of the feature. I recalled my arrival in Vietnam . . . the people, my buddies, the action we experienced together, even the Bob Hope Christmas Show. There must have been a last recon mission, but nothing came to mind. I tried to remember, but there was an incredible blackness." That blackness got even blacker when the doctors told Roy why he couldn't move his legs or his feet or his toes—he was paralyzed from the waist down.

When he tried to get answers, the doctors were evasive, unwilling to categorize his condition as either permanent or temporary. "Let's give it some time," they would tell him. "Continue with your physical therapy."

After two weeks of "physical therapy," Roy concluded that the medical staff weren't working on his *legs* so much as they were working on his *head,* preparing him mentally for life in a wheelchair. The realization sank in that his career with the Army was over. "Like a misfired round from a 105 mm howitzer, I was useless to them," he said.

A dark cloud settled in where the fog had been, and despair poured over Roy. What he called a "pity party" took him down the oldest roads of his past, where he had only flickering memories of his birth father, and his birth mother was little more than a "song in the night" that had drifted off and died. Though he remained close to his adoptive family, the Army had been Roy's life for well over a decade. It had become his immediate family; his fellow soldiers, regardless of the color of their skin, were his brothers. In the blink of an eye, all that was about to be taken away, just as his parents had been.

★

"Sergeant," a nurse said, "you've got some visitors. Let's get you into that chair."

The chair, the damned chair! Roy lamented to himself. *For the rest of my life someone is gonna have to help me into that damned chair.*

Lala and Roger wheeled Roy to the dayroom overlooking the parade ground and positioned him so he could look out. For hours they talked while Roy listened to their chitchat—a cousin was getting married, a nephew had been born, an aunt was ill. Everything was moving forward at the speed of life, including the baby. Lala was six months pregnant by this time, and Roy could barely look at her the entire afternoon she sat beside him. When Lala and Roger left, he hated himself for it. *This is no life for Lala,* he thought. He wished his pathetic, skinny dead legs were gone, that they'd been blown off his body.

Roy counted the ceiling tiles in his hospital room every day. Sometimes he did it once, and sometimes he did it over and over. The winning number was 327. If he got to the final row in the grid and counted down to the last one and it was off, he'd shake his head, or shrug, or curse, and start over. He'd keep counting until he got it right. It was his own invention, his own mental therapy, to test his ability to focus. After weeks in the same bed, he felt as if he were going insane. The counting became almost compulsive.

When the chief orthopedic surgeon visited him to check his progress, noting that needle pricks to Roy's feet and legs continued to elicit zero response and that Roy could not wiggle his toes, the topic of discharge from the Army was brought up. Roy did what any self-respecting, Army-through-and-through sergeant would do. He begged. He begged for a little more time, swore that he was feeling tingles and shocks and other indications that his legs weren't dead yet. And so he bought himself a few more days, a few more weeks.

Each time the surgeon left, he felt as if he'd dodged a bullet. He would lower his body down into the chair beside his bed, just as he'd learned in "cripple therapy," as he called it, and do the long, slow push to the little chapel at the end of the ward.

He would maneuver himself down the hall, past what he later described as "the human debris of Vietnam [that] was beginning to wash up on the shores of America." He saw wounds so severe, so grotesque—hands that looked like burnt match tips, men with multiple amputations—he wondered how it was possible they'd survived.

He would wheel into the simple chapel—the few pews bathed in the gold- and rust-colored light from a stained-glass window—and roll to a stop in front of the figure of the crucified Christ. But he never once thanked God that the mine, or booby trap, or whatever it was, hadn't exploded, that he was in one piece, that he was alive. Instead, he asked, "Why?" He would say it as solemnly as he'd recited his oath to serve his country. "Why did you do this to me? What use am I now?"

Why? Why? Why?

Roy's Catholic faith was as deeply rooted in his heart as it was with his family and in the Hispanic communities where he'd grown up. Later in life, he would say he was living proof that a devout altar boy is fully capable of wearing out the hinges on a confessional.

"When I was a little kid, just looking around in the big church taught me something about faith," Roy said. "I knew even then that there was something bigger than I was, bigger even than the adults I knew. I knew God listens, even when nobody else listens or cares. From the time I was a child and I lost my parents, I have always believed that."

Roy felt that Nicholas and Alexandria had been answers to his prayers, as was Art Haddock. Grandfather Salvador, too. They were guardian angels who had come into his life during dire times—times of intense prayer. Mr. Haddock had told him, "God makes no mistakes."

So, if God makes no mistakes, why am I being punished? Always he returned to *Why?*

As he repeated that question, he began to lose hope, until somehow the word brought him back to Berlin, when he had thought for certain his career was over. "Why?" It was the same question the West Point captain had asked him. Why?

And what had been his answer? Why hadn't he taken the easy way out and lied? Because Duty, Honor, Country—*Deber, Honor, País*—forbade it.

Here in the hospital, he knew there was no honor in giving up. He tried to imagine what his life would be if he accepted the medical discharge and went home in a wheelchair, and the person he saw wasn't the man he wanted to be. "There was no sergeant from the 82nd Airborne back in El Campo," says Roy. "Instead, there was only a Mexican pepper belly named Benavidez, a seventh-grade dropout who used to work at the Firestone tire store."

THE DISTANCE between the hospital bed and the cold, hard floor seemed great, even for an Airborne soldier; on an evening in March 1966, Roy decided that he was going to get there. The nurses had finished their rounds, and the light on the ward was dim when Roy checked to see if the coast was clear. With his arms, he was able to slide his legs to the edge of the mattress.

Holding the bed railing with his hands, he went over and crashed onto the ground with a grunt.

"What the hell?" a fellow patient called out. "Benavidez, are you all right?"

As he called for the nurse, Roy stopped him. "No, I'm okay. I'm gonna try some therapy. Just leave me alone."

Rolling onto his stomach, Roy used his chin, elbows, and forearms to pull himself toward the wall, dragging his legs behind him. He never got there. A night nurse discovered him on the floor and helped him back into bed.

Roy fell asleep with a grin on his face. Rolling out of his bed and sliding across the floor was the biggest adventure he'd had in months. The black-and-blue hip he woke up with the next morning was worth it, as was a dull ache. Feeling! There was some feeling in his lower extremities.

The day dragged by, but finally it was evening and he could give it another go. He was quieter with his dismount from the bed, and he was able to repeat the roll onto his stomach, his chin to the floor, elbows and forearms working—inching forward. His objective was a narrow section of wall between the two nightstands separating his bed from the one to the right.

He reached the nightstands, turned himself around, and raised his arms up over his shoulders. Levering his elbows against the nightstands, he pulled himself up, legs straight out before him, before crumpling with exhaustion. The nurses found him there on their next round.

He became the nightly entertainment for the men recuperating around him, who cheered him on every time he fell. It took a week of trying before he was able to raise himself all the way up between the nightstands by pressing his back against the wall and using his arms. This brought his legs almost underneath him, but mostly he was supported by his triceps and shoulders. "I was just sort of hanging there," Roy said. "I tried to put weight on my legs, and a burning pain shot through my back that felt like I'd been stabbed with a red-hot knife. I collapsed against the wall, and slid to the floor."

The nurses came running when they heard the cheers. Once they understood that he was trying to walk, they sent him to therapy.

After a week of painful therapy and his own nightly regimen, Roy stood—tears streaming down his cheeks, panting like a dog, hands hovering six inches above the nightstands. He was bearing his own weight.

Soon after, sensation returned to Roy's toes. He was able to wiggle them. He shuffled a few inches, more and more each day, until he was pushing his own empty wheelchair down the long hallway to the chapel, where he stopped asking questions of God and instead gave thanks for what he realized was a miracle.

The doctors—in particular the chief surgeon, who had originally given Roy the news that he'd most likely never walk again—congratulated him. After five months in the hospital, he had far exceeded their expectations. Then they tried to give him a medical discharge from the Army. He pleaded with them to reconsider. While many young men were doing all they could to avoid military service, Roy didn't want this get-out-of-jail-free card; he wanted to return to the 82nd and get on with his career.

EARLY IN the summer of 1966, Roy put on a crisply starched uniform and walked out of the Beach Pavilion at Brooke Army Medical Center on shaky legs, holding the hand of his wife. Lala, well into her final trimester of pregnancy, had proven herself a warrior of her vows, standing proudly by her man: "for better or for worse, in sickness and in health." They packed up the trailer and returned to Fort Bragg, North Carolina, arriving in time to watch the fireworks on the Fourth of July. On July 31, their first child, Denise, was born.

While Lala settled into motherhood at the Bonnie Doone Trailer Park, Roy began his new job as the administrative assistant to the personnel sergeant with the 82nd Airborne Division. His daily mission was to help navigate Airborne soldiers and their wives through the minefields, barbed wire, and coils of red tape that lay between them and the benefits associated with their "membership" in the U.S. Army.

Roy was good at what he did, and thankful that the Army had kept him in service, but in his heart he knew he was a soldier meant for the field. He dutifully stamped forms, typed reports, cleared the in-box, and filled the out-box, but his mind was back in Vietnam. Despite the terrible things he had seen, despite being nearly killed and paralyzed, he longed for that intense feeling of being fully alive he'd experienced in a combat zone. Now that he was a parent, he realized that the protective emotion he'd felt for his men was nothing less than paternal. Like a sidelined football player watching his team take the field, he watched the soldiers at Bragg train and deploy.

Always have an option. In a village, on a road, along a jungle pathway—and there in his office at Fort Bragg—Roy was always keeping his eyes and ears open for options. Though he was grateful to be alive, the desk, he knew, would kill him—not quickly like a booby trap or an ambush, but worse. It would kill him slowly.

GREEN BERET

THE STUFF OF Roy's childhood dreams, the Airborne paratroopers, had been the Army's most elite infantry troops in World War II. But in Vietnam, the airmobile tactic of inserting hundreds of soldiers by helicopter into precise landing zones in the jungle made parachute assaults passé. Special Forces—the Green Berets—although still airborne jump-qualified, took the front seat both on the battlefield and in popular culture as the new "most elite" ground troop, whose strength came, in great part, from unconventional tactics and individual versatility rather than from overwhelming numbers and conventional maneuvers and firepower. They were the "Swiss Army knife" of soldiers, who could be called upon for any kind of mission but who specialized in guerrilla warfare and counterinsurgency—tailor-made for fighting the communists in Vietnam.

The U.S. Army was serious about morale and esprit de corps, and the foundation for any soldier's pride came from his unit's identity and lineage. Special Forces tactics were rich in history and could be traced back to the American Revolution and the Civil War. The Green Berets' mission and organization, however, had evolved from World War II military units, including the 1st Special Service Force—aka the Devil's Brigade—Merrill's Marauders, and Darby's Rangers, and in particular the Jedburgh teams of the Office of Strategic Services.

That the OSS had trained and provided weapons to Ho Chi Minh twenty-two years earlier was still highly classified information.

Before his first tour, Roy had signed up for an opportunity to qualify for the Green Berets and been accepted. Now he wondered what it would take to get another shot. The John F. Kennedy Special Warfare Center and School was right there at Fort Bragg, so Roy helped himself to a stack of the inches-thick training manuals that constituted the curriculum of the Special Forces Qualification Course (Q Course). On the inside was a quote pulled from the address JFK presented to the 1962 graduating class at West Point: "This is another type of war, new in its intensity, ancient in its origins—war by guerrillas, subversives, insurgents, assassins; war by ambush instead of by combat; by infiltration instead of aggression, seeking victory by eroding and exhausting the enemy instead of engaging him. It requires—in those situations where we must encounter it—a whole new kind of strategy, a wholly different kind of force, and therefore, a new and wholly different kind of military training."

The Green Berets gave Roy hope, and he dreamed of joining their ranks—something he didn't dare mention to Lala. He secretly began to plan. His aspirations might have been fogged by the one thousand to fifteen hundred milligrams of Darvon he was taking daily for the stabbing pain that shot up his legs and into his back, but as a friend of Roy's says, "This was a guy who doctors said would never walk again. 'I can't' wasn't in his vocabulary."

Roy's personnel file already showed that he met all four of the requirements for Special Forces qualification: he'd volunteered for the Army; he was airborne jump qualified; he had personally requested to try out for the Special Forces (and been accepted); and, being a sergeant, he held a noncommissioned rank. The problem was that his wounds and hospital stay meant he needed to "refresh" his jump status; in addition, the documentation saying he'd been accepted for the Q Course had been sent before his tour and had since expired—or so he thought, since it was no longer in his personnel file.

The other, seemingly insurmountable, issue was the level of his physical fitness. The Special Forces training and qualification process—like that of the Navy SEALs, Marine Corps Force Recon, and Army Rangers—was as grueling as it got, with very few making it through. In order to wear the coveted Green Beret you had to prove you were the type of soldier who would die rather than quit.

Roy couldn't get the Green Berets out of his mind, reading everything he could about them, watching them train in the field; he even received permission to sit in on a few of the classes. In a military town like Fort Bragg in 1966, it was nearly impossible to turn on the radio and not hear "The Ballad of the Green Berets," written and performed by Special Forces staff sergeant Barry Sadler in honor of Specialist 5 James P. Gabriel Jr., an early Special Forces adviser who was shot in the chest during a Vietcong attack on his four-man advisory team and a group of Civilian Irregular Defense Group (CIDG; pronounced *sid-gee*) trainees near Danang four years earlier. Critically wounded, the twenty-four-year-old Green Beret continued to defend their position and had radioed for reinforcements until he was overrun and captured. The VC executed him.

> *Fighting soldiers from the sky*
> *Fearless men who jump and die*
> *Men who mean just what they say*
> *The brave men of the Green Beret*

★

THE GREEN Berets' motto is "De Oppresso Liber"—"To Free the Op-
pressed"; those words made Roy reflect obsessively on the atrocities he'd
seen in Vietnam. Staring at his daughter as she slept, watching her tiny
chest rise and fall, often brought him to tears. He would think about
the three children who were crucified by the VC. He would think about
the wailing women and the man who had mourned their loss. They
haunted him and fueled his desperation to get back into the fight.

Roy's request to update his jump status was categorically denied
because of his physical condition. Assigned to "light physical activity,"
he was, according to the Army, destined for a desk. But the desk did
provide for Roy, giving him an understanding of paper trails and how
documents get lost in them—and if they can be lost, so, too, can they
be found.

With a neatly forged, pocket-wrinkled authorization slip in hand,
Roy smooth-talked his way aboard a crowded aircraft late in September
1966. He jumped three times that day. He went home, limping and in
pain from a particularly jarring landing, with the news that they'd be
getting fifty-five dollars extra that month in "jump pay." Lala rarely
raised her voice but would call Roy by their last name when she was really upset. "Benavidez," she said sternly, "you know you're not supposed
to be jumping!"

What he didn't share with her was that this was just the beginning
of his plan. Now that he'd proven both to the Army and to himself that
he could handle the air, he would conquer the ground. Every morning
on base he walked, then jogged—gradually increasing the miles while
decreasing what had become addictive pain medication. Less than a
year after leaving the hospital, Roy had weaned himself completely off
the painkillers and could run five miles without stopping. That was
when the signed, stamped, and approved papers for Sergeant Roy P.

Benavidez to transfer into the Q Course from two years before suddenly appeared in the stack of current requests.

"I broke a few rules back then," Roy later admitted, "and it wasn't the right thing to do. It was wrong. But my time was running out. I was over thirty and still pretty badly damaged. I wanted back into that war. [It] was the most horrible experience of my life, but I was a soldier. . . . I felt my life had been spared for a reason, and I knew that I couldn't find it sitting behind a desk."

LALA WAS happy to see the fire return to Roy's eyes during those months of personal training, but in February of 1967, when he told her he had been given the opportunity to qualify for the Green Berets, she just shook her head and said, "Benavidez." The thirty-one-year-old airborne- and infantry-qualified sergeant first class was older than most of the instructors at the John F. Kennedy Special Warfare Center and School, where he was assigned. His most recent duty had been as an administrative desk jockey with the 82nd Airborne Division, and before that he'd spent almost half a year at Brooke Army Medical Center convalescing from his wounds. On paper, he was not exactly prime Green Beret material.

But if his instructors were privy to Roy's medical history, they never mentioned it. And, likewise, in a community of elite warriors where reputation is everything, Roy never spoke a word of his past wounds for fear he'd be marked as a liability among the men or, worse, that the instructors would beat him down harder than the others to be sure he had what it took.

He strove to be the gray man who blended in and never stood out. Unable to lead during physical training, he gave it his all to avoid being in the rear, consistently hanging somewhere in the central part of the tail of the group. Camouflaged naturally by his short stature and

hunched over from sheer agony, he powered through requirements that
included daily calisthenics—push-ups, sit-ups, leg lifts, squats, pull-ups,
chin-ups, dead hangs—and double-time marching, forced marching,
jogging, and running, eventually with a seventy-pound rucksack on his
back. The crux of the physical tests was parachuting with minimal gear
and five days' worth of food and water into the woods, where, teamed
up with a buddy, they were expected to both survive and stay oriented
for twelve days, during which various objectives had to be accomplished.

Still, the physical training was for Roy the easy part. It was the
MOI, method of instruction, and MOS, military occupational specialty,
training and cross-training—the classroom training in particular—
that weeded out the men unable to show their depth as a soldier, leader,
technician, and instructor. If you couldn't both master a skill and teach
somebody else that skill—such as reassembling a broken-down M60
machine gun and naming off the function of each part along the way—
you had no place on a Special Forces Operational Detachment Alpha,
an A-team. You had no right to wear the Green Beret.

An A-team is the basic operational unit of Special Forces, consisting
of two officers (at the time a captain and a lieutenant), two operations/
intelligence experts, two communications experts, two weapons experts, two medics, and two engineers (demolition experts). This twelve-
man team is capable of building, healing, and destroying. In the event
that any of the team is wounded or killed, all its members cross-trained
to perform proficiently the basic duties of their teammates. In certain
situations the unit can be split in half to operate as two six-man teams.

In Vietnam, the Special Forces mission focus was similar to Roy's
duties as an adviser during his first tour: he would be training and leading the South Vietnamese and indigenous tribes to fight the communist
insurgency. But as a member of an A-team, he would likely be assigned
to a remote Special Forces "A-camp," where twelve Green Berets oversaw
(or built) units of South Vietnam ARVN or CIDG soldiers, who, de-

pending on the region, could be ethnic Chinese Nungs or Montagnard tribesmen. These A-team–led camps could be platoon strength, company strength, or in some cases multiple companies and were strategically located near high-traffic infiltration routes from Laos or Cambodia, as well as key provincial villages likely to be targeted by the Vietcong.

The A-team outposts were the eyes and ears of the countryside, the boonies—known as "Indian country" along the border. By patrolling, reconnoitering, and assessing the locals' knowledge, they gathered information about enemy movements and strengths and reported it to intelligence headquarters in Saigon. At the same time, the camps provided protection for the local populations (from which the Green Berets would recruit, train, and ultimately build strong localized counterinsurgency forces that could handle their own anticommunist, pronational defense). This was the Special Forces mission. It was extremely dangerous work.

AFTER REVIEWING the results of a series of tests, the Special Forces training cadre would decide where best a trainee would contribute to a team. Roy qualified for both operations/intelligence and light and heavy weapons. In the field he could always manage, but he found himself overwhelmed in the classroom, especially because, as the ranking noncommissioned officer (NCO), he was expected to lead the lower-ranked NCOs while maintaining his own studies.

The training schedule was flexible, so sometimes new students cycled in to check off the boxes of their requirements. Roy found himself sinking, inundated by the workload, when a familiar face appeared, a soft-spoken fellow soldier from the 82nd named Leroy Wright.

Thank God, Roy thought when he realized that Wright, who was four years older, also outranked him. Roy handed the extra leadership duties over to Wright, who was happy to help, and the two became quick friends, having traveled similar career paths in the infantry, including tours in Korea's demilitarized zone. But while Roy had served the standard one-year billet, Wright had volunteered for a second.

The winters in Korea were harsh, the American camps spartan, and the conditions in the postwar poverty-stricken land had made it one of the more undesirable overseas duties to pull. Why would anyone volunteer for a second tour? Wright earned Roy's abiding respect when he explained that he had fallen in love with a Korean woman who lived in squalor in an off-base shantytown. He had gone through a great deal of red tape and a second deployment in order to marry her and bring her back to the United States as a citizen.

When he and Roy reunited at the Q Course, Wright was a family man with two young boys; he had also served a tour in Vietnam, where he had been wounded by a grenade blast. Like Roy, Wright felt that he wasn't done. The two men shared a strong sense of duty as well as an innate drive to better themselves and honor their family names, a purpose that was met by the Army. And they both quietly hoped for a second tour in spite of their families' desire for them to remain stateside. Somewhere down the line, they promised each other as they shared photos of their kids, they would get their families together for a barbecue.

It was common at the Special Warfare School for active-duty Special Forces soldiers, and sometimes foreigners, to join a class as a refresher or to add a skill set to their MOS. Such was the case when an instructor introduced Sergeant First Class Stefan "Pappy" Mazak to Roy's class. It was an honor to have this combat veteran among their ranks, the instructor told his students.

Mazak was a five-foot-two-inch, forty-one-year-old Czechoslovakian "Lodge Bill" soldier who had fought with the French Resistance as a teenager, then with the French Foreign Legion. He was recruited in 1952 by the newly founded 10th Special Forces Group, under the Lodge-Philbin Act of June 30, 1950, which authorized the recruitment of foreign nationals into the U.S. military. The group's mission had been to conduct guerrilla warfare against the communists in the event of a Soviet invasion of Europe.

While the invasion never came, Mazak gained fame and respect in other actions, including an emergency rescue mission to the Belgian Congo in the summer of 1960. Mazak was part of a four-man contingent tasked with rescuing and evacuating European and American citizens who were being systematically hunted down and killed by a violent rebel group. At one point, Mazak's superior, First Lieutenant Sully H. De Fontaine, requested a Belgian platoon of paratroopers for backup when he was surrounded by "a band of about fifty threatening, gun-toting rebels," according to Roy's recount of the story. "The self-styled leader informed De Fontaine that 'all whites were to die.' Fontaine produced a grenade, pulled the pin, and said to the leader, 'Okay, boss, shoot me. We will die together.'

"For two hours the stare-down continued, with De Fontaine acutely aware that he could not hold the grenade firing lever forever. . . . Suddenly, Mazak emerged from the bush holding two submachine guns [and] fired wildly into the air as he screamed profanities at the top of his lungs. De Fontaine saw the fear in the eyes of his chief opponent and tossed the grenade into the midst of his captors. The remaining live rebels ran screaming into the bush, abandoning not only the refugees in the village but their arms as well. Later, Mazak apologized to De Fontaine for his outburst of theatrics, but stated, 'I just couldn't think of anything else to do at that moment.'"

When Roy's instructor finished telling the story, the entire class rose to stand at attention while Mazak remained humbly seated. With some coaxing by the instructor, Mazak also rose, apologizing for his broken English. Roy paraphrased:

"We in this room are all men who believe that actions speak louder than words. If I can impart anything from my life as a soldier, it is this: There are only two types of warrior in this world. Those who serve tyrants and those who serve free men. I have chosen to serve free men, and if we as warriors serve free men, we must love freedom more than we love our own lives. It is a simple philosophy but one that has served me well in life."

Roy was entranced, and he approached Mazak after class to ask if he would consider pairing up as study partners. Together they struggled through and completed the operations and intelligence course, and Mazak prepared to ship off to Vietnam.

Shortly thereafter, Roy was assigned to an A-team of fellow students, who "fought" in an elaborate mock unconventional war set in the rural counties of North Carolina. This was the Q Course final exam, during which teams faced real-world scenarios to test the depth of their training and adaptability under stress and against an opposing force.

Roy and his team made the cut, and he stood at attention as Colonel George D. Callaway presented him the certificate Roy would frame and display inside the Benavidez trailer. "Be it known," stated the certificate, "Staff Sergeant Roy P. Benavidez has successfully completed the U.S. Army Special Forces Training Group (Airborne) Course of Instruction. He has demonstrated proficiency in Special Forces Tactics and Techniques, and has specialized in M.O.S. 11B/11C. Given at Fort Bragg, North Carolina this 29th day of September, 1967."

Then Roy received what he would cherish for the rest of his life; what President Kennedy had called "a symbol of excellence, a badge of courage, a mark of distinction in the fight for freedom." His green beret.

5

THE SECRET WAR

BASED OUT OF Fort Bragg, Company E of the 7th Special Forces Group became Roy's new home. There he continued honing his skills as an operations and intelligence sergeant, destined for a foreign assignment either to a South American country, because of his fluency in Spanish, to teach counterinsurgency tactics, techniques, and procedures to allied government troops—or back to Vietnam.

The war he'd deployed to two years earlier had steadily escalated, with LBJ's most recent surge in troops bringing American forces in Vietnam to more than 400,000. By late 1967, close to half a million Americans and 250,000 South Vietnamese Army of the Republic of Vietnam soldiers were fighting an estimated 400,000 North Vietnamese Army and Vietcong soldiers in a country roughly the size of the state of New Mexico. It was a war of attrition, a bloodbath in which American and ARVN forces had killed roughly 180,000 NVA/VC, and the NVA/VC had killed 16,250 American and 24,600 ARVN soldiers. These numbers did not include civilian deaths on either side.

The Americans and South Vietnamese were confident the North Vietnamese could not sustain such losses indefinitely. The key to victory would continue to be a combination of devastating airpower—tactical bombers and massive B-52 strategic bombers that targeted industrial sites in the north and enemy positions in the south—and air mobility, the use of helicopters for troop movements, resupply, medical evacuation, and tactical air support for ground troops. Massive search-and-destroy operations had become the most effective ground strategy to locate and wipe out the enemy in their jungle redoubts.

Assault helicopter companies flew combat assaults, inserting hundreds of troops into an objective area. Accompanied by heavily armed helicopter gunships, these Hueys, or "slicks," flew in formation to a landing zone (LZ), where they briefly touched down, one after the next, in a line or a staggered trail (depending on the LZ) and just one or two rotor-disc (blade length) distances apart. Six soldiers would spill out of each, yielding platoons or entire companies of men in jungle clearings, on roads, mountain ridges, or the berm-like dikes that surrounded rice paddies.

A wave of landings could systematically surround a village, section of jungle, valley, or other suspected enemy stronghold. Assaults could be small in scale—a couple of platoons pushing through a village. Or they could be much larger, perhaps employing a horseshoe-assault strategy with some troops positioned as blocking forces on the sides and others configured at the open end of the horseshoe, pushing forward. If Charlie was there, kill him, capture him, or drive him toward the blocking forces that would do the same. When the job was done, the Americans and their ARVN counterparts would search the bodies and gear for intelligence, blindfold any captured enemy, bind their hands and feet for security, call the helicopters back in, and fly back to their staging area or base camp, where prisoner interrogations would take place. Dead enemy bodies—not territory gained or held—were the measure of success.

Corpse by corpse, the Americans were winning the battles and destroying enemy weapons, food, medical, and ammunitions caches in the process. But with its population of over 16 million, the north was prepared to replace its casualties for as long as it took to create a unified, communist Vietnam. Ho Chi Minh—the aged, sickly, yet steadfastly popular revolutionary leader and president of North Vietnam, remained brazenly confident. "You will kill ten of us, we will kill one of you," he said in response to American victories on the battlefield, "but in the end, you will tire of it first."

It was difficult to judge whether or not the North Vietnamese people were tiring of the killing. Nearly 200,000 of their own people had been lost, but North Vietnam had no freedom of speech or press; all distributed information was censored. U.S. Psychological Operations dropped millions of leaflets over the north, informing the populace of the massive defeats and body counts in the south, telling them that their Uncle Ho was sending them to slaughter. Still, voluntarily or not, they came, as Ho promised they would.

A key American strategy to bringing eventual peace to the south was to deny the North Vietnamese access to the "battlefield" by closing off enemy ingress at the borders. By the time Roy earned his green beret, the combined branches of the American military working with their ARVN allies had effectively limited the communists' ability to send war matériel and replacement troops into South Vietnam via both the demarcation line between north and south (the 17th parallel) and the entire eastern coastline of the South China Sea, which wraps around the southern tip of South Vietnam and into the Gulf of Thailand.

The western border of South Vietnam, on the other hand, was abutted by the countries of Laos and Cambodia, whose representatives had signed legal declarations of neutrality during the 1954 Geneva Peace Conference, which prohibited them from joining any foreign military alliance. Nor could they allow the operations or basing of foreign military forces to occur on their territories. Representatives from the Associated State of Vietnam (the predecessor of the Republic of Vietnam, or South Vietnam), the People's Republic of China, the Soviet Union, France, Great Britain, and the United States had also signed the document, acknowledging that their countries would adhere to and respect the stated rules.

But, like water from a leaking dam, tons of communist war matériel and thousands of troops continued to flow steadily from North Vietnam, through sections of Laos and Cambodia and into the south—a direct violation of the aforementioned declarations.

This communication and supply route was known by the United States as the Ho Chi Minh Trail, and by the north as the Truong Son Strategic Supply Route. The word *trail* had become a misnomer by 1967, since it had evolved from a centuries-old smugglers' pathway, hacked out of the jungle and only wide enough for a person pushing a bike or a small cart, to thousands of miles of interconnected footpaths, waterways, and in places, multilane roads. The route was built, camouflaged, repaired, and maintained by Group 559, a transportation and logistical unit of NVA men, women, and children, whose sole purpose was to keep it passable.

The trail began in North Vietnam and entered directly into Laos, allowing the enemy to bypass American and South Vietnamese defenses at the line of demarcation. It then continued southward for more than a thousand miles: a vast and geographically treacherous journey through steep mountains, jungle, and swamps inhabited by tigers, poisonous insects, snakes, and malaria-carrying mosquitoes. At various points along the way, branches ran east as infiltration routes into South Vietnam.

The trail advanced roughly two hundred to three hundred miles south through Laos before entering Cambodia, where it paralleled the eastern border for another seven hundred miles all the way down to the Gulf of Thailand and the Cambodian seaport of Sihanoukville. Communist troops used this pipeline to stage and launch offensive operations into South Vietnam, then retreat and regroup inside the Laotian or Cambodian jungle sanctuaries that U.S. air and ground forces were not permitted to enter.

Cambodia's leader, Prince Norodom Sihanouk, publicly and adamantly denied that North Vietnam was using his country militarily. Intelligence gathered by the United States, however, suggested that Sihanouk both knew of and was profiting from the arrangement, selling rice by the ton to the North Vietnamese, who rationed out 700 grams (three cups) per day to trail builders, porters, and troops in transit to the battlefields of the south. The general wartime allotment per person per day in their home villages in North Vietnam was around 450 grams (two cups), making it a lucrative black market business.

Sihanouk also permitted communist ships from both China and the Soviet Union to dock at the Sihanoukville seaport and off-load into warehouses. At night, covered Russian trucks—their headlights off—departed the warehouses and headed north. This suspected northbound transportation system for supplies was referred to by U.S. intelligence as the Sihanouk Trail, or Sihanouk Road, which merged into the Ho Chi Minh Trail.

JUST AS the North Vietnamese and Prince Sihanouk staunchly denied the existence of communist bases and supply lines within Cambodia, so too did President Johnson deny the presence of U.S. troops in that country. "We are in Vietnam to fulfill a solemn promise," he said regularly during television and radio addresses. "We are NOT in Cambodia."

Covertly, however, LBJ had begun to authorize small-scale reconnaissance missions into Cambodia as early as April 1967, albeit with a
laundry list of restrictions. These highly classified operations were conducted under the guise of the Military Assistance Command Vietnam,
Studies and Observations Group (MACV-SOG), whose mission on
paper was to "study and observe" U.S. military operations. The name
deliberately evoked a think tank of analysts or statisticians holed up in a
reinforced Saigon basement and removed from the action.

In fact, very few high-ranking officers in the U.S. military and intelligence communities were even aware of the existence of SOG, the
Studies and Observations Group, and fewer still were privy to its ultra-
secret, anticommunist, counterinsurgency mission. In 1967, the commander of SOG was Colonel Jack Singlaub, a hard-charging Special
Operations veteran who had conducted covert ops behind enemy lines
in both World War II and Korea. As chief of SOG, Singlaub reported
directly to General Ray Peers—the special assistant for counterinsurgency and special activities as well as the conduit to the Joint Chiefs
of Staff at the Pentagon. "General Westmoreland had the authority to
veto our operations," says Singlaub, "but we had to get approval from
the White House and the Commander in Chief Pacific Command Ad-
miral U. S. Grant Sharp. It was a very short list of people; we were well
shielded. I don't believe I was ever asked to be interviewed by a reporter
while I was in Saigon. Who wants to interview the *Studies* guy?"

For the first two-plus years of its existence SOG had focused on
Laos and North Vietnam, but when LBJ finally authorized cross-border
reconnaissance (recon) teams to operate deep in Cambodia, "the intelligence was alarming," Singlaub says. "The number of communist
troops, NVA and VC, the bases, and hospitals, R & R centers, it was
alarming, and it was frustrating. Especially at first, before we could take
the fight to the enemy."

Westmoreland and his conventional U.S. and ARVN forces, both air and ground, were champing at the bit to go after Charlie in his Cambodian lair. But without the green light to cross over the border en masse, the best they could do was stretch their leashes across the rarely marked and always rugged boundary. The NVA/VC became infamous for hit-and-run-for-sanctuary tactics. But what about the grunt whose buddy just got shot through the neck? Does he stop chasing his ambusher at the border or does he push the limits for payback?

Skirmishes between U.S. and ARVN troops and communists retreating over the border were inevitable, and when Cambodians were caught in the cross fire, Prince Sihanouk was quick to denounce U.S. and South Vietnamese "acts of aggression." He made his stance clear as far back as May 3, 1965, by closing the U.S. Embassy in Phnom Penh, Cambodia, thus ending diplomatic relations with the United States. In a public radio broadcast, Sihanouk explained that this was retaliation "for an April 28 bombing-strafing attack by four South Vietnamese planes against two Cambodian border villages in which one person had been killed and three wounded," reported *Newsweek* on May 5. "Recalling his previous warnings that Cambodia would sever diplomatic ties with Washington if another Cambodian were killed in a Vietnam border incident, [Sihanouk said] 'Our warnings were not heeded.'"

There was speculation that Sihanouk's motivation for closing the embassy wasn't retribution, but instead was a means to deny the Americans a way station for spies—a diplomatic perch from which to watch over the prince as he provided for and plotted with the Soviets, Chinese, and North Vietnamese. The Johnson administration, Joint Chiefs of Staff, and CIA were all but certain that the communists had his ear while their guerrillas and soldiers had his jungle, his rice, his roads, his sanctuary.

"Once it was done, and the last of the U.S. Embassy personnel had packed their bags and left, taking their radio transmitters and other espionage equipment with them," Sihanouk wrote in his memoir, published seven years later in 1972. "I felt as if an enormous weight had rolled off my shoulders."

While the politicians bantered back and forth and pointed their fingers, and journalists clamored for the next big story on the war, never once was the Studies and Observation Group outed by its members, who stealthily roamed around enemy encampments, performed their reconnaissance duties, rescued downed pilots, raided prisoner-of-war (POW) camps, and killed quite a few North Vietnamese and VC along the way. There were no newspaper headlines, television special reports, books, memoirs, or magazine articles published in the weeks, months, even years after the war ended that exposed what SOG was about. How small teams of two or three American Special Operations warriors—predominantly Green Berets, but also Navy SEALs, Force Recon Marines, and Army Rangers—and three or four indigenous mercenaries would sneak over the border to harass the enemy, reconnoiter his sanctuaries, and provide accurate intelligence regarding his bases, weapons, numbers, and plans. The cloak of secrecy was so effective that nearly all the men recruited or assigned to SOG had never heard of it or its mission beforehand. On rare occasions, a SOG warrior leaked its existence—but only to exceptional fellow warriors, whom he respected and felt would fit in.

IN THE last week of October 1967, twenty-one-year-old Special Forces Communications Specialist 4 Brian O'Connor stood before "the big map" inside the assignment office at 5th Special Forces Group headquarters, Nha Trang, Vietnam. Bristling from the wall-size rendition of South Vietnam were eighty-four pushpins bearing different-colored flags to represent the Special Forces A-team and B-team camps and bases dotting the countryside. Fifth Group headquarters, the C-team, was on the central east coast with a big "you are here" arrow pointing at it.

A sergeant major explained to O'Connor how each flag had a dash, a dot, or an X—a symbol of some sort—penciled on it, representing the personnel needs of that particular team or detachment: weapons specialist, medic, operations and intelligence, engineer. If there had been a symbol for commo, O'Connor's MOS, on the company HQ flag, he could have stayed right there at headquarters in Nha Trang, where Vietnamese girls at the mini-PX shop around the corner sold ice-cream cones for ten cents apiece. Instead, he requested to go to the team called B-56.

The sergeant major hesitated and then pointed to the flag numbered "61" northeast of Saigon. "B-56 is at Ho Ngoc Tao," he told O'Connor. "Do you know anybody there?"

As a kid, O'Connor had learned Morse code in Boy Scouts, and along with his father—who worked on top secret radio and electronics development projects during World War II—built several radios out of bits and pieces they found around the house: cardboard tubes, wires, and the key ingredient, a galena crystal (a piece of rock used as a semiconductor to recover audio from radio frequency waves). He'd even set up an illegal FM radio station one summer with some buddies, prompting the legitimate radio stations to contact the Feds, who quickly shut it down.

Years later at a field exercise in Fort Bragg—when O'Connor was deep in his advanced MOS training—this passion for radio and communication became evident to the thirty-year-old E-6 staff sergeant who sat shoulder to shoulder with him for several days in a two-man commo rig. O'Connor was drawn to this older staff sergeant, who had just returned from Vietnam and told of his days on an A-team, when he'd set up the communications at a B-detachment and started running missions that seemed straight from the pages of Robin Moore's bestselling novel *The Green Berets*. The sergeant took O'Connor under his wing and taught him a few things about communications in war. "Like a wide-eyed kid listening to an uncle's tales," says O'Connor, "I got to hear story after story about B-56 and something called SOG."

So when the sergeant major at Nha Trang asked him if he knew anybody from B-56, O'Connor gave the name of his E-6 staff sergeant friend.

"You're sure about B-56?"

"I know what I'm getting into," O'Connor told him. "I have experience with their commo rigs, and it looks like they're shorthanded."

Three days later, on Halloween morning 1967, O'Connor joined eight other Green Berets in an Air Force C-7 Caribou as they leap-frogged from A-camp to A-camp across Vietnam, dropping Special Forces soldiers at some bases, picking them up at others, turning what would have been a two-hour flight into most of the day. Eventually, he transferred to the smaller aircraft that would be needed to get onto the short dirt airstrip adjacent to the American Special Forces camp at Loc Ninh, in Binh Long Province, South Vietnam—a few miles from the Cambodian border.

For the previous two days, entire companies of VC had attempted human-wave attacks against Loc Ninh. Now there was either a break in the battle or it was over, and engineers had bulldozed hundreds of enemy bodies off the runway. O'Connor's aircraft was cleared to land.

It was O'Connor's first look at the "real war": a fast-and-hot landing and almost immediate takeoff, the surrounding jungle filled with smoke, fires, bodies, and the enemy. The Green Berets at Loc Ninh—along with the camp's three companies of CIDG soldiers, an artillery battery, and air support—had fought off the attack from roughly 3,000 to 3,500 NVA and Vietcong. According to the after-action report, "Approximately 9 NVA battalions were believed to have participated in the Loc Ninh Attack. . . . These units were: 3 Battalions from 273d Regiment; 1–2 Battalions of 165th Regiment; plus a mortar and anti-aircraft Battalion. Each battalion, except for heavy weapons battalion, is believed to have had approx 300–400." The enemy retreated back across the Cambodian border, leaving behind 850 of their own confirmed dead. Forty-six Americans and fewer than 100 ARVN were killed.

EVEN AS U.S. generals looked to the west, knowing full well that this large-scale attack, as well as another against the Special Forces camp at Song Be, had originated from Cambodian soil, Sihanouk continued to staunchly deny any communist military presence within his borders. So confident was he in the communists' ability to camouflage their movements and bases, he challenged foreign media to prove the communist presence.

Foreign journalists in Cambodia had been closely monitored by Sihanouk's ministry of information and escorted throughout the country. They had not been free to roam. The ministry of information, however, was overwhelmed in early November 1967, when First Lady Jacqueline Kennedy arrived in Cambodia to fulfill a childhood dream to visit the ruins at Angkor Wat. From the moment she stepped off the plane onto a plush red carpet covered with jasmine blossoms, throngs of reporters and photographers from around the world were there to document her every move.

During her weeklong visit, three American journalists slipped away from the media circus, hired a driver, and headed out of the capital of Phnom Penh, following directions from an American intelligence officer in Saigon who had received the information from one of SOG's recently authorized cross-border recon teams. After a few hours on roads cut through the jungle, they pulled over at a dirt road barricaded by a bamboo gate just four miles west of South Vietnam, in a border area known as the Fishhook.

The reports of what they found hit the papers the following week and were then summarized in *Time* magazine's November 24 issue.

"[T]hree American newsmen—the UPI's Ray Herndon, the AP's Horst Faas and George McArthur—took Cambodian Prince Norodom Sihanouk up on his offer to prove, if they could, that the North Vietnamese and Vietcong were using Cambodia as a sanctuary. Armed with specific map coordinates from U.S. intelligence in Saigon, they uncovered a headquarters complex only nine miles from the South Vietnamese town of Loc Ninh, which the Communists unsuccessfully attacked three weeks ago; the complex included a well-stocked dispensary, officers' quarters, storage facilities and huts for some 500 men. Leading towards the Vietnamese border was a road paved with six-inch-diameter logs for trucks, and truck tracks were everywhere."

McArthur and Faas reported in their own AP story that "Cambodia's ruling prince reportedly regards the discovery . . . as a fabrication and part of a campaign against him by the U.S. press. We found the Vietcong camp, very recently used, on the border opposite War Zone C. It had been used for several months and was most probably a staging area for the Loc Ninh battle."

CAMBODIA WAS a "PROBLEM." So stated in the first line of the Special National Intelligence Estimate Report dossier delivered to President Johnson and his cabinet on December 14, 1967. The top secret report, prepared by the CIA, the intelligence organizations of the Departments of Defense and State, and the National Security Agency (NSA), "estimated the extent and significance of Vietnamese Communist use of Cambodian territory in support of the Communist war effort in South Vietnam."

According to the report, "During the past year, increasing Allied pressure on the Communists' military structure in South Vietnam [including combat assaults, search-and-destroy missions, defoliation efforts, and tactical bombing of enemy positions] has caused them to depend more heavily on the use of border areas. They use Cambodian territory as a sanctuary to evade Allied Forces, as a refuge for rest, training, medical care, and . . . as a route for the infiltration of personnel and military supplies from North Vietnam."

The report went on to detail specific examples and locations of the communist tactical sanctuary, troop movements, infiltration routes, supply routes, foodstuff, types of ammunition and weapons being stockpiled or moved along the Ho Chi Minh Trail, as well as chemical agents, known and mapped base areas, and the identification of specific NVA or VC units. In one instance, during a search-and-destroy mission into War Zone C (a region near the Cambodian border where Vietcong activity was exceptionally strong), "elements of the Central Office for South Vietnam (COSVN) took refuge in adjacent Cambodian territory." COSVN—the U.S. acronym for the Communist North Vietnamese political and military headquarters—was supposedly located somewhere deep within South Vietnam, but many, including General Westmoreland, believed it to be hidden within Cambodia. Pinpointing the location of COSVN became the American forces' highest priority.

The report concluded: "If the Communists continue their present strategy, the importance of Cambodia to their war effort will probably grow in 1968, particularly as a sanctuary and as a source of rice. Denial of Cambodian sanctuary would probably not cause the Communist war effort to collapse in the neighboring areas of South Vietnam, but would make it much harder for the Communists to conduct effective military operations in these areas."

Behind each word, sentence, and succinctly crafted paragraph of this and other classified reports was the gritty, often bloody story of the warriors who risked everything to obtain the intelligence the reports contained. These men in the murky shadows of the secret war didn't expect recognition. They didn't expect Secretary of State Dean Rusk, Secretary of Defense Robert McNamara, or President Johnson to consider the source. They were content to debrief after a mission and have a beer. By the time they buried their dead, the three- to four-page after-action reports of their operations were buried as well, the teletyped copies from Saigon to Washington sealed in an underground vault at the Pentagon. The originals—filed alphanumerically, with a single digit preceded by a letter for Laos and two digits preceded by a letter for Cambodia—were stored in vaults marked "top secret" and "BURN" inside the S-2 (Intelligence) bunkers at SOG bases scattered throughout South Vietnam.

The reports archived at Camp Ho Ngoc Tao recorded the missions of Project Sigma, Detachment B-56, the least-documented MACV-SOG "Special Projects" detachment operating "over the fence" in Cambodia—code-named Daniel Boone—during this period of the war. The Sigma/B-56 camp would relocate from Ho Ngoc Tao to Ban Me Thuot, two hundred miles northeast of Saigon, in February of 1969. During the old camp's breakdown, the vault—a virtual treasure chest of reports and photographs documenting many of the war's most covert missions—would remain at Ho Ngoc Tao, with a handful of guards and a couple of radiomen. It would sit in the back corner of the communications bunker to await transport to the new base.

Inside that vault, an after-action report dated May 2, 1968, outlined a daring "heavy team"—twelve men, double the standard recon team size—mission into the Fishhook. The mission objective was to capture a high-value target, an NVA officer, off the Ho Chi Minh Trail deep in the Daniel Boone area of operations. But there was another objective—a "capture" of another kind—that never made the ink on any official documents. The detachment commander had conveyed this off-the-books objective verbally and only to the team's leader and the platoon leader of the assault helicopter company that would fly the mission. These two men then filtered the verbal objective into their ranks on a need-to-know basis.

This proposed "capture" was so audacious and politically valuable that, if successful, it could represent ironclad evidence that there was a North Vietnamese military presence in Cambodia, thus potentially changing the course of the war. It was an objective that would—like one of the players in the impending events—become legend.

FOUR MONTHS and a week before that mission would launch, far from the hot and humid jungles of Vietnam, the Kingdom of Cambodia, and the politics of Washington, DC, it was Christmas '67 in El Campo, Texas. Staff Sergeant Benavidez didn't yet know he would be going back to Vietnam for a second tour. He reveled in the warmth of the house he'd grown up in, surrounded by an extended family that now included his nieces and nephews, breathing in the nostalgic aromas of his Mexican American youth: corn and tamales, turkey and stuffing. Lala, too, soaked in every second of home and family, looking on as Denise was doted on by relative after relative. These were the times that made her realize how much she missed El Campo, and how much she loved—and was proud of—her husband. Just look how far he'd come! Roy, in uniform, was the centerpiece of the celebration.

Grandfather Salvador had recently passed away, and Roy felt his spirit as he sat in the living room and told stories of the Benavidez family. He had worn his uniform not to show off, but because he remembered the message a man in uniform had conveyed to him as a boy, the respect and the dreams the uniformed paratroopers had inspired in him. It had been a gift, and what better time than Christmas to pass that gift on.

The children wanted to hold and wear his green beret, which he allowed. The younger boys asked what the men wanted to know: Had Uncle Roy killed anybody in the war? He told them simply that, yes, he had because he had performed his duty. Then he explained what the green beret stood for, in terms the young might grasp: explained how they fought when they had to, how they helped good people more than they fought bad people. And, Roy told them, there *are* bad people in the world. He firmly believed the NVA and Vietcong were bad—evil, in fact. The image of the three dead Vietnamese children was bored so deeply in his mind that he still had to shake his head to make the vision go away.

"But let me tell you about your Great-grandfather Salvador when he was a vaquero . . ." Roy ended the story of the narrow mountain pathway with his grandfather's words: "If someone needs help, you help them."

EIGHTY MILES northeast of El Campo, in a neighborhood of small wood-framed houses in Jacinto City—a post–World War II steel mill town near Houston—Cecil and Maxine McKibben were celebrating the holiday as well, though it wasn't the same without their son, Larry.

When the "Bob Hope Christmas Special" aired, they, along with their sixteen-year-old daughter, Debbie, were glued to the television set. Warrant Officer Larry McKibben was stationed at one of the Vietnam bases where Hope's USO troupe had performed, and they thought there was a sliver of a chance they'd catch a glimpse of Larry in the crowd.

When Hope called out "Merry Christmas, men!" the camera panned across the audience, and the men shouted back a resounding "Merry Christmas, Bob!"

"Did you see him? Did you see him?!" Debbie asked her parents, who shook their heads. The crowd had gone by too fast, and there was no pause, rewind, or replay button to hit. In fact, there was barely reception in Jacinto City during the winter storms.

Twenty-year-old Larry had been in Vietnam for six months and ten days of his one-year tour and Debbie was counting every single day: 193 down and 172 to go. She remembered the evening he'd informed them at the dinner table of his plan to join the Army and become a helicopter pilot. He'd barely gotten out the words *helicopter pilot* before Debbie ran into her room, slammed the door, and started to cry. She associated helicopter pilots with Vietnam, and Vietnam was the place where young men went to die.

Following Debbie to her room, Larry put his arm around her, and as calm and firm as a big brother could be, he smiled, squeezed her tight, and said, "I'm going to go fight communism there so you don't have to face it here. I'm not afraid—I want to go."

Larry and his best friend, Frank McAvoy, had it all figured out. They'd become pilots, go and fight for their country as Larry's father, Cecil, had in World War II, and this would give them the salt—the seasoning—they knew they needed to become men. They'd return from the war, each would find the perfect gal to marry, and they would move their families to Alaska and start a business: McAvoy and McKibben Bush Pilots.

That was the plan: to live a life of adventure, happily ever after.

6

ANATOMY OF A MISSION

FIFTEEN MILES EAST of Saigon, First Lieutenant Alan "Big Al" Yurman, from Kearny, New Jersey, found himself in the audience at Camp
Martin Cox, aka Camp Bearcat. He'd scored a coveted seat only a few
yards from Bob Hope, who strolled around the stage during his USO
show with his signature golf club, cracking jokes for the troops, a sea of
Army green that pushed right up to the cameramen and military police
surrounding the platform.

Hope and his writers, whose research gave every show a personal
touch, had discovered that while the VC were known to harass bases
with rockets or mortars during or just after a USO performance, Camp
Bearcat had never been attacked. The writers were also aware that a
rash of venereal disease had swept through the 9th Infantry Division,
prompting the base commander to place local villages off-limits.

"Merry Christmas, men, Merry Christmas," said Hope. "We're here
with the 9th Infantry Division at Camp Martin Cox. This place has

never been attacked. Until *today*. The Cong would like to attack this place, but they can't. Everything is off-limits here." The crowd roared. "The 9th Infantry Division is known as the Old Reliables. Funny, I thought that was mouthwash and penicillin!"

Yurman joined the throngs standing in their seats, snapping photos. He blew through half a role of film when actress Raquel Welch strolled onstage in white knee-high boots and a blue miniskirt, chatted with Hope, and then danced when the band started up. Some soldiers stared in silence with frozen grins, others whistled and hollered. All were able to forget for a brief period of time that they were in Vietnam.

But after Hope had delivered his final punch line, and the crowd had laughed their last laugh, Yurman was still at Bearcat, a new platoon leader at the 240th Assault Helicopter Company (1st Aviation Brigade, 12th Combat Aviation Group, 214th Combat Aviation Battalion), still sweating in the Southeast Asian heat. When he'd arrived in Vietnam a month earlier, a sergeant from the 240th had picked him up at the 90th Replacement Battalion at Long Binh and delivered him to his quarters at Bearcat: a tent with a pallet for a doorstep. "This is a good company you're joining," the sergeant told him. "We've been here since April and had a lot of missions and no casualties or accidents. A couple of ships got shot up, but nothing of any consequence." *Well, that's great,* thought Yurman.

Aside from its stellar luck, the 240th was structured just like the other assault helicopter companies operating in Vietnam. It consisted of four platoons. Two platoons were made up of five transport Bell UH-1H (Huey) helicopters each, known as "slicks," one of which directed the insertion slicks during missions and was called the command-and-control (C&C) slick. Sometimes the company commander would act as C&C; other times, platoon leaders like Yurman would. Every slick had an aircraft commander—the primary pilot—in the left front seat and a copilot in the right. A crew chief, in addition to being responsible for maintenance of the helicopter, also manned the door gun behind the aircraft commander on the left side of the aircraft, while a second door gunner manned the machine gun on the right. The four-man crew was often joined by an infantry or Special Forces "bellyman," whose job on board was to act as a medic, to help with loading during extractions, and in many cases to defend the aircraft with a personal weapon.

A third platoon had heavily armed Bell UH-IC gunships—known sometimes as "hogs"—with different configurations of pilot-fired rockets, grenade launchers, and miniguns, as well as two M60 machine guns manned by side door gunners. The gunships featured the same crew setup as slicks, but their focus was firepower, not troop transport, so they never flew with a bellyman.

The fourth platoon was the maintenance platoon, responsible, along with the crew chief of each helicopter, for keeping the aircraft in the air.

The assault helicopter companies were versatile units vital to the U.S. military's air mobility strategy. Morale was particularly high in the 240th; as a captain from Oklahoma showed Yurman around, almost everybody he met told him that he could not have been placed with a better company or a better company commander.

"We're called the Greyhounds," the captain informed Yurman when Yurman commented that the nose art on all the slicks looked like the greyhound logos on buses in the United States. "It doesn't *look* like it, it's the *same*. You can thank Major Hoffman for that."

Major Glen Hoffman, the first in-country commander of the 240th, had brought the company over by ship nine months earlier in March 1967. Tasked with providing a name for the company's helicopters, he and his junior officers settled on Greyhounds for the slicks, tweaking the bus company's motto to make it their own: "Go Greyhound and leave the flying to us." Playing on the company's dog theme, the gunships of the third platoon were named Mad Dogs (motto: "Death on call, VC for lunch bunch"), while the maintenance platoon (fourth platoon) got the apt title of Kennel Keepers.

In an effort to build morale, Hoffman had taken a long shot and sent a letter to the CEO of the Greyhound bus company explaining why they'd chosen the name Greyhounds, "based on the idea of speed and dependability and—in line with the famous Greyhound buses—safety and service to our passengers." The letter closed with a request: "We would be proud to have Greyhound sponsor our company."

At a time when American casualty counts and body bags were daily media fodder, and antiwar demonstrations and sentiment were steadily increasing stateside, Hoffman had not anticipated even a response from the multimillion-dollar company. To sponsor a helicopter company in Vietnam could be construed as supporting the war, and that was a big public relations risk. When Hoffman received fifty seventeen-inch Greyhound logos as part of a care package, he was stunned. Not only did Greyhound sponsor the company, its employees adopted the 240th, sending along cookies, cards, and words of encouragement for the men. Soon the Greyhound logo was plastered on the nose and sides of all the 240th's H-model Hueys, the newest, fastest, and most powerful slicks operating in Vietnam. "We're one of a few companies flying these babies," the captain told Yurman. "Everyone wants to work with us."

At twenty-five, Yurman was an old man compared to the average warrant officer piloting the slicks in his platoon; most were nineteen or twenty, old enough to be drafted, but, like the majority of the troops in Vietnam, not old enough to legally buy a beer or to vote back home.

"That kid old enough to drive?" Yurman asked the captain about one pilot they saw while walking the flight line, where the 2nd Platoon slicks were parked in a row of revetments.

"I don't know if he can drive a car," the captain said, "but he sure can fly the hell out of a helicopter. Let me introduce you."

★

LARRY MCKIBBEN had in fact learned to fly before he'd learned to drive. He had been with the 240th Assault Helicopter Company (AHC) for only a little over a month—transferred into the Greyhounds from the 162nd AHC, the Vultures, where he'd spent the first four months of his tour—and already he was known as one of the coolest, calmest, and most technically proficient pilots in the company.

As a thirteen-year-old in his hometown of Jacinto City, McKibben had rebuilt an old single-prop with his father, the area scoutmaster, for an Eagle Scout project. Eventually he flew his first solo flight, earning his pilot's license when he was just sixteen.

Every couple of weeks since the beginning of his tour, he had sent home an audiotape to his parents and sister, narrating the war to them in his relaxed Texas drawl.

"Got your letter the other day," McKibben said in his first tape, when he was based at Phuoc Vinh with the Vultures. "Ya'll had said you heard an air base got mortared and rocketed, and wondered if it was anywhere nearby.

"Well, it *was* pretty near; I would say about twenty feet. It knocked me out of bed. I just grabbed my steel pot [helmet] and my flak jacket, got out the back door, and crawled in our bunker. I wasn't hurt, just shook up a little bit, I guess, so don't worry.

"Anyway, if ya'll hear any loud booms, well, we have a couple artillery batteries here and they're always firing. When I got here, I asked, 'If we *do* get mortared, how in the heck can I tell the difference from that artillery going off and mortar rounds coming in?' They said, 'Don't worry about it. You'll *know*.' And you know what? I *knew*. There wasn't any doubt in my mind."

It had long been known that these ten-foot-long rockets, with a range of twelve to twenty miles or more, had been supplied to the North

Vietnamese by the Chinese and were knockoffs of the Soviet Katyusha rockets. With nineteen-kilo high-explosive fragmentation warheads, they were highly successful as both explosive devices and psychological weapons, and their range allowed them to be fired from over the border in Cambodia or trucked on mobile launchpads, giving reach to a wide range of targets within South Vietnam.

Thus far, U.S. intelligence agents had been unable to learn exactly how the rockets were getting into the hands of the North Vietnamese, where the NVA stored them, how many were stockpiled, and, most important, how to go about destroying them. The most likely point of entry was the port of Sihanoukville, Cambodia. CIA agents and informants in Shanghai had reported hundreds of rockets being loaded onto freighters from neutral countries such as Liberia and Panama; when some of these freighters reached Sihanoukville, however, only agricultural machinery and products were off-loaded. Either the rockets were cleverly concealed within the cargo, or the agents were missing something.

Preceding the November 1967 elections in Vietnam, Army intelligence major James Reid briefed Henry Cabot Lodge Jr., former U.S. ambassador to South Vietnam, who had returned to oversee the election. Reid, a linguist who spoke French fluently, identified these rockets as a significant security threat to both the coming elections and to American forces, and suggested using the deeply rooted French society, including French plantation owners who owned large tracts of land along the Cambodian border, to help keep watch in their regions and perhaps provide intelligence on the rockets. Also in attendance, General Westmoreland was intrigued enough to form a task force—named Operation Vesuvius by Reid. Westmoreland gave the major three months to solve the puzzle.

Upholding his oath of secrecy, Reid would not discuss Operation Vesuvius, nor his findings, for decades. More than thirty years later, he finally told retired foreign correspondent and *New York Times* managing editor Seymour Topping details of his account, which were included in Topping's memoir, *On the Front Lines of the Cold War*. Topping verified that Operation Vesuvius was the brainchild of Reid and described Reid's discovery of how hundreds of these rockets were smuggled into South Vietnam by the freighters belonging to neutral countries. While en route to Sihanoukville, the captains would anchor offshore in the night, wait for U.S. Navy patrol boats to pass, then ferry the missiles ashore via smaller boats and man-to-man lines into the surf.

This bold technique was, according to Reid, witnessed by a French plantation owner who also watched the rockets being loaded onto trucks that were driven through the plantation roads into Cambodia. CIA agents and informants within the Cambodian populace were tasked with gathering intelligence as to where these rockets ended up. SOG recon teams that had already identified numerous bases within Cambodia soon joined the effort.

Of course, these sites could not be bombed or attacked because Cambodia was neutral territory. "Isn't this a political problem?" Reid posed the question when he briefed Westmoreland on his findings. "If they're [the rockets] going into Cambodia, isn't there something our diplomats should arrange with Cambodia?"

Westmoreland's response was "I will get in touch with Washington."

McKibben's audiotape letter did not mention that in one attack that lasted about fifteen minutes, the Vietcong fired eighty rounds of 122 mm rockets and seventy-two rounds of 82 mm mortars at his base in Phuoc Vinh, killing twelve Americans and injuring sixty-eight.

Instead, he talked to his family about the high-quality stereo he'd bought at the base PX and set up on a shelf by his cot. One afternoon he flipped on the recorder to tell them that some nurses were flying over from Saigon for a party in their officers club that night. "I might even meet a girl over here," he said. "How about that?" Another time he recorded the laughter and banter going on in his tent and had his roommates introduce themselves. In Jacinto City, Cecil and Maxine McKibben listened to the tape with a smile—until they heard a loud artillery *BOOM!* Their smiles vanished, and they just stared at each other. Their boy Larry was in the middle of the most dangerous place in the world, flying a bullet magnet 140 hours a month over hostile, enemy-occupied territory.

During a month-long search-and-destroy mission in support of the 101st Airborne Division in the mountains of Binh Thuan called Operation Klamath Falls, McKibben logged 152 hours of flying for the 240th. Holding a hover at thirty-five hundred feet was exhausting work. One day he flew fourteen hours, and "the flight surgeon got real mad they had me fly that much," he said in a tape. "They set a limit—not more than a hundred forty hours in any thirty-day period."

The 240th suffered its first casualties in Operation Klamath Falls when a slick's transmission froze up and the helicopter dropped from the sky, killing First Lieutenant Haron Brown, Warrant Officer William Clawson, Specialist 5 Matthew Amaral, and Specialist 4 Ronny Kindred. It was December 14, 1967—a date Al Yurman would remember forever because it was also his first mission. His initiation into the war was watching Brown's slick crash and burn on the side of a mountain pass.

The men killed weren't in his platoon, so Yurman didn't personally know them, but he couldn't stop thinking about how the sergeant had told him that the 240th hadn't had *any* casualties and *any* accidents. He wished he hadn't heard those words—it was as if they had somehow jinxed the company. *Well, here we go,* he thought. *Welcome to Nam.*

★

THE SOG recon men working the Daniel Boone mission were not privy to higher-level strategic planning such as Operation Vesuvius. They were, however, dismayed that they were gathering so much evidence (troops, weapons—including rocket caches—and matériel) and yet the conventional U.S. military was forbidden to cross the Cambodian border and destroy the enemy and its weapons.

In the second week of January 1968, under tight security measures, Major Reid joined a team that included fellow intelligence officer Lieutenant Colonel William White, the chief of Army operations Lieutenant General William De Pugh, and veteran State Department negotiator Philip Habib onboard two T-39 jets. The flight took them from Saigon to New Delhi, where they briefed Chester Bowles, U.S. ambassador to India, on the violations of the Cambodian border by the Chinese-backed North Vietnamese, and the proposed mission that had evolved from Reid's Vesuvius operation.

From there, Ambassador Bowles flew to Phnom Penh, Cambodia. Once a diplomatic friend to Sihanouk—who had refused to meet with the United States for almost three years—Bowles was able to convince him of the importance of a face-to-face, closed-door meeting, during which he presented the first Vesuvius package. This package was filled with transcripts of radio intercepts and interrogations of captured VC, photos of the rockets and of the carnage—the aftermath of the attacks on South Vietnam—and, most important, maps showing where the enemy bases and rockets were located and how they were being trucked from Cambodia to launch sites in South Vietnam or launched directly from Cambodia.

"Sihanouk was cornered," says Reid. " 'Listen,' he said, 'you've been skipping over into [Cambodia] although international regulations prevent it, going after ground troops from the Vietcong after their hit-and-run operations. You would go across, they would go across. But I had no idea that they were using missiles.' He was genuinely astounded, or played it off that he was. So an agreement was made as follows. He said, 'If you let me know [in advance] information that you have about the location of these missiles, I will put out the word through my staff to the local villages to be out of the area pretending that they've got a festival or some agricultural event. And at two or two thirty, during the day, not in the evening when there's a danger of error, your plane or planes will come over and bomb these installations.' That was the agreement that was made."

Sihanouk requested more evidence—undeniable, concrete evidence, in addition to photographs. Reid's assumption was that Sihanouk could at some point present the evidence to his people, if necessary, to prove the communists were indeed breaking the international laws regarding neutrality. And perhaps even present the evidence to the media.

If the United States could provide such ironclad evidence, military advisers believed that Sihanouk might cooperate in both exposing the North Vietnamese as invaders of his neutral state and insisting that they leave. And if they did not vacate his country, he would accept the assistance of the United States in removing them. Ironclad evidence would also be a valuable card that the United States could reveal during the highly anticipated peace talks currently being planned.

Sihanouk had proven to be unpredictable, but Bowles and the team—including Philip Habib, who was also the Deputy Assistant Secretary of State for East Asian and Pacific Affairs—that put together the Vesuvius package made an educated guess that Sihanouk wanted the Chinese and Soviet–backed North Vietnamese out of Cambodia, but he'd gotten in too deep: "principally, because the Cambodian Armed Forces are just not strong enough," concluded the CIA, NSA, and DOD in their top-secret National Intelligence Estimate Report, dated December 14, 1967. "The army totals only 32,000 and less than 9,000 regular troops are stationed in provinces along the entire 700-mile border with South Vietnam. In the two large northeastern provinces of Cambodia, moreover, there are only eight border posts and these are manned by small para-military units. Four of these are clustered around the junction of Route 19 and the South Vietnamese border, just north of the Commu-nist Chu Pong base area. Along this sparsely manned frontier from Kon-tum to northern Tay Ninh alone are over 20,000 Communist troops."

In addition, Sihanouk was contending with the rise of an insur-gency known as the Khmer Rouge. In 1968 the movement officially became the Communist Party of Kampuchea (Cambodia) and was sup-ported by North Vietnam. Like the NVA and the Vietcong, the Khmer Rouge used terrorism as a tactic, which resulted in the deaths of tens of thousands Cambodians during Sihanouk's reign.

According to Reid, Sihanouk admitted to Bowles that he had to tread lightly with the Chinese government, which had warned him that there would be consequences if he was ever found to be working with the Americans. To keep up the appearance that Sihanouk was *not* working with the United States, an agreement was made, accord-ing to Reid, that Sihanouk "would expostulate violently each time we bombed [or there were border incidents]. Sihanouk said, 'If I sit there and do nothing, the Chinese will say I'm working with you. And in my treaty I have with the Chinese, it stipulates that there must be no cooperation with the U.S. of any kind in Vietnam or we, the Chinese, will intervene in Cambodia,' which meant an invasion. So Sihanouk did a wonderful act of 'Oh! These damn Americans! They're bombing us. It's outrageous! This must be stopped!' But it was all a game. Very few people knew about Vesuvius, even in Washington—it was kept highly, highly secret."

EVEN WHILE Bowles was presenting Sihanouk with the Vesuvius pack-age, record numbers of NVA and Vietcong fighters were sneaking from their Cambodian bases into South Vietnam, caching weapons, and staging troops in and around more than a hundred cities and towns, thirty-six of the forty-four provincial capitals, and most of the major cities, including Hue and the capital, Saigon.

They were the final preparations for what would be the single largest military operation of the war—a coordinated attack by more than eighty thousand North Vietnamese troops against key military and government bases and offices across South Vietnam. The North Vietnamese belief was that the U.S. and South Vietnamese military, after years of defending the population against sporadic, small-scale attacks, would crumble under such a massive onslaught, triggering the population of South Vietnam to spontaneously rise up to aid and join their brothers and sisters from the north to overthrow the "puppet government" of the United States.

On January 30, 1968, the Vietnamese lunar New Year—Tet—the NVA and Vietcong launched their attack, in what would become known as the Tet Offensive. The NVA and VC swept into the heart of the south, briefly seizing dozens of ARVN installations and inflicting significant casualties, prompting the U.S. media to initially report the attacks as a communist victory. But the U.S. and South Vietnamese forces quickly regained almost all the ground the North Vietnamese had taken and killed more than thirty-two thousand NVA/VC in the first seven days of the attack, taking another six thousand prisoner. (U.S. losses numbered around one thousand, the ARVN just under three thousand.)

The Tet Offensive would be considered a military victory for the United States and South Vietnam, but the subsequent fallout among the American people (arguably due to the media's reporting of events) deemed it a political defeat. Many would say the nail in the coffin was CBS news anchor Walter Cronkite's broadcast on February 27, 1968. "To say that we are closer to victory today is to believe, in the face of the evidence, the optimists who have been wrong in the past. To suggest we are on the edge of defeat is to yield to unreasonable pessimism. To say that we are mired in stalemate seems the only realistic, yet unsatisfactory, conclusion."

Peace protestors marched on college campuses and in Washington to bring the troops home, while the pro-war citizenry demanded that the job be finished. And the North Vietnamese returned to their safe haven in Cambodia to regroup and prepare for the next offensive, punctuating the need to expose, once and for all, the communist base of operations, supply, and sanctuary in Cambodia.

7

WELCOME TO DETACHMENT B-56

WHILE THE TERM *SOG* was never breathed outside the gates of the unit's top-secret bases, the effects of its missions became increasingly known—and feared—by the NVA and VC based in Laos and Cambodia: patrols along the Ho Chi Minh Trail were found dead or went missing. These attacks were silent and unpredictable, executed by SOG teams that seemed to materialize from the jungle to wreak havoc, and then just as quickly disappear.

The records that made their way into the file cabinets at SOG headquarters and the secret archives of the Pentagon documented the one hundred or so missions of the SOG recon teams that launched into the Fishhook area during the last six months of 1967. In November and December the teams—tasked to remain hidden, observe enemy movements, bases, and storage facilities, and to avoid enemy contact unless absolutely necessary—captured two enemy and killed more than one hundred in Cambodia. They mapped more than 150 infiltration routes and trails and just under 100 enemy installations, as well as huge caches of weapons and ammunition along the Ho Chi Minh Trail.

Combining psychological operations with ground operations in a project code-named Eldest Son—whose goal it was to create among the NVA and VC distrust of their weapons—the teams began to sneak sabotaged ammunition into the enemy's storerooms, causing NVA rifles to blow up when fired. They planted thousands of self-destructing mortar rounds that would explode when launched, killing entire mortar teams. Company-size SOG assault missions were assigned to investigate known enemy strongholds and plant anti-personnel mines in and around enemy installations; if discovered, they had the firepower to fight back and, in some cases, overrun communist bases.

The added benefit of these cross-border missions was the hamstringing of thousands of North Vietnamese troops, who were forced to remain within Laos and Cambodia to defend the Ho Chi Minh Trail against attacks. Postwar records show that more than fifty thousand NVA and VC troops stayed off the South Vietnamese battlefield to focus on fewer than a dozen U.S.-led SOG teams.

At the same time, these teams were not untouchable. As they became wise to the Special Forces tactics, the North Vietnamese employed hunter-killer teams whose job it was to watch for the SOG teams. They patrolled the roads and various installations on the Ho Chi Minh Trail and kept a close eye out for potential helicopter landing zones, LZs, that the United States might use for team insertion, especially those LZs near key bases and installations.

In 1967 and 1968, SOG recon team members were reported to have a nearly 100 percent casualty rate, meaning that if you were on SOG recon, you would eventually be wounded or killed on a mission. Purple Hearts weren't a ticket home; they were a routine addition to a SOG man's uniform and so commonplace that most were never even written up. These soldiers held to a strict code: fight to their death protecting one another and their indigenous counterparts. Being captured was not an option.

That code, and the fact that these teams were being systematically hunted, led to increasing numbers of cross-border teams vanishing in Cambodia and Laos. Some had final radio transmissions marked by gunfire and static before their radios went dead; others seemed to be swallowed by the jungle, with no indication of trouble—nothing but radio silence. Were they victims of hunter-killer teams of equal stealth and tactics? Had double agents within their indigenous ranks turned on them? By the war's end, over fifty SOG operators would go missing in action, including ten entire teams. Not a single one of these men was ever reported as a prisoner of war.

COMMUNICATIONS EXPERTS, or commo men like Brian O'Connor, were the lifelines for these teams. His first few weeks at Ho Ngoc Tao, O'Connor had remained mostly inside the wire at the base, but he quickly found that being a good commo man with Project Sigma was much like being a trusted barber in a small town. He became privy to everybody's business—from the recon team leaders to the officers, agents, and politicians in Saigon and Washington—and the short radio bursts of information were like strokes of a brush, gradually painting a picture of what exactly was going on in his corner of the war.

Besides playing a deadly game of hide-and-seek with the enemy—and harassing him and killing him in his own backyard—these SOG teams were bringing some clarity to an enemy that had for years been invisible. Recon was exciting, albeit dangerous, and all of it intrigued O'Connor. He was respectful of the danger, but he also sensed he would perform just fine under pressure. The only way to find out for sure was to get out in the field, either as a remote relay for a team, or as the radioman on a reaction force or recon team. Less than a month into his tour, he got his chance. A team was being inserted into a known enemy area west of Nui Ba Ra ("White Virgin Mountain")—the southern "sister" mountain to Nui Ba Den ("Black Virgin Mountain") in Phuoc Long Province—and he would be their radio relay to the nearby Special Forces camp at Song Be and to headquarters at Ho Ngoc Tao.

Shortly before Thanksgiving 1967, O'Connor was flown from the Special Forces camp at Song Be with six CIDG soldiers to the top of Nui Ba Ra. Mountaintop positions in Vietnam were predominantly "owned" by American forces, while the bottom and middle of the mountains were "owned" by Charlie. About fifty to seventy-five yards across and somewhat square, the crest of Nui Ba Ra was surrounded by a four-foot-wide, earth-filled bamboo wall topped by barbed wire built near the edge of the cliffs that sloped down steeply into the jungle tree line twenty to thirty yards below. Within the spartan perimeter were a helicopter pad, a few bamboo hooches, and some trench lines and fighting positions. Set along the outside of the barbed wire, the perimeter defenses included an early warning system of trip flares/pop flares and anti-personnel weaponry such as grenades, Claymore mines, and Bouncing Betty mines, which popped out of the ground when stepped on and exploded in the air, inflicting maximum damage at waist or head height.

This station was where O'Connor was to be relay to the recon team of six men camouflaged on the floor of the jungle no more than five miles away in a remain overnight position—most likely only yards from an enemy base or trail, and with no fortified walls or defenses beyond their own stealth and the firepower they carried. During the day, such teams were monitored by forward air controllers (FACs), who flew small prop planes at higher altitudes and maintained line-of-sight radio contact. But at night, the FACs were replaced by radio relays who represented, in an emergency, help or deliverance just a call away.

The few men making up a small radar unit on the mountaintop left shortly after O'Connor was dropped off, leaving him and the six CIDG to defend this critical high ground. At first everything ran smoothly. They set up the commo gear and made contact with the team and the headquarters—and would continue to do so every three hours. The panoramic views were "splendid," says O'Connor, "and it all seemed so peaceful." Then the sun went down.

Trouble began with shouts from below, the VC taunting the men with obscenities in English, followed by scattered gunfire and total darkness. Around 2:00 a.m., a trip flare went off below one wall, alerting them to an approaching enemy. Not long after, another. Each time, O'Connor and the CIDG systematically handled the situation by activating Claymore mines, tossing grenades over the wall, firing their AK-47s down into the jungle. Screams of pain from the darkness below were the measure of their success.

For O'Connor, this was his first time under fire. For the CIDG who guided O'Connor on dos and don'ts (do spread out the team's ammo and grenades, stockpiling half on the crest for everyone's easy access and the other half at a few locations near the perimeter walls; don't keep it all in one place), it was not. The CIDG were battle-hardened soldiers, whose ethnicity O'Connor was not certain of. They were South Vietnamese (not Montagnards or Nungs), but his eighteen- or nineteen-year-old Vietnamese interpreter, Tuan, also seemed to have some Chinese in his facial features.

Over the next hour, the VC triggered most of the flares and large sections of defenses. "They were probably angry as well as motivated," says O'Connor. "The flares had worked really well to signal their presence, but now most of them had been used, and it was pitch-black. You could not see three feet in front of you."

More shouts came from below, this time very close to the top of the wall, and a barrage of grenades sailed over the barbed wire, invisible in the dark. The men were far enough above that they were able to use flashlights to help them dodge the explosives without giving away their positions; they returned fire by tossing their own grenades back.

O'Connor called in gunship support, but before it arrived, another hail of grenades wounded two of the CIDG, one severely. A slick quickly medevaced the wounded, and the remaining men repositioned themselves at the center of the perimeter and out of range of the grenade attacks, Tuan acting as the link between O'Connor and the other three CIDG. All took shifts along the perimeter walls, tossing grenades and mines off the side to keep the enemy guessing. At one point the VC attempted to mortar their position, but the rounds sailed overhead and exploded out of range. Through it all, O'Connor was able to keep the vital communication link open with the recon team.

When the sun began to rise, Charlie faded with the night, and O'Connor returned to Song Be with a deep respect for the CIDG fighting men, and especially Tuan, who had reinforced the reputation he had around Ho Ngoc Tao for being trustworthy and battle savvy. Without the CIDG, O'Connor knew, Nui Ba Ra would have been overrun and he would have likely been killed.

Likewise, Tuan had seen this new radioman perform well in battle. For the CIDG, the man with the radio was the key to survival. He was the one who would call for the "taxi" ride home at the end of a mission, or when things got too hot to stick around. An American, like O'Connor, who was calm on the radio but also good with a rifle was a desirable teammate.

OVER THE course of several missions together, Tuan and O'Connor became friends. O'Connor learned that Tuan, who was from Saigon, had attended university for a while and planned to return. He was well-read and a staunch anticommunist, but he also complained about corrupt Saigon politics. Tuan's appreciation of Vietnam really shone through while talking about the food, the traditions, the culture, and history. "He enjoyed being a 'tourist' and a 'guide' in his own country," says O'Connor, "an idealist of sorts—an intellectual who also had courage."

Eventually, Tuan invited O'Connor to dinner at a woman's house in Saigon he introduced as his "sister," a longtime friend rather than a blood relative. Though her apartment was adorned with photos of the South Vietnam president and a South Vietnamese flag, she and Tuan seemed more interested in O'Connor's plans and dreams rather than his political bent or military aspirations. He talked about his lifelong love of the arts—inspired by the words and works of Shakespeare—and how he was an artist himself, sculpting, painting, and creating pottery. The military had been a tradition in the O'Connor family dating back to World War I, but for O'Connor it wasn't a lifelong career; it was a means to an end. He believed in what the United States stood for, its freedoms, the importance of the Constitution. They espoused a way of life he was willing to fight for, and when the war was over, he dreamed of having a life, a family, and a house with a well-stocked bookshelf and a little art studio out back.

Tuan agreed. Fighting and killing the communists was a temporary situation. The war would end and life would go on.

THE SECRET war in Cambodia was in full swing, with neither side reporting their losses, because neither was officially supposed to be there. Though isolated and unreported, these battles raged as bloody as any fought within Vietnam. As the years stretched on—not only in the sanctuary regions, but also within South Vietnam—both sides evolved and adapted their military and intelligence tactics to stay one step ahead. The United States and the South Vietnamese would, for example, perform false helicopter insertions with recon teams and combat assaults to throw off the enemy's ability to ascertain when a team actually hopped off a helicopter. And the NVA and VC set up early warning systems, watching flight paths and anticipating landing zones, sometimes with deadly accuracy and suspicious timing.

While working a combat assault mission near Dong Tam on March 8, 1968, the 240th "stepped into" one such "trap," Larry McKibben told his family in an audiotape. "We got in a lot of trouble down there the other day. Got eight helicopters shot down. I was one of them. We only had two pilots killed, and the rest of us were pretty lucky. We went into this LZ, and they were waiting for us with fifty-calibers and all kinds of stuff. Ran into an NVA battalion, landed right in the middle of a trap. I don't know where they got word that we were coming in there, but they knew it. Got hit on approach, got hit on short final— they really opened up on us."

McKibben was able to get his helicopter, Greyhound One, back in the air but was forced to land a couple of hundred yards away for a quick engine check. As his crew chief, Specialist 5 Paul "Frenchy" LaChance, jumped out and gave the aircraft a once-over, a distress call went out over the radio: one of their Mad Dog gunships was going down near the LZ. LaChance jumped back in, McKibben pulled pitch, and moments later was over the gunship, which was in flames on a dike surrounded by rice paddies. Running around the helicopter was a man on fire.

Greyhound One started taking hits as it came in, landing fifty yards from the burning aircraft, and LaChance called over the intercom, "I'll go get him." He left the slick and sprinted along the dike, bullets kicking up all around him from machine-gun emplacements concealed in the jungle to his left, at the far side of the water-filled rice paddy. Another Mad Dog swooped down and launched rockets over his head toward the machine guns, then hovered, its side door gunner providing cover while LaChance reached the burning man, whose screams he heard even over the roar of the guns and helicopters. He tackled the man and lay on top of him, pressing his body into the earth to extinguish the flames. He could feel the heat as he picked the man up and ran back with him over his shoulder, unaware that the jet fuel had caught his own pants on fire.

Greyhound One was hovering close by. The second LaChance threw the injured man in back and dove on board, McKibben raced forward over the wreckage—the bodies of both pilots were in their seats and engulfed by flames; the missing fourth crewman had presumably perished as well. As the door gunner blasted LaChance's legs with a fire extinguisher and covered the burned crewman, LaChance couldn't stop staring at the man's name tag: "Warr."

"When we got off the ground," McKibben narrated on the tape, "they got us again. This darn old Huey is unbelievable; it kept flying, took a fifty-caliber right in the engine. Dad, you know what a fifty-caliber does to things. God must have kept those blades spinning, I'm not kidding, 'cause I took a hit right in the damn motor. Went right through that thing, cut my fuel control. All my gauges went, my instruments were shot out, and I figured I better keep on going and see if I could make it to Dong Tam, which was about fifteen miles away. It started losing altitude—I lost my power and went down. I was lucky, though, made it to a little ARVN Special Forces compound, shot toward that, and made it just outside a couple hundred meters. Another ship came in and pulled out that crew chief and my crew chief, Frenchy, who got fuel all over him and got burned, too. Our ship was shot up pretty good though. I don't know when I'll get it back. I just hope I don't have to go through that again. I'm telling you, it scared me to death."

MCKIBBEN RETURNED to Bearcat the following day and learned that the two men killed in that fiery crash were his good friend Warrant

Officer Guy Eisenhart, who had come with him from the 162nd to the 240th, and the aircraft commander, Captain Charles Jilcott Jr. Specialist 5 James Warr died in the burn unit of a hospital in Japan three days later.

Then there was the missing door gunner. "We never saw him," McKibben continued in his recording. "We thought he burned up in the crash, but he was thrown clear from the aircraft as it was going down. Broke his pelvis. Charlie was all around him, and he couldn't get up or Charlie would have shot him, so he just crawled into the water and stayed under some straw all night. Infantry found him the next morning, took him to the hospital, and he'll be okay. I felt real bad, didn't know he was down there. I could have picked him up."

After a few days, McKibben's trusted Huey came back from maintenance. It had taken a hit to the tail rotor, and McKibben asked to keep the rotor blade for a souvenir, which he leaned up in the corner of his hooch, bullet hole prominently displayed. A week later, LaChance returned from Long Binh; his eyebrows, eyelashes, and arm and chest hair had been burned off, and his legs—from his boot tops to his knees—were covered in third-degree burns. He had snuck out of the hospital with an armload of bandages and ointment so he could rejoin his buddies.

McKibben finished his recording to his family with "I've been getting a little homesick lately. I've been thinking a lot about all the places I'd like to see again, that I'll be seeing again pretty soon. I guess I'm growing impatient in my old age—twenty years old now. No teenager no more. Oh well, I guess it's kind of hard growing up. I know when I was younger, I always wanted to grow older, but now that I'm starting to grow older, I kind of wish I was younger again. People expect a lot more out of an older person than they do out of a kid."

He sent off the tape in the second week of March, right before the 240th Assault Helicopter Company was assigned to work with a Special

Forces unit at a small base camp just a five-minute flight from Bearcat. None of them had heard of Project Sigma, Detachment B-56.

LIEUTENANT COLONEL Ralph Drake—the cigar-chewing commander of Project Sigma, Detachment B-56—was responsible for carrying out SOG recon missions in the Daniel Boone area of operation, a task that had become increasingly more difficult due to increased enemy strength and movement, especially in the Fishhook area.

Detachment commanders such as Drake and his subordinates were responsible for both the lives of the men they sent into harm's way, as well as the tangible results of their reconnaissance missions. If a team was compromised—the enemy had spotted the men—the standard operating procedure was to immediately extract them. The interpretation of "compromise" was usually left to those on the ground. SOG teams were a highly professional and intrepid lot, men like Jerry "Maddog" Shriver, whom a SOG recon man and eventual historian of the unit, John Plaster, would describe as "a walking arsenal with a sawed-off shotgun or suppressed submachine gun, pistols, knives and grenades [who] . . . teased death scores of times."

It was Shriver who coined what Plaster would credit as "the most famous rejoinder in the history of the Studies and Observation Group." During a reconnaissance mission in Cambodia, Shriver found his small team outnumbered and completely surrounded by the enemy. He radioed the situation to his superiors and told them not to worry. "I've got 'em right where I want 'em," he said. "Surrounded from the *inside*." Shriver and his team made it out alive that time. He was severely wounded on a future mission, but his body was never recovered and he is listed as MIA.

In the spring of 1968, Drake had a solid group of recon men assembled at Ho Ngoc Tao, but B-56 headquarters was having a difficult time keeping teams on the ground long enough to gather the intel being requested. In March, the area of interest was the Fishhook area.

The recon company commander reporting to Drake was twenty-three-year-old Green Beret first lieutenant Fred Jones, who had been with B-56 for nearly nine months. One of the most experienced officers at Project Sigma, he was well liked by the team leaders because he spoke their language, having personally led numerous recon missions along the Cambodian border himself.

In March his teams had encountered heavy infiltration coming down the Ho Chi Minh Trail southeast through the old French War Zone C toward Saigon. Keeping Drake apprised via radio from their forward launch site—the brigade base camp of the First Infantry Division at Quan Loi—Jones had inserted a handful of teams thirteen times in ten days at various locations in the Fishhook border region, and every one of them was either visually compromised or took fire upon or immediately after insertion and had to be pulled out. His teams were exhausted—mentally and physically—and Jones decided to make the fourteenth the final attempt to keep a team on the ground.

This team "was led by two of my best NCOs," says Jones, "and it seemed to be the perfect insertion spot. They went in, got off the helicopters, and came under fire immediately. We called in gunships to suppress the enemy fire, barely got them out, and they came back to Quan Loi, shut the choppers down, and I said, 'No more.' It was a really hot area, just lots and lots of bad guys on the ground, and I wasn't going to send anybody in before we went back to Ho Ngoc Tao, regrouped, and looked at the maps."

Jones radioed his decision to temporarily abort insertion attempts back to command at Ho Ngoc Tao. He heard back directly from Drake, who told him to put a team on the ground that afternoon: "That's a direct order."

"Sir," Jones replied, "as soon as you get on a helicopter and get up here, you and I will take a team out. But I am not sending anybody else from my company on a recon mission today. Sorry, can't do it."

In response to Jones's refusal to obey his order, Drake ordered Jones on the next helicopter back to Ho Ngoc Tao, where he relieved him of duty as the recon company commander. He later gave him the only negative Officer Efficiency Report Jones would receive in his thirty-plus-year military career: "LT Jones eagerly sought this combat command," wrote Drake in the OER. But "he was greatly influenced in his performance of duty by senior NCOs in his command and seemed unable to reject or overrule suggestions that did not serve the accomplishment of the mission. He did his best work while actively engaged in field operations."

"Drake accused me of letting the enlisted men influence me," says Jones. "He thought that they were telling me they didn't want to go out. It was *my* decision. I could see the tension they were under, the physical condition they were under; nobody was sleeping. These people had to get a break, and so I made that determination."

The next morning as Jones was eating in the mess hall, Drake approached his table. "Lieutenant," he said, "finish your breakfast and get your gear. You're going back to Quan Loi. You're now the launch officer; you're the assistant S-3. You're *running* the operations."

In Jones's opinion, Drake realized Jones was the most experienced guy he had to launch these missions. "So he slapped my wrist by taking away my command of the recon teams, but then kept me doing the same thing as the launch officer [but] with more responsibility."

Meanwhile, the Pentagon, the White House, the CIA, and SOG headquarters were clamoring for intelligence in that area. "You could feel the pressure to perform," says Jones. "I'm sure Drake felt that pressure."

ON MARCH 19, 1968, Special Assistant for National Security Affairs Walt Rostow delivered to President Johnson a list of recommendations compiled by the members of the Southeast Asia Coordinating Committee, the same group that had organized the delivery of the Vesuvius package to Sihanouk two months earlier. The list "emphasized the great importance of the collection and exploitation of specific hard intelligence on the Vietcong/North Vietnamese Army use of Cambodia, as well as of circumstantial evidence which is convincing by dint of its quality and quantity. Collection of all types of intelligence on Cambodia should be given higher national priority than heretofore. Use of more aggressive intelligence collection methods should be authorized where necessary to obtain such intelligence. Movement of supplies to and through [the seaport of] Sihanoukville is a particularly important area for an increased intelligence collection effort."

The need for Special Forces–qualified Green Berets for a range of assignments was so great in Vietnam that many were being sent straight to the war upon graduation from the Q Course. For his part, Staff Sergeant and Vietnam War veteran Roy Benavidez and his bad back remained poised in purgatory at Fort Bragg, uncertain as to whether he would return to Southeast Asia or be given the South American assignment he half-expected and that Lala prayed for.

Roy received orders at the end of March for deployment to Vietnam, and he moved Lala—who sighed at the news but never complained—and twenty-month-old Denise back to El Campo the first week of April. He leveled the trailer in the lot beside Lala's parents' house, kissed his wife and daughter good-bye, and on April 20 was at the 5th Special Forces Group headquarters in Nha Trang, standing in front of the "big map" bristling with the flags of fate.

IT HAD been six months since Brian O'Connor had stood in front of that same map, and with half of his tour behind him, he had garnered a solid reputation as a technically sound, battlefield-calm radioman. He'd worked the larger company-size reaction and assault missions along the border, and pulled a recon mission or two with Stefan Mazak, who, O'Connor noted, "had an uncanny ability to lay low and still and wait for an hour or two or more for the NVA/VC to come to us, rather than hunt them down. He crawled very, very slowly. Could be still like a lizard on a hot rock, and was able to sense the nearby presence of the enemy before we could."

That was what O'Connor witnessed firsthand as Mazak's radioman on April 18 when Mazak set up an ambush on a trail, reportedly in Long Khanh Province. According to the citation written to award Mazak the Silver Star, "SFC Mazak led his force to a known enemy-occupied area and began preparing an ambush position for the night. As his men dug in, a Vietcong force attacked their perimeter from the left and rear with intense automatic weapons and grenade fire." Says Jones—who as launch officer listened to events unfold over the radio and later debriefed the team members—"One indigenous troop at the very lead end of the ambush position got nervous and opened fire early, thus alerting the enemy to the ambush. That allowed the bad guys to flank the ambush position and assault their position."

Mazak was wounded, but refused treatment, moving instead to assist a wounded teammate, and then, "With bullets striking all around him," reads the citation, "he led part of his force in a furious counterattack to prevent the envelopment of his patrol. The Vietcong began to withdraw. SFC Mazak directed [his teammates] to take cover and attacked the enemy alone. He was mortally wounded while fearlessly leading his men in close combat against a determined enemy."

O'Connor fought back the enemy alongside the CIDG while manning the radio throughout the bloody engagement. "Brian O'Connor earned the respect of everyone for the way he handled himself during that op," says Jones. "He made sure Mazak's body came with them as they fought to break contact and made it to a location where they could be extracted.

"I identified Stefan Mazak's body at the hospital morgue at Long Binh post. He had volunteered to go recon even though he was encouraged to take a less dangerous position. He had a wife and a young child back home. He'd fought in World War II, Korea, the Congo—and Vietnam is what got him."

Back at Fort Bragg, Roy had done some reconnaissance work at the noncommissioned officers club, speaking with some of the returning Green Berets, and here in Vietnam he was friends with the sergeant major in charge of assignments. When Roy told the sergeant major he wanted to go to the same place where Stefan Mazak and Leroy Wright were assigned, the sergeant major informed him that Mazak had been killed two days before.

It saddened Roy but did not dissuade him; his friend Wright was there as well as a couple of other guys he really respected, and he felt more comfortable going to a place with a few people he knew. At first the sergeant major declined Roy's request, but Roy persisted and eventually the sergeant major consented, saying, "All right, Roy, go ahead. But goddamn it, if you get killed, I don't want Lala blaming me for it. I tried to keep you from going to that outfit."

When Roy passed through the gate that separated Camp Ho Ngoc Tao from the rest of the war, he left behind the army he'd known for most of his career and entered the realm of MACV-SOG: a turnkey interpretation of sixties-era soldier/author Jean Lartéguy's "real one" army.

"I'd like to have two armies," Lartéguy wrote in *The Centurions* in 1970. "One for display with lovely guns, tanks, little soldiers, staffs, distinguished and doddering generals, and dear little regimental officers who would be deeply concerned over their general's bowel movements or their colonel's piles, an army that would be shown for a modest fee on every fairground in the country.

"The other would be the real one, composed entirely of young enthusiasts in camouflage uniforms, who would not be put on display, but from whom impossible efforts would be demanded and to whom all sorts of tricks would be taught. That's the Army in which I should like to fight."

"Welcome to Detachment B-56" was the first typed line of paragraph one on a single sheet of paper handed to Roy after he was assigned his billet, a steel-framed bed inside a metal-roofed, plywood-walled hooch. "By the time you read this you will probably be hot and tired from the trip from Nha Trang. Please bear with us for a short time while we process you into the Detachment. It will be practically painless, and a cold beer or soda awaits you at the club shortly. There are a few things you should know." A couple of paragraphs outlined the camp's location (between Saigon and Long Binh on Highway 1) and added some props about the excellent meals prepared at the mess, plus its hours of operation:

Room maid service, laundry, haircuts, and some tailor services are included with your membership in this detachment. Your Mess fee covers these services. There are movies practically every night. . . .

After-dark travel on Highway #1 is banned because of the ever-present danger of ambush. Weapons should be carried at all times when leaving this camp. . . . Use good judgment in the display of weapons in the city of Saigon itself. NEVER LEAVE A WEAPON IN A VEHICLE. Do not travel alone. Generally, a "shot-gun" rider is necessary.

The mission of Detachment B-56 is highly classified. Just about everything we do here is classified. Do not write home about your operational activities. Watch your conversation, especially when you are off-post. DO NOT TALK SHOP! We frequently have visitors from other units and from Saigon, both military and civilian, American and otherwise. They should not learn from you what you are doing or what the detachment is doing. Your life could depend on your conversational discretion, especially among indigenous personnel.

We hope you will thoroughly enjoy your assignment here. You are now a member of a very closely knit family and we are very glad to have you on board. If you have any questions about anything, our operational and administrative personnel will be very glad to help you. Welcome once again to Detachment B-56.

"HELLO, HELLO," Roy heard Leroy Wright sing out the lines of the recent Beatles hit, "I don't know why you say good-bye, I say hello . . ."

The two friends embraced, and Wright invited Roy to his hooch in a nearby building, where they caught up with recent photos of their families and shrugged at the fact they hadn't found the time for that barbecue. Taped to Leroy Wright's locker were some drawings by his two young sons. Their father was also an artist; he loved to draw cartoons and planned to work that into his life after the war.

The following day, Roy accompanied Wright, who was on the recon company, and fellow recon man Lloyd Mousseau on some McGuire Rig training, where he learned how to be a bellyman on a slick, hoisting men out of the jungle on long ropes when a landing zone could not be found. On April 30, 1968, when Roy had been in-country for ten days and at Ho Ngoc Tao for barely a week, he was told he would be sent to a forward launch site to help keep tabs on teams in the field from the base tactical operations center (TOC). The base he was heading to was as close to the Cambodian border as it got, a place called Loc Ninh.

8

OVER THE FENCE

Around 5:00 p.m. on April 30, Larry McKibben, aircraft commander of Greyhound One, heard Big Al Yurman's New Jersey accent come in loud and clear over the radio. "It's a bust, guys."

McKibben and his wingman, Greyhound Two aircraft commander Jerry Ewing, had been sitting standby with two other slicks on the tarmac at the Quan Loi Army supply base near the Cambodian border for nearly three hours, ready to insert a Project Sigma B-56 recon team west of Loc Ninh. "We'll take these guys home to their headquarters," Yurman continued, referring to the recon team. "Then we can sleep in our own beds at Bearcat."

But on the final approach to B-56 headquarters at Ho Ngoc Tao, some forty miles from Quan Loi, Yurman was summoned by radio to land and shut down. The detachment commander, Lieutenant Colonel Ralph Drake, wanted to see him.

What the hell is this all about? Yurman thought as he hopped into the back of a truck with the recon team and was driven from the helipads at the camp's back gate into the perimeter at Ho Ngoc Tao, where Drake awaited him outside his command office. Drake began the conversation by thanking Yurman for the work the 240th had accomplished for B-56 the previous five weeks. This had included some hot extractions that left quite a few bullet holes in the assault helicopter company's slicks and gunships. Drake was particularly grateful for the water drop and medevac mission of March 28, for which Yurman had recommended and Warrant Officer Jerry Ewing had received the Distinguished Flying Cross. His copilot, Warrant Officer William Armstrong, received the Air Medal with Valor.

The B-56 distress call that Ewing had responded to on March 28 was from what was described as a reconnaissance-in-force search-and-destroy mission utilizing two of Project Sigma's reaction companies. One company (six Americans and approximately 150 CIDG) led by Special Forces captain Russ Proctor had taken heavy casualties while assaulting a "heavily fortified, entrenched enemy base camp," just across the Cambodian border. The other company of six Americans and approximately 130 CIDG, led by Special Forces captain Jerry Ledzinski, was to reinforce and quickly extract Proctor's company.

Upon insertion, Ledzinski says he was ordered by B-56 Command to "abort the extraction, stay in, and capture a prisoner." Both companies were subsequently surrounded, resulting in one of the bloodiest battles of B-56 history. The American-led forces ran out of water after the first day; by day three, some of the men were delirious with thirst and even drinking their own urine. Heavy enemy anti-aircraft machine-gun fire had beaten back attempts at resupply, and the canteens and cans of juice dropped from high-flying and fast-moving helicopters became deadly projectiles that exploded on impact, the men trying to suck the moisture from the dirt wherever they hit.

Proctor's and Ledzinski's companies had killed between two hundred and three hundred NVA, but not without heavy losses of their own. Virtually every American and CIDG was wounded, and at least fifty of the CIDG had been killed. Because of the smell, the bodies, in body bags or rolled up in ponchos, were moved away from their fighting positions and laid out in rows.

Toward the end of the third day, after two of the 240th helicopters had been shot down, Ewing and copilot Armstrong volunteered to attempt a resupply. The laboring helicopter was so weighted down with water that it began to sink into the jungle canopy while hovering over the American perimeter. Ewing held the helicopter steady, taking fire from the enemy and trimming a few treetops as he descended into the foliage and his crew frantically kicked out hundreds of pounds of water in specially designed water bladders that would not burst upon impact. This resupply sustained the men on the ground until a reaction force was able to extract them on the fourth day of battle.

"It's what we do, Sir," Yurman responded to Drake's commendations.

"We've got something for you tomorrow," Drake said. "But it's a little different than what you've been doing. I need you to return to your base and have all your aircraft and crew sterilized—remove everything from uniforms, patches, names, and strip the ships. Nobody will carry personal effects, wallets, wedding rings, ID, nothing. Pass that along to your CO in person—no radio. Have the whole package back here at 0700 tomorrow. I'll tell you more then."

Yurman had briefed his own pilots at the helipad before the fifteen-minute flight back to Bearcat, where he advised his boss, the new 240th company commander, Major Jesse James, of the mission, as well as the Mad Dog gunship platoon's leader and ranking officer, First Lieutenant Rick Adams. Adams chuckled and shook his head. He'd just been listening to the Armed Forces Network radio, where he heard President Johnson repeat his almost daily message: "My fellow

Americans, we are in Vietnam to fulfill a solemn pledge. We are *not* in Cambodia."

Not in Cambodia, thought Adams. *Yeah, right.*

IT WAS past 9:00 p.m. and already dark when Adams briefed the Mad Dog gunship pilots and crew about the vague yet ominous plans for the following day. Among them was Mad Dog Four crew chief Specialist 5 Pete Gailis, who listened carefully as Adams ran down the list of exactly what he and the other four crew chiefs and five door gunners—most of whom had yet to eat dinner or complete their post-flight inspections—would have to cover, paint, or remove from their aircraft. The order to "leave all your identification behind" sat about as well with Gailis as a priest delivering last rites. They'd been, as he put it, "working the line" between Vietnam and Cambodia for weeks— launching missions with B-56 up, down, and around Tay Ninh and Long Binh Provinces, from Quan Loi to An Loc to Loc Ninh. The one constant across the board was the overwhelming numbers of Charlie the recon teams encountered right on Cambodia's doorstep. He couldn't fathom how many of them they'd encounter once they were actually inside the front door.

When Warrant Officer Roger Waggie checked on his slick, Greyhound Three, before hitting the rack around midnight, he found his twenty-year-old crew chief, Michael Craig—the remains of his C ration dinner atop the revetment—still at it, giving their aircraft a thorough going-over. Specialist 4 Craig might have been the youngest Greyhound crew chief, but Waggie openly bragged that he was the best he'd ever worked with, as well as the hardest worker. Four years older, Waggie thought of Craig as a younger brother. "You take care of me," he'd told Craig when he became his crew chief, "and I'll take care of you."

Craig had been in-country since October 14, 1967, becoming a crew chief in just two and a half months, an unusually quick promotion he detailed in a letter to his parents and sister: "Yesterday our flight went down into the Delta to insert some infantry guys," he wrote on January 11, 1968. "We sent twelve ships down and we have six left that can fly. My ship was in maintenance . . . so I wasn't flying. I guess there was Charlie all over the place. Two of our crew chiefs got shot through the head. One died and the other one is coming along fine. By the way, I'm a crew chief now."

Craig and Waggie had flown more than two hundred missions together. They had been shot down four times in the past four months. During the first phase of the Tet Offensive, Craig had seen dump trucks full of dead Vietcong. While he'd witnessed his share of American body bags, he had yet to see them stacked up like cords of wood. Contrary to the post-Tet statement by CBS news anchor Walter Cronkite that the United States was "mired in stalemate," Craig's experience was that there were dozens, if not hundreds, of Charlie killed for every American killed in action. "Don't believe what you hear," he told his parents in a letter.

But Michael Craig didn't discuss the impending mission as he chatted with Waggie. Instead he talked about his parents and his sister and brother-in-law and niece—even their rescued puppy, Zelda.

GREYHOUND SENIOR pilots Larry McKibben and Jerry Ewing were preparing for the mission in their hooch when Al Yurman stopped by to give them the lineup for the following day.

Yurman "hated like hell" to send his men on a mission like this when they were so close to going home: McKibben was only six weeks shy of the end of his yearlong tour, while Ewing was just under two months. The unwritten rule was you'd keep the "short" guys off the risky missions, but in this case he didn't have a choice. The 240th had had a couple of slicks shot up the week before and they were still in maintenance, plus their pilots were already past their limit for flight hours the previous thirty days.

"Mac, Jerry—you guys will be primary on this one, a two-slick insertion," he said to them. By simple seniority, that meant McKibben would be lead, flying Greyhound One, and Ewing would be his wingman, flying Greyhound Two.

"Will do," McKibben replied. He'd been on so many missions that the news caused him no more concern than he'd felt preparing to fly his single-prop over the farmland outside Houston when he was sixteen. He trusted his Huey to fly even when it was full of bullet holes and he also trusted the safeguards and procedures employed by the Special Forces recon teams, as he'd told his folks on his latest audiotape. "We've got four slicks, four gunships, and one command-and-control slick. We fly in low-level, he vectors us, we drop them off. Actually there's just two slicks—the infil/exfil slicks are loaded—I'm one of the infil/exfils. The other two are just standby: in case we go down, they come in and pick us up. We go into these places without any gunships or anything, just try to drop them in as quiet as possible, and then go out. We keep the gunships on-station, just in case. And if they do make any contact, we call that position compromised, and we'll go in and extract them right away.

"It's real interesting work, and real different than what we've been used to. If we receive any fire going in, we abort the mission right away, or if we miss the LZ, like we're going too fast to slow down for it, or miss it, we won't go back to it—there's an alternate LZ already picked for us. It's pretty tight security, you know, 'cause when you put in a small team, they aren't really equipped to take any large-scale-type attacks—they're just there for recon. They just carry enough weapons for defense, and anytime they get into trouble, they call us up and we go and pick them up. Their job is to find Charlie, not to fight him. They do a good job, really outstanding."

★

JERRY EWING, McKibben's good friend and wingman for the past several weeks, had always been impressed with how devoted Larry was
to his family. He'd listen in sometimes, with McKibben's permission,
to the tapes he received from home. The last one, from McKibben's
mother, was still in the tape player. "It sure made us all feel a lot better
to get your tape, Larry, and hear that you're all right. That day that you
got shot down made the cold chills just thinking about it. I sure was
sorry to hear the bad news, the bad part of it, but I'm glad you came out
of it as good as you did. I don't see how you did. But I guess you learn
how to do a lot of things that you really don't know how to do, or want
to do sometimes. I just hope the Lord keeps on protecting you and be
real careful."

Hearing their voices—and reading his own letters—often launched
Ewing into memories of home and his childhood. He had spent count-
less hours playing war with his older brother while bouncing from military base to military base. His father was a career Army officer who
made sure his sons understood that true superheroes wore uniforms,
not capes.

The Ewing brothers also understood the significance of the different medals for valor, as well as specific examples from World War
I and World War II of service members who had earned them. This
was critical information in understanding bravery under fire—ignoring
wounds, storming enemy bunkers, saving fellow soldiers' lives—as they
played war. Several times his brother bestowed upon him the highest
honors, posthumously, for sacrificing his life for his men, usually for
jumping on an enemy hand grenade.

Jerry Ewing would lie there and wait for his brother's verdict.

"He was the bravest soldier I ever saw. Thanks, kid: you saved the
lives of four men." Or "Wait! He's still alive! Get a medic over here

fast!" in which case Jerry would regain consciousness, ask for a rifle, and fight on until dinnertime.

Ewing's older brother would go on to graduate from Notre Dame, his education paid for by their parents. For Ewing, who took a little time off to figure things out after graduating from high school in 1964, his father had other aspirations. "I think if you learn a trade," his father told him while handing him a brochure for barber school, "you will always be able to look out for yourself. I can pay your tuition. It's honorable work. You have a lot of potential."

Whether his father was serious about barber school, or whether the brochure had been strategically delivered genius designed to motivate Ewing into action, within a few months he joined the Army and was accepted into helicopter flight school, his sights set on serving his country just like his dad.

Ewing reveled in every minute of the training. The conflict in Vietnam was already being touted as the "Helicopter War," and he was in the vanguard of the future of warfare. Many of Ewing's flying instructors had been wounded during their tours in Vietnam, and they wore their scars proudly. Glass eyes, prosthetics, and back braces were viewed by the students as badges of courage, along with the actual service medals delivered to these larger-than-life heroes at on-base ceremonies each Friday:

"With complete disregard for his own personal safety, Warrant Officer James flew his damaged aircraft into the withering enemy fire to rescue . . ."

"Ignoring the enemy fire, Lieutenant Thomas, his pilot mortally wounded, and grievously wounded himself, nonetheless gained control of the aircraft and attacked the enemy with rockets . . ."

The graphic descriptions of battle, the walking wounded on base, and the flag-draped coffins on the evening news could not penetrate the fog of testosterone and bravado that enveloped Jerry Ewing in a force field of confidence.

The Army had trained him well.

THE MORNING of May 1, 1968, Yurman flew back to Ho Ngoc Tao with four Greyhound slicks that had been stripped of identification. Their crews were equally anonymous.

At the base, Lieutenant Colonel Drake ordered him to load up the recon team members and transport them to Quan Loi for a future brief. All he would divulge to Yurman was that an American unit up north in the A Shau Valley had captured a Russian truck a few days before and intelligence needed to know if the same types of trucks were coming up from the south. If the recon team could capture a truck—not just the driver but the actual truck—they'd find a way to get it back to Vietnam.

Yurman's eyes widened. Though Drake didn't identify Cambodia by name, he clearly had said, "Get [the truck] back to Vietnam."

Before returning to the slicks to brief his crews, Yurman stepped into the Special Forces communication bunker to radio Major James, who would send the gunships over to Quan Loi from Bearcat. On the occasions when he thought something was BS, Yurman used a certain colorful phrase to express his skepticism. He used it that morning as he briefed his men. "Here's what we're doing," he said. "It sounds like a John Wayne picture to me and I got a case of the ass about this, but we're going to drop these guys off, then they're gonna capture a truck and drive it out."

He received only silence in return, and a few nods. Everyone knew that this was, in Yurman's words, "very secret shit."

★

AROUND 11:00 in the morning, five slicks, including McKibben's and Ewing's Greyhounds, each carrying half of the twelve-man recon team, landed at Quan Loi. A half-hour flight from Ho Ngoc Tao, this 1st Infantry Division base camp and Army supply base surrounded by the forest of an old rubber tree plantation, was one of the busier aircraft hubs in South Vietnam. It serviced predominantly American forces up and down the Cambodian border and had a runway built by Army engineers to handle the giant C-130 Hercules cargo airplanes, dozens of which flew in and out weekly. The war matériel and supplies were then loaded into, or hoisted up by, the big dual-rotor, heavy-lift Chinook helicopters, whose pilots and crews hauled everything out to resupply the American camps and bases spread across the countryside.

Amid this buzz of activity, the unmarked slicks of the 240th slipped in and settled their skids on one of the large rectangular tarmacs off the main flight lines—a helicopter "parking lot" reserved for combat assault and search-and-destroy mission staging, medical emergencies, and the increasingly frequent special-mission assignments.

From this tarmac the pilots, crew, and fully loaded recon team were led by a Special Forces sergeant into a wooded area adjacent to the runway. This was the location of the base camp of the 1st Infantry Division's 3rd Brigade: a grid of wood-framed tents of various sizes, underground bunkers, and latrines.

A block of tents fenced off by a few coils of barbed wire and guarded by two Chinese Nung from Ho Ngoc Tao's Camp Defense Company served as the B-56 Special Forces compound. Inside its tactical operations center—a heavily sandbagged tent with an array of wires that trailed up to antennas extending above the treetops—B-56 assistant S-3 Launch Officer Fred Jones, the man in charge of the mission, was reviewing topographical maps when Yurman walked inside and shook his hand.

The two had worked together previously, and Yurman recalled that

Jones was competent and a straight shooter, as well as the same rank, which meant that Yurman felt he could speak candidly.

While the men of the 240th AHC settled into temporary billets in the B-56 compound, Jones and Sergeant Leroy Wright—the "one-zero" or recon team leader—proceeded to show Yurman the "area of interest" on the map and, within that area, a specific branch of "the trail." Jones tapped his finger on the spot, clearly on the west side of the line representing the Cambodian border, although how far, it was hard to tell. But it was at least a few miles in, maybe five, "deep in bad-guy country."

THE REST of the 240th had been shuffled into a mission-planning tent, where their uniforms were inspected for names or insignia. Next the men put their ID cards inside envelopes to be held in an ammo box until the mission was completed. Each pilot and crewman had also signed an affidavit when they started flying for B-56 that stated they understood that they could not speak or write about anything they heard or did for thirty years. Any slips or leaks would be considered treason and would result in a dishonorable discharge, a ten-thousand-dollar fine, and a long trip to Kansas, with room and board at Fort Leavenworth military prison.

Yurman slipped into the tent to grab his copilot, Warrant Officer Thomas "Smitty" Smith, and his crew.

"What are we doing, Big Al?" Smith asked.

"Don't tell anybody," Yurman replied, "but we're going to Cambodia."

"Right now?"

"Right now."

A visual reconnaissance flight was standard operating procedure for any recon mission. The dual goal was to get eyes on the objective and to pick a primary landing zone and two alternates. The team leader, the launch officer, and either the insertion helicopter pilot or the command-and-control (C&C) pilot all needed to agree that these landing/potential pickup zones were okay for both the men on the ground and those in the air.

Aboard the C&C slick, recon team leader Wright sat in the right jump seat behind the copilot, Smith, while Jones was in the left jump seat behind Yurman, the pilot.

All were familiar with the insertion tactics for recon teams, but Yurman wanted to be sure that this one didn't deviate. In this insertion the platoon would be running only two slicks—staggered with a couple of rotor-blade distances between them and just above treetop level—with no gunship flanking support; it was all about stealth and surprise. Yurman would fly two hundred or three hundred feet above and a five- or six-rotor-blade distance behind the two slicks. That extra altitude would allow Yurman to "steer" them from above with directions such as "Turn left—stop; turn right—stop; descend—stop; climb—stop."

At about one mile out from the LZ, Yurman would give them warning: "Slow; slower; LZ straight ahead; it's all yours." From his higher altitude, Yurman would be able to see the opening on the jungle horizon and bank away, not wanting to overfly the LZ. The lead slick pilot would provide visual confirmation, then the two slicks—which would have been flying so close together they would sound like one helicopter to those on the ground—would separate slightly on final approach to six or eight rotor blades apart. One after the other, they would drop into the hole in the jungle, flare, and hover while the troops piled out. In no more than a few seconds, both slicks would rise back into the air and return to base.

For the visual recon, Yurman maintained an altitude between fifteen hundred and three thousand feet. He was linked up via intercom with Jones and Wright in the backseat, listening to their conversation as he flew northwest to Loc Ninh—a Special Forces camp a mere ten minutes from Quan Loi and a five-minute flight from the border. Jones identified Loc Ninh as a potential staging area from which to launch the mission across the border and where the slicks and gunships would sit standby after the insertion.

At Loc Ninh, Yurman turned due west, flew past a deserted French fort and toward the border. Though the border was ambiguous and difficult to determine on the ground, from the air, the large scorched slashes of jungle and B-52–bombed wasteland dimpled with water-filled craters gave it away. Just as Yurman crossed the area, a voice cut in over the emergency radio guard channel to say, "Aircraft entering Pepper Pot—be advised." Air Traffic Control had picked him up on radar; he was now in Cambodian airspace.

Helicopter pilots in Vietnam had for a time sought out bomb craters as opportune landing zones. But the enemy quickly learned this tactic and began to devise ingenious spotting and ambush tactics, constructing platforms from the splintered, blown-up trees beside the craters, then covering the platforms with thick soil from the craters' centers. When the craters filled with new plant growth from monsoonal rains, the earthen roofs of these platforms sprouted as well, rendering them—and the enemy-manned PKM machine guns beneath—invisible to the American and South Vietnamese air forces that dominated the sky.

Now Yurman left this pockmarked border region behind, and the Cambodian jungle stretched out before him like a carpet. There was little relief to the terrain, few hills with which to mask a helicopter's approach. The only option the American helicopter pilots had was to fly low and fast. At a speed of eighty or ninety knots, a helicopter passed over before the enemy beneath the canopy could react; as a result, the chance of dropping into a pack of "sharks" within this vast green sea was slim. At least that's what Yurman kept trying to convince himself.

In his mind, the sharks were potentially anywhere and everywhere. Flying in was a crapshoot.

On previous missions, he'd always dropped the patrols a good distance from areas known to host the enemy—areas such as the giant, snaking road he could see from three thousand feet: the Ho Chi Minh Trail. He made a slow, orbiting bank so that Wright and Jones could take a closer look with binoculars. But even without binoculars, the trucks streaming down what Yurman called the "Ho Chi Minh Turnpike" were clearly visible, reminding him of the heavy traffic on the New Jersey Turnpike back home.

Thinking that photographs would answer the question of whether there were Russian trucks on the trail, Yurman asked Jones if his crew chief should get out the camera he kept with him, the one with the zoom lens.

Jones thought it was a good idea, and Yurman banked again for the photo op, maintaining his altitude well above small-arms fire, but making the C&C completely vulnerable to a surface-to-air rocket. He took another slow bank back at three thousand feet when Wright vectored him in on a section of jungle east of the road, a small green fingerprint within the darker forest green. The clearing was, by his estimate, less than a half mile from the Ho Chi Minh Trail.

"Mark that," Jones said as he leaned forward into the cockpit. "That's our LZ."

"That?" Yurman asked. "Right next to the road that looks like the Jersey Turnpike?"

9

THE LAUNCH

CREW CHIEF PAUL LaChance, who had transferred from Greyhound One to Mad Dog Three, was up before the sun on the morning of May 2, 1968, grabbing a cup of coffee in the 1st Infantry mess. He and the rest of the 240th currently attached to B-56 at Quan Loi were, as of 0600 hours, on twenty-four-hour alert.

Coffee in hand, LaChance headed out to the flight line, where his right-door gunner, Specialist 4 Jeff Colman, was ready to perform the daily inspection of their aircraft, including the M21 armament system—miniguns—and rocket pods. Today, the two gunship teams were Mad Dog One and Two, piloted by chief warrant officers William Curry and Michael Grant, and Mad Dog Three and Four, piloted by Chief Warrant Officers Louis Wilson and Gary Whitaker.

All was quiet except for the pulsing drone of the generators. As he walked, the light-blue dawn rose into the inky darkness of the eastern horizon. To the west, all was still black in the forbidden zone. Cambodia.

LaChance was a big James Bond fan, had seen *You Only Live Twice* shortly before his tour began, and he thought the feeling that morning was very Double-O-Seven. If he went down in Cambodia and was captured, he'd be considered a spy—they all would. But his goal was the same as that for every mission: "get the team in, get the team out, and get home alive."

A LITTLE after 11:00 a.m., Yurman approached his C&C slick, which was parked within a revetment beside the rest of the Greyhound slicks, and found his copilot, Thomas Smith, already waiting by the door, his flight helmet on the seat. Yurman's boss, the 240th's new company commander, Major Jesse James—who Yurman had thought was back at Bearcat—was there talking to Lieutenant Jones and another Special Forces major.

Yurman soon realized that the Special Forces major had been sent over from Ho Ngoc Tao, by Drake, to ride along and "observe" the mission and that James had come over to fly it. "Who's your copilot?" James asked Yurman, who nodded toward Smith.

"Tell him you're taking his seat," James said. "I'll take yours."

James then pulled a stack of black-and-whites from a folder he was carrying and showed Yurman an aerial photograph of a convoy of trucks and a close-up of one particular truck. "These are the photos your crew chief took at the objective. The major here says it's Russian—the same model as the one they captured up in the A Shau Valley last week."

The photos, it turned out, had been developed at Ho Ngoc Tao's new photo lab right after the recon flight. "So they saw the photos that confirmed the trucks were on the trail and they still need to send a team in to try and get one?" Yurman asked.

James nodded.

If Yurman had known James well enough to be candid, he would have replied: "Sir, I think this whole thing is a bunch of John Wayne, Hollywood bullshit. You don't steal a truck off the Ho Chi Minh Turnpike and *not* get compromised."

Instead, he informed Smith he had the afternoon off and climbed into the right seat. While waiting for the green light to launch, Yurman felt the weight of his impending duties. If James flew this mission, Yurman would be responsible for both identifying the LZ and directing the insertion slicks to the location. James had only been with the company a few weeks and was not yet familiar with their insertion tactics, nor had he been on the visual recon flight and seen the LZ. The formation would be tight, the flying tricky: low level and high speed.

Yurman had no idea how Major James, his new commander, would react to his planned proposal that he—a lower-ranked officer—do the flying.

BACK INSIDE the B-56 compound, the twelve-man team assigned to the mission was assembled and waiting for a truck to shuttle them over to the helicopter pads. It was led by Team Leader (TL) Leroy Wright and consisted of seven CIDG that included Tuan (the interpreter), Bao (the point man), and Chien (the grenadier), two South Vietnamese Special Forces warrant officers, the radioman, Brian O'Connor, and the assistant team leader (ATL), twenty-four-year-old Staff Sergeant Lloyd Mousseau, who was four months into his second tour in Vietnam and in his seventh year in the Army. Mousseau had begun his first tour in an administrative role in Saigon, but had been—like many of the best recon men—recruited by SOG team leaders in-country. His training had been almost entirely on the job, and after another mission or two, he'd get his own team.

Each man checked his own and each other's gear, making sure anything that might rattle was either taped or strapped down. "They'd done this so many times," says Jones, "that the pre-mission planning amounted to little more than going over the map, pointing out the LZ, objective, and alternate LZs, and then launching. It wasn't like Hollywood, with scale models of the objectives and weeks of training. That happened, but it was rare. This mission was like most: a couple of hours prep, a few questions, and they're good to go. The guys who knew what they were doing, knew that everything changed once they were on the ground."

There was no formal formation pre-launch; they did not stand at attention while Wright walked the line. They mingled, then loaded onto a truck and drove to the tarmac.

Daily temperatures in Vietnam ranged between 80 and 95 degrees Fahrenheit with 80 percent humidity, and Crew Chief LaChance was soaked with sweat by the time he finished the preflight checklist for his Mad Dog Three gunship. Glancing up at the sound of a vehicle, he saw the B-56 recon team arrive, dressed "like the VC or NVA."

As they neared the helicopters, a transformation occurred among the team members. "Any and all talk or chatter between us ceased, as did any last-minute adjustments of a strap or harness," says O'Connor. "Silence and a form of stoic stillness set in. We were no longer a group of men preparing for a mission, and a few simple hand signals verified the fact—we were now on it."

LaChance watched the men climb onboard the two lead slicks, with "one or two of the CIDG wearing those NVA helmets; the Americans carried shortened machine guns, AK-47s, camouflaged faces, and big rucksacks. I rode a helicopter to work and didn't hoof it on foot, so any rucksack looked big and heavy to me. I was in awe of those guys, and they looked to me like they were either packing a lot of ammo or going in for a while."

★

"READY ON the P, Chief?" Louis Wilson's voice came over the onboard intercom. LaChance checked power and confirmed, "Ready on the P," and Wilson reached to the control panel between himself and his co-pilot to start the auxiliary power required to crank the engine. There was a brief *whoosh* as the engine ignited, and the rotor blades began to rotate and whir.

One Greyhound slick carrying half of the Special Forces team lifted off, then the other, while the Mad Dogs held at flight idle—a united whine of turbines. Jet fuel exhaust fumes filled the gunships' interiors as their pilots awaited clearance, and for a moment LaChance could have imagined he was driving behind a real Greyhound bus back home in New England on a humid summer day—if it weren't for the potpourri of sewage, cookfires, and the sweet rot of decaying jungle.

He slid down off his seat behind his M60, which hung from the doorway on a bungee cord, and hopped over the skid to the ground. As the pilot pulled pitch and the helicopter lifted slightly off the ground and began to inch ahead, he and his gunner, Jeff Colman, moved forward alongside it. The crew chiefs and gunners on the other three helicopters were doing the same, taking their Mad Dogs for their daily walk. It was a necessary ritual; their gunships were so weighted down with fuel, weaponry, and ammunition, they could not get off the ground without the weight of these men removed while the pilots coaxed their aircraft into the air by literally skidding and bouncing down the runway.

Watching a fully loaded or overloaded Huey take off was nothing like the catapulting of a jet off an aircraft carrier or the nimble, featherweight launch of a reconnaissance plane. Even the lumbering C-130 could somehow find grace two-thirds of the way down a runway. Helicopters—in spite of being the ground warrior's best airborne friend in this jungle war—were not only awkward at takeoff, they were ungainly, their crews running alongside, bouncing them up and down off the runway as the skids threw sparks. At the right moment, LaChance and Colman hopped lightly onto the skid and into the back and the helicopter picked up speed and gradually ascended.

"You can't help but have the feeling that there will come a future generation of men . . . who will look at old pictures of helicopters and say, 'You've got to be kidding,'" said ABC news correspondent Harry Reasoner, reporting from Vietnam in the late sixties. "The thing is, helicopters are different from airplanes. An airplane by its nature *wants* to fly, and if not interfered with too strongly by unusual events or incompetent piloting, it will fly.

"A helicopter does not want to fly. It is maintained in the air by a variety of forces and controls working in opposition to each other. And if there is any disturbance in this delicate balance, the helicopter stops flying—immediately and disastrously.

"There is no such thing as a gliding helicopter.

"That's why being a helicopter pilot is so different from being an airplane pilot, and why in generality airplane pilots are open, clear-eyed, buoyant extroverts. And helicopter pilots are brooders, introspective anticipators of trouble.

"They know if something bad has not happened, it is about to."

THE C&C slick fell in behind and just above Greyhound One and Two with James in the left pilot seat. Though lower in rank and seated in the right copilot position, Yurman was still the acting aircraft (and airmission) commander, focused on the controls while scanning the surrounding airspace, an unusual rank arrangement that James had been receptive to when Yurman proposed it.

Shortly after entering Cambodian airspace, Yurman made contact with his Greyhound slick commanders on one channel; another allowed him to converse with the team's forward air controller. Trailing behind the slicks as they approached the border were the accompanying gunships Mad Dog One and Two, piloted by William Curry and Michael Grant.

The other four helicopters, Greyhound Three and Four and Mad Dog Three and Four, flew five minutes northwest from Ho Ngoc Tao to the Loc Ninh Special Forces camp, where they powered down and sat on alert on the helicopter tarmac adjacent to the camp's artillery battery—call sign "Deadly."

Louis Wilson had felt a certain eeriness as he'd set his skids down on the tarmac at Loc Ninh. He'd heard from an engineer who had helped build the jungle airstrip back in November of 1967 that the blacktop was the lid for a mass grave of Vietcong who'd attacked the camp in late October. The fighting had been fierce and lasted for days; bodies were bloating in the sun where they'd fallen, from the rubber tree plantation at the far end of the strip all the way down the dirt runway to the Special Forces camp. "Deadly" had, on various occasions during the course of battle, leveled its massive guns horizontally and fired anti-personnel "beehive" rounds (packed with metal darts, or "flechettes," they represented a swarm of buzzing death for ground troops) down the runway to repel the Vietcong's charges.

When the VC had finally retreated back into Cambodia, Army engineers first bulldozed the enemy bodies into the trees. The stench became so bad, however, that the mass grave with its blacktop lid was ordered.

Mad Dog Four crew chief Pete Gailis made himself a cup of instant coffee by filling a C ration can with a handful of dirt soaked with jet fuel that had dripped from his gunship's fuel tank drainage valve. Once the dirt was lit, it turned the can into a ministove that heated a cup of coffee in a minute.

It was pretty late in the day for a covert mission, thought Gailis, but making insertions at all hours kept the enemy guessing. And while the cover of darkness would in future decades be the norm for special ops, when every operator would use night-vision goggles, soldiers in

1968 had only an early generation of night vision. An entire team would share a "starlight scope."

The general wisdom was that "Charlie owned the night," especially on the Ho Chi Minh Trail. Yurman, in the C&C slick, had believed it as well—before yesterday's recon flight, when they'd found the road bustling with traffic in the middle of the day.

He had expected a sleepy, inactive road—and a sleepy, inactive, unsuspecting enemy. *One can still hope,* he thought. *One can still hope.*

WRIGHT, O'CONNOR, Tuan, Bao, Chien, and other CIDG were inside Greyhound One; Mousseau and five CIDG had piled into Greyhound Two. The "heavy" team—double the size of a standard recon team—was the maximum number of American personnel permitted by the Johnson administration to operate as a single unit "over the fence."

They crossed the Cambodian border, where the accompanying gunships went into a holding pattern to lessen the air activity near the insertion point. McKibben and Ewing dropped their Greyhounds to treetop level west toward the LZ. Flying a few thousand feet above Yurman's C&C slick, which was just above and behind Greyhound One and Two, twenty-six-year-old Air Force captain Robin Tornow, the B-56 team's forward air controller (FAC), announced over the radio of his O1-F Bird Dog Cessna that vehicle traffic on the Ho Chi Minh Trail a half mile west of the LZ was light. *Insanity,* thought Yurman. He still couldn't believe they were inserting guys this close to the road.

Roughly 150 yards by 100 yards, the kidney-shaped LZ tapered to a narrow arm that jutted into the jungle to the northwest; the main clearing was a wide-open meadow to the east. Knee- to waist-high grass dominated the eastern half of the clearing, with a few bushes scattered here and there. Just west of center were two clumps of trees, small thickets or "islands" of cover surrounded by a sea of waving grass. Running east to west through the middle of the twenty-foot-tall wispy trees in the larger southernmost thicket was an oblong anthill, ten feet long and waist high. Farther west of these thickets, the grass was joined by thicker concentrations of bushes and small trees.

Once Yurman had talked the two slick pilots in close enough to have eyes on the landing zone—seventy-five or one hundred yards—he peeled off so as not to overfly the LZ, while McKibben dropped into it, flared to a hover a couple feet off the ground; seconds later Wright, O'Connor, and the four CIDG were running toward the northern edge of the clearing. McKibben lifted off and was just clearing the treetops when Ewing came in to drop Mousseau and his five CIDG. Banking low and hard, both slicks reversed direction and were gone by the time the team had traversed the forty exposed yards and disappeared into the jungle. While the men checked their equipment, Wright did a quick head count and made radio contact with Tornow, flying overhead at four thousand feet—a speck barely visible against a light-blue sky scattered with high clouds.

Tornow confirmed with Wright that the team was at the correct insertion point and undetected, then initiated a high, lonely orbit to monitor the mission far below. Nearly half of his ten months in Vietnam had been with B-56, and these clandestine recon missions were the most fulfilling of his career. He held the SOG (Studies and Operations Group) brotherhood in the highest regard, and while he wasn't on the ground beside them, he was their overwatch, their lifeline, and he felt responsible for their safety. But his ability to provide it was severely handicapped the moment they crossed into Cambodia. Per the current rules of engagement, if a team was compromised or fell under attack across the border, they could only call for helicopter extraction with helicopter gunship support. Under no circumstances could they call in support from fixed-wing aircraft such as fighters, bombers, or the C-130 gunships.

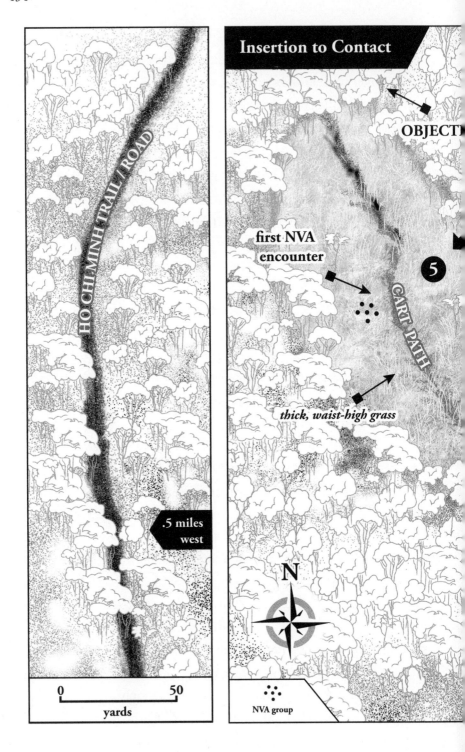

HO CHI MINH TRAIL / ROAD

.5 miles west

0   50
yards

Insertion to Contact

OBJECTI

first NVA encounter

CART PATH

5

thick, waist-high grass

N

NVA group

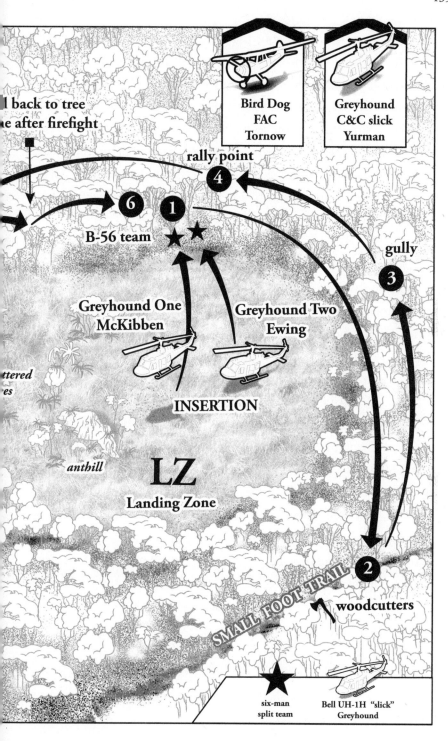

The majority of the missions that had infiltrated Cambodia before 1968 had used small reconnaissance teams of six to twelve men crossing the border on foot and penetrating less than a half mile. By early 1968, a few teams had been taken in by helicopter, but almost none had gone this deep. Tornow knew of the teams that had simply vanished into this no-man's-land and that the men were not reported as prisoners of war. He knew the code—that Wright, Mousseau, O'Connor, and the CIDG would not allow themselves to be captured. They would fight to their deaths protecting one another.

THE TEAM lay silently in the jungle on the northern edge of the clearing, each member watching a section of the enemy's backyard. Some of the men were responsible for monitoring the clearing; the others faced the shadowy unknown beneath the triple-canopy ecosystem spreading out before them like the edge of the world.

The uppermost layer of the canopy, the tallest trees, topped one hundred feet, their branches soaking in the sunlight that filtered down to the second canopy of tree-sized ferns that required less sunlight. The lowest canopy of vines and tangled, thorny "bush" was the darkest. In addition to the enemy, it concealed all manner of dangerous fauna, from poisonous snakes to man-eating tigers to monkeys. In fact, the .22 caliber silenced pistols recon men carried to kill, or incapacitate and capture, enemy soldiers on the trail served a double purpose of shooting the male monkeys whose screeches could pinpoint their position.

The team waited, hearing little more than the creaking of tree branches and a gecko's repetitive *geh-ko, geh-ko*. After a half hour, when it appeared that the helicopters had not attracted any enemy activity, Wright and Mousseau reviewed the map. If the intelligence report was accurate, there would be a small foot trail approximately one hundred yards to their south, beyond the far side of the clearing. The trail angled east to west-southwest through the thick jungle about three-quarters of a mile before intersecting a well-maintained section of the Ho Chi Minh Trail.

The team moved out to circumvent the northeast end of the clearing, with Bao at the point and Mousseau just behind him. Wright was in the center behind Tuan, and O'Connor was toward the rear with another CIDG as the rear security "tail gunner" for the column. It was slow going as they, quietly as possible, pushed and picked their way through the dense vegetation. After nearly fifty yards of slow, hot bushwhacking they passed a gully that offered a little cover in the otherwise flat, spongy ground.

Fifty yards beyond the gully, the team reached the foot trail. Now a decision had to be made: follow the trail, opting for speed, or take the more tedious route through the jungle, opting for concealment. Both routes would ultimately reach their main objective, the gravel road, where they would set their trap to capture an NVA officer or, if the opportunity presented itself, to hijack a supply truck; the question was whether they would reach it in one hour or several.

The plan to steal a truck was at best theoretical: target a supply truck traveling alone or trailing far enough behind a convoy to not be seen in a rearview mirror. A bend in the road would be required for concealment; a bend in the road with a side road, preferably heading east, would be ideal. One member of the team, a CIDG, would act as if he were injured, carried or helped along by two other CIDG, who included Tuan. The trio would emerge from their hiding place and start hobbling down the road, with Tuan hailing its driver for help. The driver, and if need be, passenger, would then be incapacitated.

A year before, the commander of SOG—Chief SOG Jack Singlaub—had requested the inclusion of tranquilizer darts in the rules of engagement to "incapacitate enemy prisoners ambushed on the Trail," he later explained. "Washington denied the request, saying such darts were risky because, without knowing the subject's exact body weight, we might administer a fatal overdose. Therefore, the darts were unnecessarily 'cruel.'" Singlaub tried to convince Washington that "a bullet . . . was infinitely crueler than a tranquilizer dart, and that, given a choice, the NVA soldiers in question would no doubt vote for the dart. But they held their ground."

And so Wright's team would "incapacitate," deciding on the spot to capture or kill the driver and potential passenger with a bullet or two fired from a silenced pistol. The team members would dispose of the body or bodies, or bind and blindfold the prisoner(s), drive the truck off the road, and conceal it. Then, according to O'Connor, "we'd have a moment of discovery" as to how, exactly, they were going to get the truck back to South Vietnam—either by driving it or hoisting it with a heavy-lift helicopter.

This was all distant speculation. First the team had to make it to the road undetected, and there was work to be done along the way—mapping the network of suspected concealed paths and reporting any enemy encampments or movement.

After ten minutes, Wright signaled O'Connor forward. He whispered that Mousseau had spotted a small group of people moving toward them along the trail. "Watch the rear," Wright said, "and be ready to reverse in case of trouble."

A BIG part of SOG's mission in Cambodia was PSYOP—psychological operations devised to demoralize and cause the NVA and VC traveling on the Ho Chi Minh Trail to defect. Operation Camel Path had, in November 1967, begun dropping millions of leaflets from aircraft over the border areas. Recently, Leaflet 95-T showed a photo of dead and rotting NVA soldiers with text that read: "During the Communists' Tet Offensive, the Army of the Republic of South Vietnam and the Allies killed more than 65,000 Communist troops and captured more than 12,000. You are being sent to replace them. Most of you will be killed. . . . Seize the first opportunity to leave your unit and come over to the ranks of the Republic of Vietnam." Another leaflet, chillingly poetic, warned the NVA operating in this region that their future was destined for the "fate of the unmarked grave on Cambodian soil, of preying beasts [that] await your dying breath."

Mousseau and Bao, their faces camouflaged, were those beasts, as still as the vegetation surrounding them as they crouched a few feet off the trail, monitoring the three men who approached their position. Charged with widening the footpath using machetes and hatchets, these "woodcutters" were also armed with AK-47s slung across their chests, marking them as North Vietnamese.

Wright was a dozen yards behind Mousseau, deeper in the undergrowth, while O'Connor was poised for retreat a few yards behind him. At this distance—some twenty yards off the trail—O'Connor couldn't see the work crew, but he could hear them hacking away with their machetes, tossing aside cut branches and vines. The noise increased, and O'Connor tried to discern when the sounds of breaking branches began to recede, indicating the work crew had passed them by.

It was not to be. A muffled scream was accompanied by a quick succession of "clicks" that were the reports from a silenced pistol. It was followed quickly by a short burst of gunfire from an AK-47.

O'Connor paused momentarily, confirming that there was no follow-up to the gunfire—no firefight. Wright signaled with his hand to reverse, and O'Connor with the CIDG quickly backtracked to the gully he had identified earlier as a rally point. He directed the CIDG into the cover, where they formed a hasty defensive perimeter, their rifles and carbines pointed back down their route, prepared to cover Wright, Mousseau, and Bao if they were pursued.

A few minutes later, Wright appeared; he reported that the woodcutters had begun chopping out the narrow spot of the trail where

Mousseau and Bao were hiding, clearing away some of the foliage that concealed their position. Then a woodcutter had looked right at them, the trigger for Mousseau and Bao to eliminate the threat, swiftly and quietly. One had gotten his finger on his AK-47 trigger as he went down.

Moments later Mousseau and Bao, their hands and arms smeared with blood, crawled into the perimeter.

"We hid the bodies," said Mousseau, "but the gunfire may have compromised us."

The entire team knew how damning the gunfire was but held on to hope that since it had been both brief and from an enemy weapon, it could be interpreted as an accidental discharge. If the helicopters were also heard, however, the gunfire would be investigated. The men had to assume the worst—that their role was shifting from hunter to hunted.

"They chopped right up to us," said Mousseau, "we had no choice."

THE TEAM members hastily dug in, concealing themselves within the undergrowth of the gully, while Wright quietly discussed options with Mousseau and O'Connor. Then they heard voices from the general direction of the insertion point—a disturbingly quick response to the gunfire.

In late 1967, the NVA had converted an entire brigade into "hunter-killer" forces, their mission to track down and capture or kill American and South Vietnamese recon teams on the Ho Chi Minh Trail. Intelligence would eventually learn that these large, company-size "counter-recon" units of a hundred and fifty men were assigned to conventional forces based at intervals on the trail. After a recon team was detected, the North Vietnamese counter-recon force split into squads or platoons and swept the suspected area, often employing tracker dogs. The search was orchestrated by radio, with the conventional forces called in to ensure that superior numbers could encircle and overwhelm the recon team and thwart any rescue attempts. They would also shoot down the helicopters they knew would attempt an extraction, multiplying the casualties.

Concentrating on the voices, Wright came to the conclusion that this was an enemy patrol sweeping across the clearing, looking for signs of a recent insertion—trampled grass, footprints, perhaps a carelessly dropped piece of equipment—while heading toward the foot trail to investigate the gunfire. If the patrol avoided the thick jungle to the north, instead crossing the clearing to the trail, it would pass right by the team's current location.

The brief conversations among members of the patrol provided snippets of information that indicated they were moving into the wood line and away from the team. But it was impossible to know if there were others lying in wait, monitoring the clearing—the only LZ within a mile where a helicopter could land.

Once he was convinced the patrol had passed them, Wright attempted to radio Tornow to request a standby alert for possible extraction. The thick jungle canopy, however, prevented contact. Knowing the enemy was close and might at any moment find the bodies of the woodcutters, Wright then turned the radio off while backtracking to the first rally point, a location near the clearing where they'd had a clear radio signal. There they monitored the clearing, which appeared void of any enemy movement. They could barely make out the faint sounds of voices and machetes chopping through the jungle off its southeastern end.

Perhaps the group had been another work party, crossing the clearing en route to the trail they were enlarging. Or perhaps they *had* been sent to investigate the gunfire. If so, where were they sent from? Was there a nearby NVA base camouflaged from the air patrols? That, of course, was part of their reconnaissance mission: to get a good sense of what this jungle held beneath the canopy or, deeper still, dug into the ground. The NVA were masters at constructing underground tunnel systems. The team could be standing on top of an enemy base right then and there and not even know it.

The group continued to move away from the men to the southeast; the team's objective—the Ho Chi Minh Trail—was in the opposite direction to the northwest. While O'Connor changed out the antenna on his radio, the CIDG gave conflicting reports on what the enemy had been saying, and their type and unit size, which ranged from a squad of six to twelve NVA to a large detachment of woodcutters. Tuan listened attentively to the CIDG as they reported the enemy conversations. One word they agreed on hearing was *truc thang,* Vietnamese for helicopter, and Tuan concluded that it had most likely been the NVA looking for an American recon team or a downed helicopter—but he couldn't be sure.

Wright tried to decide whether to call in that they had been compromised and request extraction, or to continue with the mission. "It was a difficult decision," O'Connor later wrote, "because the objective was close to being a one-time try, and if we reached it we would have total and full support; but if we got compromised or made hot contact on our way to the objective, the enemy's guard would be up and it might be too late to try it again at another time."

Wright proposed to Mousseau and O'Connor that since the team had not been detected, they should inform command of their situation and hopefully get the okay to continue toward the objective. The men agreed. They had begun to discuss an alternative route to the objective, and Wright was preparing to call in a report when they again heard voices. Everybody froze.

The mystery group was returning from the eastern side of the clearing and coming toward the north side, their location. On the southern side, across the landing zone, were more voices.

A decision was quickly reached. Wright contacted Robin Tornow, explained the situation, and requested immediate extraction.

★

STILL ORBITING high above, Tornow received Wright's transmission loud and clear. He could see the LZ out the side window of his banking Cessna, a light-green crescent. The Ho Chi Minh Trail, a prominent line a half mile to the west, was speckled with vehicles.

Tornow told Wright to stand by, then relayed the communication to Jones, who was in the C&C slick just as Yurman was approaching Quan Loi to land. Jones asked Yurman to remain airborne and return to the LZ. Minutes later, they came within range of the team's PRC-25 radio, and Jones was able to speak directly to Wright, who confirmed three points: they had been compromised by three armed men, there had been gunfire, and the team had killed the men and hidden the bodies.

"Stand by for extraction," Jones informed Wright.

At that moment, the Special Forces major tapped Jones on the shoulder and said, "No, no, they have to stay in."

"No, Sir, that's not the way we do this," replied Jones. "I'm the launch officer; we're gonna go in and get them, come back, and refuel, regroup, and then we'll put them back in on their alternate LZ. We have to get them now." He told Yurman to get his slicks on station to extract, and Yurman relayed this to his Greyhounds and Mad Dogs, poised to launch at Loc Ninh.

But the Special Forces major told Yurman to cancel the launch. "They're not in contact," he said. "They're going to stay in."

It was unusual to override standard operating procedure for extraction in such instances, but not unprecedented. Ultimately, it was the call of the officer in charge.

At Loc Ninh, Mad Dog Three gunship copilot Jesse Naul, who was monitoring the radio, spun his finger in the air to signal to his aircraft commander, Louis Wilson, and crew chief, Paul LaChance, that it was time "to crank," says Naul, who wasn't surprised. "Our unit [the 240th] had inserted and extracted several teams prior to [this]. The area was so heavily patrolled that we simply could not keep the teams on the ground long enough to accomplish their mission."

Then they got the call to abort the launch and stand by.

In the C&C slick, Jones and the Special Forces major argued back and forth—Jones stating several times that it was standard operating procedure to extract a team at compromise, and in this case there had been gunfire, so it was much more than compromise. The major, according to Jones, argued that unless the team was still in direct contact, they were to stay on the ground.

Hearing this, Jones assumed the major had been sent not to "observe" but to make sure he kept the team on the ground as long as possible. While Jones and the major argued in the backseat, Yurman hit the privacy button on the intercom and spoke to James privately.

"Sir," he said, "when there's contact, we pull them. I agree with the lieutenant."

Finally James leaned back between the seats and bellowed at the major, "Look! The lieutenant knows what he's doing. Let's go in and get them now while we can, before they get into any more trouble."

"Sir," Jones pleaded, "if we wait, we're going to lose the team, or we're going to lose helicopters. This isn't the time to discuss this."

"But he was insistent," says Yurman. "He had his orders and was sticking to them. He told Lieutenant Jones he outranked him and [Jones] was off the mission. He was in charge now."

Tornow knew the protocol and was surprised when he received orders for the team "to evade and stay concealed until the threat passes. [Then] move on with their mission." He relayed the communication to Wright, who gave the order to continue to the objective, adding that they would "take a shortcut in order to leave the LZ area before the enemy swept through."

Following Wright's lead, the team members shouldered their ruck-sacks, checked their weapons, and moved away from the LZ as silently and quickly as possible, pushing rather than cutting a route through the foliage—a technique that was quieter than a machete and didn't leave behind an obvious trail.

PER THE directive of the Special Forces major, the C&C slick returned to Quan Loi to refuel and wait. Upon landing, Jones immediately headed for the headquarters of the First Infantry Division's Brigade Commander—the ranking officer at Quan Loi—while Yurman headed for the B-56 compound to monitor the radio.

Approaching the TOC, Yurman recognized Larry McKibben's tall, lanky frame standing on a rise just outside the sandbag walls that surrounded the tent.

"Contact," Yurman said, and McKibben nodded, staring off into the distance. When a team announced they'd made contact, the next call, in their experience, was for extraction and both Yurman and McKibben suspected this was going to be a hot one.

As long as Yurman had known him, McKibben had never shown an ounce of trepidation. Less than two months before, on March 8, his part of a combat assault mission near Dong Tam had earned him a recommendation from his commander for a Distinguished Flying Cross award, currently under consideration.

Today, Yurman sensed a change in McKibben—in his eyes, in his mannerisms. He had seen it before, especially when a pilot was as short as McKibben was, only a few weeks shy of going home.

"Even the coolest pilots have a limit," Yurman says. "They've been holding it together for three hundred days plus, and whatever day it is they cross that line and they start to think, and up till then they hadn't done that. At the beginning of your tour, maybe you think you're not gonna make it home, so screw it, just fly the guts out of the helicopter, make it do things the manufacturer says it can't do, why not? Then you hit that magic number and you start thinking the opposite, like 'Holy shit, maybe I *will* make it.' And your mind starts playing games."

Knowing that McKibben had never questioned any order, never even hesitated before, and would never ask to be taken off a mission, Yurman decided to give him a break if he could. "Larry, everybody knows you're lead, but listen, I want you to be my reserve for extraction. Waggie, Armstrong, and Ewing will be primary. You sit tight in reserve."

"Sir—" McKibben started to say.

"What are they gonna do to me?" Yurman said. "Send me to Vietnam? You and Ewing head to Loc Ninh and sit standby with the rest of the guys. If I don't call you, we don't need you. Keep your skids on the ground. That's an order."

BACK ON the north side of the clearing, O'Connor was the second man in the column, just behind Bao. He scanned their flanks as they moved west, looking for anything that didn't fit the landscape—a horizontal line that could reveal a bunker, a shape among the branches of a tree that might betray a sniper.

Mousseau was positioned in the center of the patrol, and Wright took the tail, warily monitoring their rear. All were on high alert, relying on their intuition and training as they crept west toward the main road, through progressively thicker vegetation, catching occasional glimpses of the clearing far to their left. Every step they took away from their insertion point was distancing them from where the enemy would most likely start to track them. After more than a hundred yards and just as the jungle's darkness was beginning to cloak the team in a degree of invisibility, light filtered more brightly through the layers of cover—the telltale sign of thinning vegetation.

They had reached the far end of the clearing where it curved and tapered into an arm—the narrower side of the kidney. Pausing to survey the distance needed to cross the thirty or forty yards of the opening, they noted a few scattered trees and bushes at the near end, and a cart path heading north to south. Both the clearing and path appeared devoid of any movement, and Bao moved quickly forward. He was approximately a third of the way across when O'Connor followed, the rest of the team behind him and just inside the edge of the tree line.

At that moment, eight to twelve NVA soldiers, fully armed and in their signature green uniform, emerged from the jungle on the other side of the clearing.

Both units stopped abruptly in their tracks.

10

AS BAD AS IT GETS

Jones entered the First Infantry Division, brigade headquarters tent, and asked to speak with the commanding officer. Three days before, Lieutenant Jones had briefed him about the impending mission they were to launch from his base camp across the border into Cambodia.

Much of the B-56 recon missions had, in the early months of 1968, been focused within South Vietnam and on the infiltration routes along the Cambodian border. The May 2 mission was the deepest B-56 had probed into Cambodia; the strategy, according to Jones, was to fly over the enemy that was massed and entrenched along the border and insert the men where they were not expected.

Now Jones found the colonel in his office, along with his S-2 (intelligence) officer, a First Infantry Division major, up to their elbows planning San Diego (search-and-destroy) missions. They looked up from the map they were studying.

Anticipating that the team on the ground was about to get into trouble, Jones said to the colonel, "Sir, we have a Daniel Boone Emergency."

"He looked at me like I had three heads," says Jones. "He had no idea what I was talking about."

"Sir," the S-2 officer interjected, "they've got troops in contact in Cambodia. Across the border, Sir."

That got the colonel's attention. He walked around the desk, faced Jones, and with a thick, reassuring Southern drawl said, "Well, now, what do ya'll need, Lieutenant? What can I do to help?"

"They're far beyond your artillery range," Jones replied. "I just wanted you to be aware of the situation, and if you have any extra gunships on alert, we might need them real soon."

"I think we can spare a light-fire team [two helicopter gunships]," the colonel said. "You can count on that."

"Thank you, Sir," Jones said, feeling he had done all he could as he hurried out of the office and to the B-56 TOC to monitor the radio.

THE NVA squad and the B-56 team faced each other in the clearing. Then Bao moved confidently ahead and began talking loudly to the NVA squad leader.

Looking down at his boots to hide his face, O'Connor casually pulled a piece of paper out of his pocket. He continued to stare at it while walking a few steps backward to stand beside Mousseau. The two men kept their heads down, studying the paper as if it were a map. Tuan came up beside them. "They think we're from the other unit," he whispered.

"Tell them we're looking for a chopper that was shot at, that we heard go down," Mousseau whispered back. Tuan nodded, but before he could move ahead and deliver the message, Bao turned around and commanded the team to search the thickest jungle area, as if he was in charge.

Mousseau and O'Connor immediately obeyed, but as they headed toward the clearing's edge, Mousseau quietly said to O'Connor, "I think they might have seen your face. When Bao is clear, you take the left and I'll take the right, but only if things look bad."

Bao continued to bark orders, and the NVA leader waved what appeared to be a parting "good-bye." Suddenly, the enemy officer called out harshly to Bao.

"They know!" shouted Tuan.

What happened next was instantaneous as Mousseau, O'Connor, and Bao went on autopilot: Mousseau targeted the enemy soldiers to the right, O'Connor took those on the left, and Bao, not privy to the impromptu plan, joined them in sending a hail of bullets into any still standing. Their marksmanship under pressure was astounding: all but two of the twelve NVA were dead within seconds. The two survivors dropped to their knees and returned fire. One let loose a rocket-propelled grenade (RPG) that passed over the team's head and exploded in the trees.

Mousseau, O'Connor, and Bao continued to fire while back-stepping into the jungle, where the rest of the team remained concealed, and Wright was calling for immediate extraction. Once the three men were clear, their CIDG teammates opened fire and killed the two remaining NVA.

Twenty or thirty yards into the jungle, the team formed another perimeter, and Wright informed Mousseau that the extraction slicks were "on the way and ready for a hot one." Reaching into his shirt, he pulled a few documents from the waterproof pouch he kept secured by a lanyard around his neck and handed them to O'Connor. "Destroy these," he said. "They're no good to us now."

As O'Connor and Mousseau ignited a chunk of C-4 explosive and lit the papers on fire, Wright motioned for the team to head back east toward their original insertion point. It was a risky move, but there were no other clearings in the vicinity, and the helicopters were inbound.

Between their own firepower and the cover fire of the extraction slicks and their gunships, with any luck they'd be picked up and gone before a large-scale NVA reaction force converged on the area.

INSIDE THE Forward Air Controller's Bird Dog, the radio sprang to life with the sound of gunfire, and the firm voice of Leroy Wright declared the obvious: "We are taking fire. Request immediate extraction. We are in heavy contact. What is your ETA?"

Almost an hour had passed since Jones had been relieved of his command of the mission. Yurman did not wait for an order, but immediately radioed the 240th reaction force on standby at Loc Ninh, telling aircraft commanders Jerry Ewing in Greyhound Two, Roger Waggie in Greyhound Three, and William Armstrong in Greyhound Four to launch immediately as the primary extraction team. McKibben would be reserve.

"Be advised," Yurman said, "it's going to be a hot one."

The pilots at Loc Ninh, including McKibben, ran to their slicks and gunships that their crew chiefs—having anticipated what was to come—had prepped for takeoff. Jumping into his seat, McKibben got on the ship-to-ship radio and told Armstrong and Waggie to stand down, and told Ewing to crank. "We put them in," he said. "We'll get them out."

But when he attempted to fire up the engine, there was no juice. His battery was dead, perhaps from monitoring the radio. Throwing his arms up in frustration, McKibben radioed back to the other pilots, "I've got a dead battery here—you'd better launch. I'll catch up."

Waggie's crew chief, Michael Craig, piped in with the line he used whenever his aircraft got the green light for an extraction: "Let's go get 'em, then."

On the ground, the B-56 team was concealed just within the trees beside the clearing. As O'Connor and Mousseau divided the men into two groups of six, Wright contacted Tornow to reconfirm that they were ready for extraction and standing by at the "exact location" they had been inserted at nearly two hours prior. A hush had enveloped the jungle, an eerie calm after the explosive firefight. This quiet did not mean the men were alone. They waited, ears tuned for any sound—the creaking of a tree, the snap of a branch, the sudden cry of a monkey— that might betray the enemy's approach. The harder they listened, the longer the minutes seemed to stretch.

WAGGIE AND Armstrong had launched from Loc Ninh a few minutes after Yurman's order. They didn't take the time to gain altitude; instead they flew low and fast, a couple of hundred feet above ground level, Waggie in the lead, his copilot, Warrant Officer David Hoffman, beside him. Behind Waggie, his crew chief, Michael Craig, pointed his M60 machine gun down toward the jungle canopy to cover the seven to eleven o'clock of the aircraft. The right-side door gunner was covering the five to one o'clock.

Fifteen minutes after they'd taken off from Loc Ninh, Yurman got a visual on both slicks, flying in a staggered trail formation with Armstrong about thirty seconds—or half a mile—behind Waggie. While James held the C&C slick in a wide clockwise orbit, giving Yurman an open view of the clearing—no longer considered the LZ, it was now referred to as the pickup zone (PZ)—he vectored the two Greyhounds in from the east, northeast. Standard operating procedure called for both aircraft commander and copilot to have their hands on dual controls that moved in unison; the commander kept a firm grip on the stick and did the actual flying, while the copilot "covered" the controls with a light hand, ready to engage the controls and operate the aircraft at a moment's notice if the commander was wounded or killed.

In the event that either the pilot or copilot *was* wounded or killed, the crewmen behind could yank on a red lever on the back of each of their seats, reclining them. This allowed the crewmen to pull a wounded or dead pilot backward into the cargo area of the helicopter, clamp a spurting artery, or climb forward to assist the surviving pilot. If both pilots were dead, a crewman could take the stick himself—the stuff of crew members' nightmares.

Greyhounds Three and Four were joined by their gunship support, Mad Dogs One and Two piloted by William Curry and CW2 Michael Grant. Curry, the gunship fire team leader, had—during the insertion—remained airborne at the border with his wingman, Grant, ready to provide close air support with their full complements of four thousand rounds of M60 ammunition, six thousand rounds of minigun ammunition, and fourteen rockets. After the first half hour of quiet, Curry and Grant had flown back to Quon Loi to refuel. They had been on their way to stand by on alert at Loc Ninh with Mad Dog Three and Four when the B-56 team's emergency call for extraction came in.

Still concealed at the edge of the clearing, the team heard the faint but distinct *whop, whop, whop* of the approaching helicopters. Wright held off throwing a smoke grenade that would help the pilots identify their position because it would also reveal their location to any enemy in the vicinity. If the slicks hit the original insertion point, the men— now divided into two teams of six—would have a twenty- or thirty-yard sprint to the open side doors. A half hour later, they'd be sipping a cold one back at Quan Loi.

"Two miles out, Greyhound Three. Stay on your current heading," Yurman radioed, vectoring Waggie toward the PZ at shorter and shorter intervals.

The B-56 team had readied themselves to sprint across the clearing when they heard what O'Connor described as "the roar of small-arms and heavy autofire" to the east that "intensified as the slicks approached." In Greyhound Three, a half mile out, Waggie saw Mad Dog One lurch to one side, then start trailing black smoke.

enemy
reinforcements

HO CHI MINH TRAIL / ROAD

enemy
reinforcements

.5 miles
west

0   50

yards

Daniel Boone Tactical Emergency

sounds of
heavy track vehicle

CART PATH

tac air strikes

FAC shoots
white phosphorus
rocket
to mark enemy

N

NVA group   machine gun .50   tree nest
(elevated machine gun)

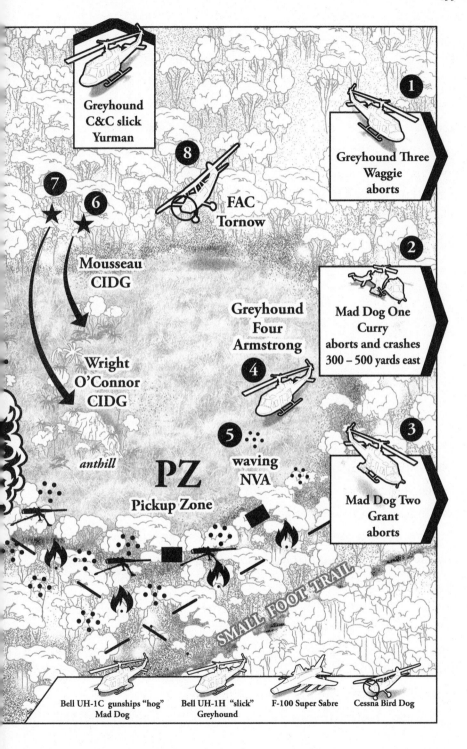

Greyhound
C&C slick
Yurman

1 Greyhound Three
Waggie
aborts

8 FAC
Tornow

7 **6**

Mousseau
CIDG

Wright
O'Connor
CIDG

**Greyhound
Four
Armstrong**

4

2 Mad Dog One
Curry
aborts and crashes
300 – 500 yards east

5 waving
NVA

anthill **PZ**
Pickup Zone

3 Mad Dog Two
Grant
aborts

SMALL FOOT TRAIL

Bell UH-1C gunships "hog"   Bell UH-1H "slick"   F-100 Super Sabre   Cessna Bird Dog
Mad Dog   Greyhound

The platoon sergeant for the Mad Dogs, Sergeant First Class Pete Jones, was so "short" he could almost taste the cold beer he planned to order on his freedom bird home in two weeks. But his crew chiefs had been flying so much the previous week, he'd decided to give one of them a break by volunteering for the mission, aboard Mad Dog One. Now the gunship was bucking through the air, and he was peppered by fragments of bullets as they ripped through the floor and bounced around the cabin. His gunner—a guy everybody called Swisher because his fake front teeth made a swishing sound when he talked—was blown off his M60 and lay motionless on his back, his eyes closed.

Jones looked for a wound, then found it: a bullet had hit the edge of Swisher's helmet and entered his forehead, leaving a tiny hole from which blood oozed. The impact had cracked the helmet from front to back. Jones barely had time to register that Swisher was dead before he smelled the burning oil, saw the smoke, and heard the change in the tone of the engine. The helicopter banked away from the PZ, leveled off over the trees, and began to gain altitude as it accelerated west.

An instant later, Waggie flew Greyhound Three into the same wall of anti-aircraft fire. He could hear the bullets coming up around his feet, distinct thuds and pings that penetrated the Plexiglas nose bubble, ripped through the thin metal skin of the aircraft, and impacted with the underside of their armored seats.

Leaning over their M60s, the gunners returned fire into the jungle, but the deep, stuttering roar from Michael Craig's gun stopped abruptly as a bullet cleared the underside of his "chicken plate" (ballistic armor worn by air crews) and tore into his ribs and chest. The impact from the round flung him up and backward onto the cabin floor. "Your crew chief is hit!" yelled the Special Forces bellyman on board to assist with the extraction. He reached over to help Craig just as the door gunner was spun backward by a bullet to the shoulder.

Copilot Hoffman instinctively gripped the controls and yelled,

"Breaking right!" as Waggie radioed Armstrong, who was hot on their tail in Greyhound Four and about to fly into a wall of fire. "Bank right, Greyhound Four, bank right! We're taking hits! Abort extraction! Abort extraction!"

O'CONNOR THOUGHT it sounded as if the slicks "had the whole jungle firing at them," yet the area surrounding the team remained silent. Suddenly Greyhound Four raced into view over their left shoulders, skimming the treetops from the northeast. Its nose flared upward to arrest its speed and the slick dropped into the clearing, whipping and flattening the grass below in the hurricane created by the rotor wash. The helicopter hovered there momentarily about a hundred yards away from the men, close to where the team had originally encountered the woodcutters.

There was no time for Wright to signal Armstrong—smoke or mirror—because a half-dozen NVA immediately emerged from the trees adjacent to the helicopter. They approached Greyhound Four, waving. The slick's skids tapped the ground, then settled into the grass, ready for the team to board.

My God, thought O'Connor, *they think that's us!* At the same moment, the team's CIDG came to the same realization and fired on the NVA that were nearing the helicopter. From within Greyhound Four, Specialist 4 Robert Wessel, the right-side door gunner, identified the CIDG's fully automatic gunfire as enemy fire and strafed the B-56 team's position.

"Cease fire!" Wright yelled at the CIDG. The guns fell silent, and Wright shouted into his radio, "Get that chopper back in the air!" There was no response, and he switched channels, attempting to reach the forward air controller, the C&C slick, the extraction pilot across the clearing—anybody who could get the message that Greyhound Four was about to be ambushed by the NVA: "Get that chopper back in the air! Get them out of there! That is Charlie, I repeat . . ."

GREYHOUND FOUR's pilots and crew were watching the approach of what they assumed was the American-led team dressed in their NVA-disguise uniforms when Mousseau and O'Connor took aim and dropped the lead NVA soldier. In response, the remaining five NVA raised their AK-47s and charged, opening fire on the helicopter. Gunner Wessel leveled his M60 at the group, their bodies flung backward thirty yards from the aircraft.

Wright ordered Mousseau to try to signal the helicopter with a mirror. If that didn't work, they would risk a grenade of red-and-green smoke in front of their position. As O'Connor flipped switches on the radio, holding the antenna overhead, cursing, and praying for a signal, Wright tapped him on the shoulder and pointed across the clearing.

Within the tree line, a column of some thirty NVA was rapidly nearing the helicopter.

MAD DOG One, mortally wounded and hemorrhaging—oil, hydraulic fluid, and fuel spraying out over the jungle—continued flying west, farther into Cambodia. Curry fought the gunship's controls to gain altitude and mileage, willing it into a bank that would bring the helicopter back on an eastern bearing. At the same time he scanned the ground below for a place to set down. There was the Ho Chi Minh Trail with its stream of enemy trucks, the PZ he'd just been shot out of, and the green of the jungle. So much green.

Alone in the backseat with the dead gunner, Swisher, Jones gripped his M60, acutely aware of the unnatural sounds of the laboring aircraft. He kept glancing down at Swisher on the floor—his closed eyes, the speck of blood in the middle of his forehead, and that perfect vertical crack down the center of his helmet. Out the window, the horizon receded while the gunship shook, rattled, and fought to gain altitude— two hundred feet, three hundred, four hundred; from hell to purgatory they climbed. They were no longer taking fire, but this was dangerous air, low enough to be reached by enemy small-arms ground fire and high enough to be spotted and tracked by anybody looking up.

And then there was a very distinct quiet of an engine suddenly stopping. "Hang on," Curry said calmly over the intercom. "We're going down."

Curry had managed to gain enough altitude that he could initiate the helicopter's version of a glide, autorotating so that its blades can catch the wind as it falls like a rock; if the pilot is able to conjure up the necessary "glide," a powerless helicopter can land without certain death to all those on board.

This is something all the pilots had done during training over a big clearing or a runway, but not over solid jungle full of enemy forces. Jones, who felt as if his stomach was pressing up against his tonsils, could make out plenty of them through the trees below as they fell. He also caught a glimpse of a bomb crater, and then Curry flared from his autorotation glide and hit hard on the skids, landing in a postage stamp–size clearing. Somehow, he had brought them down in a barely visible speck that would have been hard to hit with full power.

Jones went to unlatch his M60, then realized he had spent his last bullets on the pass over the PZ. Grabbing his rucksack, which held grenades, a couple of C rations, and extra ammo for his M16, he jumped from Mad Dog One and hurried to the front of the helicopter to help Curry and his copilot, David Brown, both with .38s in their holsters, carry Swisher.

As Jones leaned over the body, Swisher opened his eyes, startling all three men. What appeared to be a bullet hole was actually a small gouge from shrapnel, Jones realized, as he examined Swisher's head. The impact of the shrapnel had split his helmet and knocked him out cold. Though awake, he was dazed, looking around blankly while Jones and Brown carried him from the wreckage of the helicopter to the bomb crater some twenty yards away and settled inside its berm. There they waited, scanning the green around them for NVA while Curry called in a report over his emergency radio. A second later their wingman, Grant in Mad Dog Two, swooped overhead, marking the spot but passing them by, not wanting to further alert the enemy to the location of the downed aircraft.

GREYHOUND Four—turbines still whining at full power, M60 barrels still hot—sat in the grassy PZ, empty except for the six dead NVA soldiers to its right. Inside, the pilots and crew were electric with post-firefight adrenaline and feeling uncomfortably exposed without gunship support; per standard operating procedure, Mad Dog Two's pilot, Michael Grant, had chased after Mad Dog One as soon as he saw it was in trouble, while his copilot, Chief Warrant Officer Ron Radke, attempted to reach them on the radio.

In Greyhound Four, Specialist 4 Gary Land and Robert Wessel, crew chief and right-door gunner, guarded their flanks and searched for the B-56 team while Armstrong and his copilot, Warrant Officer James Fussell, scanned in front of the aircraft. Armstrong's grip—slick with sweat—was closed tightly on the controls, ready to pull pitch and exit at a moment's notice.

"Where the hell *are* they?" Armstrong said aloud into his microphone. The slick had been on the ground too long already. He asked if anyone could see a panel—a bright orange-colored fabric square used to identify U.S. and allied forces. "Smoke?" came his voice over the radio. "Anything?"

"Negative," Land and Wessel reported back. The glint from the opposite side of the clearing, where Mousseau was working his signal mirror, was not visible to them. Nor was the large group of NVA moving in at the helicopter's twelve o'clock.

Thirty seconds more, Armstrong told himself. He counted down as he tried to reach the FAC for a situation report on the team. Had they been killed? Were they lying low? Were they on the run and ready to burst from the trees any second? He didn't want to leave them, but he had to get some sort of signal, ETA, or radio contact ASAP.

WATCHING THE NVA column press forward, Wright waited a full minute before he was certain the aircraft commander had not received his communication to get the slick the hell out of there. A hundred yards was too far to run to the helicopter; the risk was too great that his team would get cut down halfway through.

Wright tried the slick's crew on the radio one last time. Nothing. He ordered Mousseau to fire a light anti-tank weapon into the NVA column; the rocket-like projectile streamed across the clearing while Wright and O'Connor pumped out grenades from handheld launchers, lighting up the distant tree line with a series of explosions.

The NVA broke loose from the jungle and charged the front and right side of the helicopter. To the left of Greyhound Four, another cluster of enemy soldiers charged out from where they had been lying in wait.

Unarmed except for the .38 revolver he kept strapped to his thigh, Fussell could only watch the attack from his copilot seat inside the helicopter. He heard the spray of enemy bullets hitting the slick and the hammering automatic fire of dual M60s as crew chief Land on the left and door gunner Wessel on the right opened fire, targeting the lead NVA. At his feet, green-colored movement under the nose bubble caught his eye. A soldier was trying to aim his AK-47 upward into the cockpit, but the space between the ground and the helicopter was too short. Fussell shot down through the glass, feeling the kick of the revolver three times as he yelled into his mic, "Let's go! Let's Go! Let's go!" Armstrong was already bringing Greyhound Four off the ground.

Glancing back into the rear of the helicopter, Fussell saw Land working his M60, laying down fire into what appeared to be dozens of green uniforms rushing from the trees through the grass, bayonets fixed on their AK-47s. The crackling thunder of the incoming and outgoing weapon reports and rounds was deafening. NVA bodies were flung haphazardly in the grass—several with their faces torn off by the 7.62 mm bullets—but the charge was relentless.

It took a moment for the sudden buzz in Fussell's ears to register as silence from behind him. Both gunners had stopped firing. Pushing against his seat restraints, Fussell lifted up and looked over his left shoulder. He could see Land sprawled behind his gun, his boot blown open, revealing the raw meat that had been his foot. Blood pooled on the floor from a severed artery farther up his leg. Over his right shoulder, he glimpsed Wessel pulling himself back up to his gun. His cheek and neck were ripped open, his jaw hanging loose, dripping blood.

A higher-pitched *tat-tat-tat* joined the enemy fire as James Calvey—the Special Forces medic who was bellyman on the flight—grabbed his carbine and pumped rounds into the chests of two NVA soldiers a few feet away from climbing on board. Though severely injured, Land managed to pull his legs back up into what little cover the open doors of the helicopter afforded. He manned his weapon and rejoined the firefight while Calvey applied a compression bandage and tourniquet to his leg to stop the bleeding.

Calvey moved to Wessel, who had been shot through the neck but stayed on his gun; he pushed Calvey away as he attempted to bandage the wound. Picking up his M-4 carbine, Calvey began providing suppressive fire. He was alternating between the right and left doors when a bullet hit his elbow, traveled up his arm, and exited behind his shoulder. After quickly checking his wound, Calvey continued to fire, taking out the lead elements of the relentless enemy charge.

Another flash of motion drew Fussell's attention forward just in time for him to shoot the NVA behind the bayonet-fixed AK-47 coming through the side window. To his left, Armstrong leaned forward in his armored seat, then sat back upright, blood pouring from under his flight helmet and down his forehead and neck.

Fussell gripped the controls, but they jerked in his hands.

"I got it!" Armstrong barked. The tail boom drifted lazily, nose pointing toward the tree line to the southwest. The controls felt heavy to Armstrong—like when a car loses its power steering—and he fought them for every inch of slow, steady, vertical climb. For the past few minutes he had been concentrating so fiercely on getting the helicopter launched that he had barely heard the gunfire or seen the attacking enemy. He knew from the initial kicks he'd felt on their descent into the clearing that their hydraulics had been shot out. He didn't realize, however, that he'd been shot in the back of the head. He was unaware of the blood that soaked his shoulders and restraining straps, or of the fact that Fussell was poised, ready to take over the second Armstrong succumbed to his injury.

The turbines labored and the rotors beat at the thick, humid air. Brass bullet casings rained from both sides of the helicopter as the wounded door gunners blasted away at the NVA, who were firing on full automatic up into the belly of the aircraft. Seventy-five feet up, the ground fire became so intense that Armstrong could no longer wait for the blue-sky horizon; he plowed forward into the wall of green near the treetops, branches disintegrating as the slick's main rotor cut a channel. At any moment an old-growth hardwood limb could drop the aircraft from the sky.

Fussell was shocked to find himself eye to eye with an NVA soldier who was more than a hundred feet off the ground in a tree stand, or nest, mounted with what looked like a heavy-caliber machine gun. The man likewise seemed shocked, frozen into paralysis by the sudden appearance of the helicopter tearing apart the jungle in front of him. If he opened fire at all, it was after Greyhound Four passed his position.

An instant later, the slick broke through the canopy and raced away, a mist of finely chopped leaves, vines, and branches drifting down in its wake. That was when Armstrong realized that he was seeing his instrument panel through a narrowing tunnel, and then he was seeing double and felt, for the first time, *not quite right.*

"Take the controls," he said to Fussell. "I can't focus."

Tightening his grip, Fussell set his course east, back to South Vietnam. "What's your heading?" Armstrong asked, rubbing his eyes to try to clear his vision. His hands came away covered in blood. Out the front of the Greyhound, the horizon looked different. *Am I in shock?* he wondered, peering at the pancake-flat jungle beneath him. He wasn't picking up the landmarks he'd noted on the way in. *No, not shock. Just confused. Something isn't right.*

The radio finally came back to life and Fussell was able to broadcast their SITREP, situation report: "My AC [aircraft commander] and entire crew are wounded; hydraulics are out. I'm coming in."

Unbeknownst to Fussell, the magnetic compass had been damaged. They weren't heading east; they were flying due west—deeper into Cambodia.

11

DANIEL BOONE TACTICAL EMERGENCY

As Greyhound Four lifted off under fire, the B-56 team moved a few yards deeper into the jungle.

The CIDG held security in a tight perimeter while Wright pulled his American teammates into a huddle to plan for an alternative extraction. Tuan crept over to inform them that the two CIDG guarding the north-northwest rear of the perimeter had heard heavy-vehicle movement—possibly tanks or armored vehicles—from the west and north, the direction of the main road and the smaller cart path.

Known for his nerves-of-steel calm, a skeptical Wright suspected the CIDG were perhaps hearing things. He radioed for confirmation from Tornow. By the time the report from the air came back, the men could hear commands being shouted from NVA units to the west, south, and southeast moving in through the forest.

Wright whispered to O'Connor, Mousseau, and Tuan that the CIDG had been right about the vehicles. "The big shit *is* coming,"

Wright said. "But we still have time before they get here . . . another extraction team is coming in with gunships."

If the extraction failed, they would have to try to outrun the enemy by heading east, the one direction from which they had heard nothing. Of course, the quiet alley through the jungle could be a beckoning ambush. This deep behind enemy lines, was evasion a solution or was it simply prolonging the inevitable? These NVA troops would employ tracking dogs and their superior numbers to locate the team. And if they were captured . . . "That wasn't an option," says O'Connor. "There was an understanding, we'd each fight to our last bullet."

The four men agreed that the only alternative was to make themselves highly visible to their helicopter extraction teams so there was no confusion as to their location. The team would also have to maintain at least some cover and concealment from the NVA—and secure the PZ, defending both their position and the slicks as they landed.

The two thickets of trees located toward the center of the clearing offered a possible solution. They provided some protection, and the large anthill within one offered more. Their position could allow door gunners to send cover fire into the jungle on either side of the clearing as the helicopters landed in the twenty yards between the two thickets—as well as rocket fire or 40 mm grenades from the gunships, keeping the enemy's head down long enough for the team to board.

The closer northern thicket was about thirty yards away. Mousseau and his half of the team would dash across the PZ, then provide cover fire as Wright's team skirted the northern thicket and took cover in the southern thicket with the anthill. Mousseau's team would also have a field of fire into the edge of the trees where much of the noise was coming from, and Wright's team could lay a field of fire through the open meadow and roadway intersection where they had previously encountered the NVA.

Mousseau and five CIDG, including Bao, entered the clearing and reached the first thicket without incident, where they set up a defensive perimeter. On Mousseau's go-ahead, Wright's team moved out through the thigh- to waist-high grass, hunched over, and running in a staggered-trail formation. They were short of the second thicket, just beginning to slow their sprint to a trot, when the jungle to their front exploded with automatic AK-47 fire and the slower pounding of a heavy machine gun, the type mounted on a tripod. No first signal shot had been fired, no command had been heard—the team just ran headlong into a wall of steel. One or more bullets slammed into Wright, stopping him in his tracks. He stumbled, spun around, and collided with O'Connor, who took a round to his left wrist as they went down together.

Beside and behind them, two CIDG took multiple hits and crumpled into the grass, twitching as bullets continued to pound their bodies. Tuan and Chien were flat to the ground but still visible. Wright felt his shoulder and his leg and gave a thumbs-up to O'Connor, who applied a hasty tourniquet to his own wrist as gunfire continued to pour in on them—obviously coming from over the top of the waist-high anthill some fifteen yards ahead.

"We gotta move," said Wright. "Let's go! Get to the hill!" A few feet into their mad scramble, another concentrated strafing hit them and Wright's body bounced and jerked.

O'Connor crawled up beside Wright, who was flat on his back, and asked where he was hit.

"I don't know," Wright said. "I can't move my legs. I can't feel them."

A hit to the back or spine, thought O'Connor. He glanced over at Chien and Tuan, whose eyes showed no fear, but beckoned for an order—or word from the man with the radio that help was on the way. Says O'Connor, "Although far from being out of ammo, we had expended a lot and the enemy could access an endless supply . . . and was out of sight. Was help on the way? We thought so. Would some of us be sipping an evening brew while mourning our losses? Nobody knew for sure."

What O'Connor did know was that shock was setting in on Wright; there was no outrunning that beast, and this was not the place to treat their wounds. They had to get Wright to the anthill.

"Leroy, are your arms working?" asked O'Connor, whose left hand and forearm were in severe pain and barely functional. "Can you still hold your AK?"

"Yeah," Wright responded. "Roll me over. Help me up."

Putting his hand against Wright's chest to block his attempt to rise, O'Connor said, "You gotta stay down. Hold on, we'll get you going."

He motioned Tuan over and handed Wright the translator's AK-47. "We're going to pick you up and move, but you've got to hold our weapons. Can you do that?"

"Yeah, yeah," said Wright. "It's good."

O'Connor grabbed Wright under his left shoulder with his good right arm while Tuan did the same on his right. Chien made sure Wright held the weapons secure and then rose up from the grass and yelled, "Go, go, go!" He fired into the tree line with his AK-47 on full automatic, covering what was a five- to ten-second pick-up-and-go as Tuan and O'Connor half carried, half dragged Wright. Bullets slapped the ground and snapped through the grass overhead, in front of, and behind them—a hail of lead.

Then they were all lying flat beside Wright, behind the meager anthill, panting, mouths open and eyes wide. Back where they'd come from, O'Connor could see the two dead CIDG sprawled in the trail of flattened grass, bullets thudding repeatedly as they continued to hit their bodies.

Looking away from the dead men, O'Connor needed only to point for Chien and Tuan to position themselves so that the four men made a ragged four-cornered defensive position using the anthill and thicket of trees, as well as their rucksacks, for cover. They watched as squads of NVA rushed from the jungle into the clearing and dropped, disappearing into the grass. Automatic-weapons fire intensified from positions within the tree line, covering enemy soldiers as they crept toward the team's two locations. In return, the team laid down consistent fire into the grass.

O'Connor nudged Wright up a bit onto the slope of the anthill and pointed out fields of fire to him. Wright's rucksack remained on, which helped him to stay propped in a semi-seated position. He had carried the boxlike PRC-25 radio inside the top of his pack, which wasn't unusual for a team leader to do, even with an experienced commo man on his team. "Just set me up good," Wright said as O'Connor lined up extra magazines of ammunition at his side, then slid his own rucksack off to access his medical gear.

The bullet that went through O'Connor's wrist had shattered bone and torn muscles and tendons, but the bleeding was kept under control with a tourniquet fashioned from a stout branch he found on the ground of the thicket. He tore Wright's shirt open to look for wounds, and Wright grabbed the bandage from O'Connor's hand and said, "I got it; I just gotta find it. Everything is numb."

There were some lulls in the incoming gunfire, and in those moments of quiet O'Connor heard "an increased crackle of branches and limbs and movement behind the tree line," but there was no attack, which was "eerie," he says. "The NVA seemed to be going about their business without too much concern." A few volleys from weapons, including machine guns, continued, and from where they were hitting the ground, O'Connor could tell the enemy was also firing from up in the trees, from the south and southwest down toward their position behind the anthill and through them to Mousseau's position in the northern thicket.

Certain help was on the way, O'Connor's main concern now was making contact with the FAC or C&C slick—neither of which he could see overhead. He passed Wright the handset and powered up the radio. Wright made repeated attempts, then gave it back to O'Connor. "I can't get through," he said. "It's all garbled—I don't think it's English; they're jamming us. Can the NVA do that?"

Listening in, O'Connor quickly identified the problem. "Two, three, or four people in the air were trying to talk at the same time on a radio system designed for only one voice to be heard at a time," he says. "I picked up hints and bits of a conversation; some crisis was in play." Knowing his attempts to join the conversation would only add to the garble, O'Connor asked Wright to continue listening, wait for a break, and try to jump in.

The volume of enemy fire increased again, and squads of NVA began to assemble in the field. The gunfire from the two thickets took them down, one at a time.

Wright and Chien were covering the tree line, Tuan and O'Connor, the open PZ, when a thunderous roar of firepower erupted, hinting to O'Connor that there was a commander out there coordinating the enemy movements. They pressed themselves against the ground, and during a slight lull O'Connor heard Mousseau call out, "I'm hit!"

A group of at least eight NVA broke from the edge of the clearing and charged Mousseau's position, supported by at least two heavy automatic-weapons crews. O'Connor, Wright, and Tuan shifted fire and raked into the NVA with both AK-47 fire and M-79 grenades, perfectly aimed by Chien.

Mad Dog Three and Four roared overhead with fast, low-level passes that scattered and dropped many of the NVA soldiers who had moved into the open. Wright gave O'Connor a thumbs-up. He'd gotten through to somebody on the gunship and directed them to the areas where the enemy fire was strongest. Rockets from the helicopters exploded in the trees, but the enemy continued to maneuver forward in far greater numbers now.

★

A COUPLE thousand feet overhead, Tornow could hear the incredible volume of gunfire over the radio and knew the situation on the ground was dire. Then he heard the report that Mad Dog One had gone down somewhere to the east.

Taking his Bird Dog Cessna into a shallow dive for a closer look, Tornow was dismayed by the number of NVA converging on the team's position. Everywhere he looked, there were green uniforms, around two hundred fifty NVA visible in the PZ. It was impossible to tell how many were in the surrounding jungle, but it was obvious that this was not just a patrol: this was an enemy base camp.

Taking a deep breath, Tornow took quick stock of the facts. Mousseau had managed to report that two of the original twelve team members were dead and three were seriously wounded. That left seven men against all those he could see—and likely double or triple that number. Enemy vehicles were arriving on all visible roads to bolster the siege.

The first extraction attempt had narrowly escaped disaster, with two slicks limping back to base and six of the eight crewmen critically wounded. One gunship had been shot down and was in enemy-occupied territory. The other was too shot up to fly. It was as bad as Tornow had ever seen it for a team, probably "as bad as it gets," he later told a friend.

"In an impulsive reaction," Tornow proceeded to risk his career by breaking the explicit rules of engagement. "I turned my radio to the international emergency frequency and called, 'Mayday, Mayday, Mayday. Any fighters in the area, I need anything I can get. Vector ten miles southwest of Loc Ninh. I need to put you in immediately. Troops in heavy contact. This is a Daniel Boone tactical emergency.'"

This "Daniel Boone tactical emergency" or "TAC-E" was a coded distress call that cut in on all radio frequencies across Vietnam. It meant that a team was about to be overrun, and it summoned all available aircraft to converge immediately, especially "fast movers" such as jet fighters and tactical bombers—which were forbidden to cross into Cambodia, even in support of teams that were in heavy or overwhelming contact. What Tornow had just requested in order to save the team had all the makings of an international border incident, and maybe even a court-martial.

"I repeat," Tornow continued to call out over the radio, "this is a Daniel Boone tactical emergency."

AROUND 1:30 p.m. on May 2, Sergeant Roy Benavidez awoke in a steam bath known as the Hilton—a sandbag-and-canvas-walled, dirt-floored tent designated for "visiting campers" at the Loc Ninh Special Forces camp. His T-shirt was soaked with sweat.

Having worked a late shift the night before—monitoring a team that had been inserted near the border at dusk—Roy had no orders for the day and would have slept longer but for the heat. He rose from his cot, pulled on his fatigues, jungle boots, and bush hat, and tightened his belt, which held his sheathed SOG recon knife with its eight-inch blade. Then he stepped outside, his mind set on coffee and chow. Whatever culinary surprise awaited him would be doused with a dozen drops from the bottle of Tabasco sauce he always kept in a pocket of his pants.

Roy walked away from the barracks, easing out the stiffness in his body, residual pain from his first-tour wounds. "Mind over matter," he liked to say. "If you don't mind, it doesn't matter." He paused when he saw a chaplain, Bible in hands, sharing the Gospel with a group of men who had gathered in front of a makeshift altar: a white cloth spread across the hood of a jeep. At its center was a small cross.

Removing his hat, Roy made the sign of the cross and listened to the sermon: no matter what trials they might be confronted with, God would always be beside them.

"Amen," Roy said as the service ended. He crossed himself again, and the chaplain said, "May the peace of God be with you."

Roy saluted him, as he often did chaplains, regardless of rank, turned, and continued his journey to the mess hall. He'd only made it a few more steps when two pilots carrying flight helmets burst from a side trail onto the path, running toward the helicopter pads. He changed direction to the tactical operations center, where he found a Special Forces radioman he recognized sitting alone at a desk, dwarfed by the equipment before him.

"What's going on?" Roy asked.

"Heavy contact in Daniel Boone," the radioman said with a forlorn look. He flipped a switch, and Roy heard the discord of battle from a small speaker that buzzed with static: the sharp, repeated crack of rifle fire, the muffled impact of explosions, and, most unnerving, the cursing and urgent calls for air support and extraction.

"Who is it?"

"Don't know," said the radioman, "but they're catching hell out there."

Hurrying from the tent, Roy climbed the embankment onto the tarmac and headed to the group of uniformed soldiers and airmen huddled around a radio and keeping watch on the western horizon.

"A team is taking a beating," a crewman explained to him. "Two slicks got shot up trying to pull them out. Lost a gunship, and they're trying to pull that crew out now. The FAC called a Daniel Boone TAC-E on the guard channel—I never heard anybody call that before. It's bad."

"Any idea who it is?"

The crewman shook his head. Daniel Boone meant Cambodia, and if it was Cambodia, then it was likely somebody from B-56. They were all his fellow Special Forces brothers, and Roy hated hearing they were in it that bad, but knowing "who" it was meant that he could add specific names to the prayers he was repeating in his head.

Nine miles to the west, the two split teams continued to get hammered by the concentrated small-arms fire and RPGs that whooshed in from the jungle wall to the south—some sailing overhead, some exploding as they hit trees—and to the north, where the cart path began to cross through the PZ. It was not a cross fire, but if the NVA continued to push to the east on both sides of the clearing, the teams would be flanked. Through the hail of fire, they had to resist the urge to return fire unless they had a clear and lethal shot. Ammunition had become too precious.

A half-dozen NVA rose from the grass and ran toward the southern thicket, their AK-47s chattering on full automatic, and Wright, O'Connor, and Tuan aimed from the perimeter they had formed behind the sloping shoulders of the anthill and took them down. The men dropped in the grass a few yards away.

Two stick grenades simultaneously flew through the air toward their position. The lower one landed directly in front of Wright, who leaned forward, grabbed it, and threw it back. The grenade exploded before hitting the ground, peppering them with burning hot shrapnel. The second came in on a high arc, accompanied by shouts of "Grenade!" in both English and Vietnamese. The high toss meant it had been timed to explode at any second, depending on how long the NVA had held it after pulling its pin.

O'Connor watched it land in the middle of their tiny perimeter, almost hitting Chien. "Get down!" Wright yelled, and then, says O'Connor, "Leroy rolled himself over, and in a heroic but futile attempt, he tried to move and pull himself toward the device. He reached for it with an outstretched arm, but it was just beyond his grasp."

In a flash of movement, Chien scrambled toward the grenade, outstretched his leg while lying on his side, and kicked it a yard or two away—but not far enough. It had been an expert toss from the enemy.

The grenade exploded "in a brown-gray cloud," says O'Connor.

"Wright's legs flew into the air and Chien sailed upward with an arched back, while on the periphery Tuan lifted and began a lateral roll." Almost immediately upon hitting the ground Tuan and Chien were up on their knees firing in the direction the grenades had come from. All four men were wounded from the blast, but "Wright was the worst of the lot because of his proximity to the grenade. If Chien had not kicked it away, Wright would have been decapitated. As it was, his wounds were severe. I thought he was dead."

Rising to his knees, O'Connor joined Tuan and Chien, firing over Wright's body, then he crawled toward Wright to retrieve the radio, "but the twisted and tangled straps of his gear and his body position posed problems. I rolled him on his stomach, reached for my boot knife to cut the straps—and he moved, and not a small twist or a lift of the head."

Though his body was torn up from grenade fragments, his clothing bloody and shredded, Wright rose up on his elbows and asked for his weapon.

At that instant another grenade sailed over O'Connor's head and exploded out of lethal range, and a familiar voice shouted, "Get down! Get down!" Mousseau had left his position in the northern thicket with a CIDG at his side. Seriously wounded, with a bandage or a dressing on his head and face, he limped forward toward the southern thicket. He chucked a grenade and dove for the dirt still yelling, "Down! Get down low!" As it exploded, Mousseau and the CIDG sprayed a burst of fire over O'Connor, Wright, and Tuan, and the enemy grenades temporarily stopped coming.

Crawling toward the body of a CIDG, Mousseau grabbed the shoulder-fired light anti-tank weapon that was strapped to the dead man's rucksack, and headed back to the northern thicket, leaving a trail of blood in the matted grass. Wright—who was fading in and out of consciousness—shouldered his AK-47 and joined O'Conner and Tuan as they covered Mousseau. At the same time, O'Connor was on the radio, ready to coordinate air support. Instead he was dismayed to hear segments of a heated conversation—Major James on the C&C slick berating the Special Forces major for not pulling the team out earlier, when they'd first made contact. While the major defended his decision, saying he had direct orders to keep the team on the ground, the FAC, Tornow, was unable to break into the argument that was jamming the public channel instead of going on over the onboard intercom.

Finally there was a pause, and O'Connor, who had become increasingly frustrated, was heard shouting obscenities along the lines of "Fuck you guys! We're getting wasted down here!" and "Boy, if you assholes could work that out later, we could sure use some tac air!" His garbled cursing, accompanied by the *tat, tat, tat* of gunfire in the background, sounded very much as if the team was in the process of being overrun. They weren't yet, but—without air support—they would be soon.

When O'Connor heard Tornow come back on the station, he quickly directed Tornow to go "up ten" to a private frequency, skillfully detouring the radio traffic jam and, after fifteen-plus minutes of frustration, O'Connor was able to report the situation on the ground.

"We have a gunship down," Tornow told O'Connor. "Support is on the way."

"Roger that," O'Connor confirmed.

Even as he listened to Tornow, O'Connor was keeping his eyes on the grass. Wright was a few feet in front of him, leaning against the anthill and doing the same. Suddenly Wright's head "bobbed up" and a bullet hole appeared in his forehead.

The team leader was dead, O'Connor reported to Tornow. Mousseau was the new team leader.

"Air support is two minutes out," Tornow replied. "I need your position and target identification."

O'Connor could now see Tornow's Bird Dog banking wide to the east and coming in for a pass. He took out his signal mirror "and as he neared," says O'Connor, "I angled and hit him with a flash, or two, or maybe three. He replied with the most beautiful of sights—he tipped his wings."

On another channel Tornow was tracking the jet fighter-bombers, the "fast movers" that were converging from all over South Vietnam; on another, he talked to Mousseau and O'Connor, who vectored him in on the team's dual positions and identified where the most imminent enemy threat was developing. On still another, Yurman updated him on the ETA of slicks for the next extraction attempt. Then there were the two Mad Dog gunship pilots, Louis Wilson and Gary Whitaker, whose leashes Tornow had to yank to keep them from going straight into the fight on yet another run.

Tornow dropped his plane in altitude and lined himself up to fire a white phosphorous rocket at the enemy-occupied tree line approximately forty yards west-southwest of the team. The rocket would mark the target for the first two fast movers, F-100s, that carried napalm bombs, cluster bombs, and strafe (miniguns).

The trick was to place the marker at the immediate edge of the PZ so the fighter-bombers had a visual on where to drop their napalm, to eliminate the enemy and not the team. Tornow would need to fly moderately fast at a low-altitude, low-angle dive; when the Bird Dog appeared above the clearing, every NVA in the area would fire directly on him.

But enemy ground fire was the least of his concerns.

"We have two teams down here," O'Connor started to repeat into the radio as Tornow prepared for his final approach. Before he could complete the sentence, a bullet slammed into his right thigh. Another shattered his left ankle.

"I'm hit," O'Connor groaned.

"Stay with me," Tornow said. "I'm coming in to slow them down."

O'Connor was writhing in agony, barely conscious, slipping into shock from the blood loss and pain, but he kept on the radio. Somebody tugged at him, and he turned to see Tuan; his arm hung at his side, barely attached to the shoulder by muscle and skin. Tuan pointed at Mousseau in the other thicket. He was clasping his bloody cheek with one hand and holding the emergency radio to his ear with the other.

"Ammo?! Ammo?!" Mousseau shouted to O'Connor. "Grenades?!"

O'Connor gave himself a morphine injection and crawled to the two dead CIDG lying between the thickets. He pulled the rucksacks off their bodies, pocked with bullet holes, and stripped them of their ammo. He dragged the ammo and grenade pouches a few yards and threw them to a CIDG lying prone at the edge of the northern thicket, who in turn crawled back and tossed them to Mousseau.

AT LOC NINH, Roy Benavidez watched a slick come into view over the rubber trees west of the tarmac. Instead of taking a standard longer approach, it came straight in as if the helicopter pad was a hot PZ, dropped down fast, and flared just off the deck. The moment the skids hit the ground the left door swung open and the pilot frantically waved over the ground crew.

Roy joined them, rushing forward through the red dust in a crouched run. "Medic!" he could now hear the pilot, Roger Waggie, shouting. "Medic!"

Like all Special Forces, Roy was cross-trained as a medic. He could handle battlefield trauma and even perform minor surgical procedures to sustain life while transporting a wounded soldier to a hospital. But when he saw the extent of Michael Craig's chest wound as he lay on the floor of the slick, which was awash in his own blood, Roy knew there was virtually nothing he could do.

Roy spoke to him with encouragement, as he'd been trained, to

ABOVE: Roy Benavidez, age seven, First Communion in Cuero (front row, fourth from left). *Benavidez Family Archives*

RIGHT: Roy's grandfather, Salvador Benavidez.

BELOW: OSS Deer Team members pose with Ho Chi Minh and General Vo Nguyen Giap near Hanoi, Vietnam, August 1945. (Left to right, standing) Lieutenant René Défourneaux, Ho Chi Minh, Major Allison Thomas, Giap, Private First Class Henry Prunier and Private First Class Paul Hoagland. (Front row kneeling) Staff Sergeant Lawrence Vogt and Sergeant Aaron Squires. *U.S. Army Photo*

Roy, age eleven, El Campo Elementary School. *Benavidez Family Archives*

Roy, age fifteen as a migrant worker. *Benavidez Family Archives*

Art Haddock (Mr. Haddock), Roy's boss at the Firestone tire store, El Campo, Texas. *Haddock Family Archives*

Private Benavidez, age nineteen, Fort Ord, California. *Benavidez Family Archives*

Roy, military police school, Fort Gordon, Georgia, 1958. *Benavidez Family Archives*

Uncle Nicholas and Aunt Alexandria, Roy's adoptive parents, at Roy and Lala's wedding. *Benavidez Family Archives*

Roy and Lala were married on June 7, 1959. *Benavidez Family Archives*

RIGHT: Airborne qualified, Roy at Fort Bragg, North Carolina, 1959.

BELOW: Roy, with his trousers "bloused" into his boots, a tradition allowed only to Airborne-qualified soldiers.

Both: Benavidez Family Archives

Roy descending into the Sicily Drop Zone at Fort Bragg during training (center).
U.S. Army Photo

ABOVE: The helicopter was to Vietnam what the jeep was to World War II. *U.S. Army Photo*

RIGHT: First Lady Jacqueline Kennedy and Prince Sihanouk on her November 1967 visit to Cambodia. *Don Kirk Photo*

BELOW: Welcome to Project Sigma, Detachment B-56, at Ho Ngoc Tao. *Nick Godano Photo*

Warrant Officer Larry McKibben next to his 162nd Assault Helicopter Company (Vultures) slick. *McKibben Family Archives*

One of the 240th Assault Helicopter Company "Greyhound" slicks, whose motto was "Go Greyhound and leave the flying to us." *Yurman Family Archives*

LEFT: Major James Reid, the man who organized Operation Vesuvius. *Reid Family Archives*

BELOW RIGHT: Specialist 4 Brian O'Connor atop Nui Ba Ra ("White Virgin Mountain"). *O'Connor Family Archives*

Larry McKibben carrying the rotor blade that had been shot through. *McKibben Family Archives*

First Lieutenant Al Yurman flying the C&C Greyhound slick. *Yurman Family Archives*

Specialist 4 Michael Craig,
Greyhound Three crew chief.
Craig Family Archives

RIGHT: First Lieutenant Fred Jones, the
launch officer for the May 2, 1968, mission.
Jones Family Archives

BELOW: A Greyhound slick on a mission.
Yurman Family Archives

fight the shock and try to instill in him the will to live. "We got you now, buddy, you're going to be fine," Roy said. "You're going home." Craig, who was taking short, shallow breaths, looked up at Roy as he lifted him down carefully onto a stretcher.

Throughout his tour—which began October 17, 1967—Craig had written biweekly letters to his sister, brother-in-law, baby niece, and his parents, both of whom were retired Navy. His father had served on a sub tender (submarine support vessel) in World War II and had survived the attack at Pearl Harbor.

While he'd kept them updated on the reality of the war, admitting in one letter how scared he'd been when he was shot at, Craig always remained in good humor and tried to temper their fears. "We took another hit yesterday," he'd written in a recent letter. "You know we do wear armor plating and a ballistic helmet so even if I do get shot, I probably won't even get a scratch. The armor plating works real good. So don't worry about me."

In the next letter home he told his sister, Sherry, that he had decided to order his mother a "bouquet of flowers for her birthday as there just isn't any time to go out and buy her anything over here. I sure wish there was more time. I tell you, I wish I could buy you all the world. I sure do miss all of you. Why don't you borrow a tape recorder and make me a tape? I really want to hear your voices. I figure it's the next best thing to being there with you."

Smiling down at Craig, Roy did his best to convey that there wasn't a care in the world. The crew chief was only twenty years old—he had his entire life before him.

But Michael Craig knew, as only the dying do.

He opened his mouth, and the last words he spoke before he passed away were "Oh, my God. My mom and dad."

★

THE WHITE phosphorous rocket Tornow fired from his aircraft impacted the tree line behind the most heavily concentrated group of NVA crouched in the clearing. White smoke billowed up from the jungle like a fog, from which the steady gunfire persisted, splintering the branches above the team's positions and kicking up dirt in the anthill where O'Connor, Chien, and Tuan covered their fields of fire.

As Tornow climbed in altitude, he switched to O'Connor's frequency. "On target?" he asked.

"Roger," O'Connor confirmed. "On target."

"Stay low," Tornow said. "They'll be coming in close."

"Roger," O'Connor said again. He signaled to Mousseau in the northern thicket, who pointed up to the sky and flat-handed down. He'd gotten the message too.

Every second seemed to drag, the voices of the NVA loud as they maneuvered toward the team. The men pressed themselves as flat into the earth as possible, unsure what would come first: the charge of the enemy or support from the air.

The answer was like a thunderclap, the prelude to the drawn-out concussion from multiple impacting incendiary bombs. The roar of the jets' afterburners was heard almost simultaneously as a bright flash engulfed the tree line, followed by a blast of heat so intense O'Connor thought his hair would catch on fire.

These guys are pros, marveled Tornow, who watched the two F-100s arc away from the PZ, leaving in their wake parallel walls of protective flame between the split teams and the advancing enemy troops. "How's that?" he radioed O'Connor.

"Beautiful!" O'Connor replied. "Thanks."

There was a lull in the gunfire, during which O'Connor injected Tuan with morphine and tied off his mutilated arm with a tourniquet. Weak from blood loss, O'Connor ran an IV of serum albumin into his own arm, while the remaining two CIDG on his team—also wounded, but not critically—watched for enemy movement.

In the northern thicket, Mousseau and the three of his five CIDG who had survived the firefight were also injecting themselves with morphine and patching their wounds—mostly bullet holes through soft tissue with no major bleeding—as best they could. Mousseau had taken the worst of it. A bandage was wrapped tightly around his left elbow and biceps, and a CIDG now wrapped Mousseau's head with a battlefield dressing, attempting to cover the new team leader's mangled eyeball, which had been blown from its socket and was hanging down his cheek.

The backdrop to the carnage within the team's bloody perimeter was a plume of black-and-brown smoke that swirled as it rose off the ground, allowing glimpses into the clearing's edge, where fires glowed red-hot and the screams of dying and burning men echoed. The NVA soldiers who had been assembling in the open to overrun the team were motionless, smoldering heaps.

GREYHOUND ONE had gotten a new battery and was now airborne and full pitch as its pilot, Larry McKibben, tried to catch up with his wingman, Jerry Ewing, in Greyhound Two.

"I'm inbound," McKibben heard Ewing report to Yurman, who diverted Ewing from an extraction attempt in order to intercept and escort Greyhound Four—piloted by the critically wounded Armstrong and copilot Fussell. Greyhound Four had continued deeper into Cambodia for two or three minutes before Armstrong realized there was no Nui Ba Den mountain in the distance. They discovered the compass was broken, and immediately Fussell initiated a long, banking turn and headed back toward the border and the airstrip and field hospital at Quan Loi.

McKibben did not announce he was inbound to Yurman, who assumed he was still sitting in reserve back at Loc Ninh. In fact, Yurman had done everything he could to keep McKibben out of the fight, calling for any other available Greyhound slicks and even checking the inventory of their sister platoon, 1st Platoon, at the 240th.

"What's the status on Greyhound Three?" Yurman radioed back to Loc Ninh. "They're trying to patch it back together," said a ground crewman, "but there's a lot of holes—a big one on the cover of the tail rotor driveshaft. And Waggie doesn't have a crew."

With Waggie's aircraft shot up and unable to fly and Ewing escorting Greyhound Four to Quan Loi, McKibben knew he was it. If an opening presented itself, they needed a slick to pull the team out. And so he continued to fly west, into Cambodia.

There was no need for vectoring; he could see the billowing smoke from miles away. McKibben heard the call that Mad Dog One was down and requesting emergency extraction and saw Mad Dog Two, piloted by Michael Grant, racing back and forth above the jungle, covering the gunship on the ground.

McKibben switched over to the Mad Dog frequency and was receiving a situation report from Curry when Mad Dog Three and Mad Dog Four announced their presence beside him, ready to provide cover. Grant vectored McKibben over the tiny clearing that Curry had managed to set the helicopter down in, and McKibben and his crew chief, Specialist 4 Dan Christensen, were able to identify the downed gunship below, sitting upright on its skids. Twenty yards off to its side was the bomb crater where Curry's crew had formed a defensive perimeter.

On his second pass, McKibben flared at treetop level above the clearing and began to descend "like an elevator," according to Christensen, who watched a Mad Dog streak past his left-side door as they sank downward. A moment later one of the gunship pilots reported NVA fifty yards—half a football field—away.

Christensen gripped the handles of his M60, relaxing into the intensity of the situation; he'd done this enough times to know that it did no good to get worked up. He felt the weapon's weight; even mounted, it had a distinct heaviness as he moved it through its arc. He dreaded the need to use the weapon yet yearned for the kick and deep-voiced *thud, thud, thud* that ripped holes in the jungle and the enemy. Letting his eyes do the work, he searched the trees for a shape, a sign, any reason to engage, until the helicopter hovered just off the ground.

The crew from Mad Dog One poured into Greyhound One's cargo area behind Christensen, who counted the men as they came on board—pilot, copilot, crew chief, and gunner—a full gunship crew. "We've got 'em. Let's go! Let's go!" he said over his mic, and they began their vertical exit, Christensen still fixated on the trees.

Crew chief Pete Jones on Mad Dog One would remain forever grateful to Curry for his "beautiful landing" and to McKibben for his no-nonsense extraction. "We weren't on the ground more than five minutes when McKibben and his crew pulled us out. The NVA were looking for us, but he beat them to us. He never asked if we were taking fire; he just wanted to know our position, and that was that. He was coming in to get us, and I knew it. For a few minutes I got to feel like a grunt, waiting for that slick, knowing if it came I was fine, but if not, I was dead."

AT THE PZ, the reprieve from enemy gunfire lasted only a brief time before the screams of misery were joined by heavy automatic-weapons fire announcing that the NVA had dug in and was determined to win this battle. It was approximately 3:00 p.m. in the afternoon, about three hours since the B-56 team had been inserted.

O'Connor heard the explosions hitting the jungle floor almost the same time that Mad Dog Three and Mad Dog Four passed overhead, the smoke from their just-fired salvo of rockets hanging in the air, miniguns spinning. Picking up the gunships on a direct channel, Mousseau directed them to hit the trees to the southwest of the clearing, but it seemed that the jungle held enemy soldiers all around.

On Mad Dog Three, crew chief Paul LaChance manned his M60 as his pilot, Louis Wilson, came around. With a deadly arc, Wilson leveled the gunship's nose and let loose with rockets while his copilot, Jesse Naul, saturated the tree line with his miniguns. LaChance and Jeff Colman, the right-door gunner, were picking up the gaps, hitting everything that moved, "knocking them down, ripping them to shreds," says LaChance. "We'd come around and more were coming, a steady flow of replacements. They were stepping over the dead, and we'd just add them to the piles. Jesus, though, talk about discipline. But they were doing their best to knock us down. It's hard to see tracers in the daylight, and you can't really hear much, there's so much noise, but there's this static—you don't need to take a bullet to know you're getting shot at. We had bullets hitting us galore, hot lead and tracers coming through the doors, in one side and out the other. And that's okay, you just keep returning fire, and you know if they're shooting at you, that's taking a little heat off the team on the ground."

Mad Dog Four, piloted by Gary Whitaker, took his run just as Mad Dog Three was pulling out, a figure-eight pattern in the air that kept continuous suppressive fire on the jungle that surrounded the team. Crew chief Pete Gailis on Mad Dog Four could never get used to the smell after a napalm run. It was horrible as they passed over the clearing, a sweet, foul medley of burning flesh, burning trees, and cordite that he could only describe as a wood-fire barbecue, with crap barbecue sauce.

Monitoring the battle in progress on the radio, Jerry Ewing in Greyhound Two escorted Greyhound Four back across the Cambodian border and to the base at Quan Loi. He heard Armstrong telling the tower they were coming in to land, and watched the slick line up with the runway and then almost get taken out by another helicopter also coming in to land. "Bastard!" Armstrong shouted over the radio.

Without hydraulics, there would be no hovering or flaring in Greyhound Four's bag of antigravity tricks—they were going in on a shallow dive, hot and fast. The skids hit the blacktop, sparks flew, and the aircraft slid more than a couple of hundred feet before stopping. Ambulances were rushing toward it as Ewing banked to the west, dropped the nose of Greyhound Two, and headed back into Cambodia.

The smoke rising from the PZ was horrendous. A slight breeze kept it from blowing away more quickly, and it looked like "doomsday on the horizon," according to Ewing, who continued to monitor the situation on the ground through the C&C: reports of both dead and wounded, and there was gunfire, lots of gunfire. Greyhound Two was on-station, Ewing reported to Yurman; he was ready to go in. The fast movers had just finished a run, and Yurman cleared Ewing to try for an extraction.

"Identify smoke?" he heard the team below request.

Visibility was very limited, making it difficult for Ewing to orient himself within the context of the clearing he'd flown into during the insertion, so he and his copilot, First Lieutenant Bob Portman, relied on their crew to spot the team's position through the wafting smoke. The crew chief, Specialist 5 Paul Tagliaferri, leaned out over his M60 on the left, scanning the ground through the open side door while the door gunner handled the right side. They were across the PZ in what seemed like the blink of an eye.

Ewing banked hard into a tight sweep back over and into the smoke. He could see glimpses of grass and some clumps of trees, but no colored smoke to identify the team's location. Something nicked his pant leg, and then his microphone casing jerked an inch away from his mouth—a bullet had ripped through the floor and glanced off the microphone.

The microphone still worked, and the close call hadn't broken

Ewing's concentration. He continued to fly, alternating glances at the horizon and down through the bubble beneath his feet.

"I can't see them," Ewing said. "Anybody see them?"

"I see them," Tagliaferri said. "They're directly below us!"

"I can't see them!" Ewing yelled. "And we're taking hits." He wasn't about to put the brakes on to hover and drop straight down into a smoky void without eyes on the team; he'd circle back around.

"We are not taking hits!" Tagliaferri said.

"I just got hit in the leg!"

Immediately Tagliaferri leapt into action, moving forward and grabbing the lever on Ewing's seat in order to yank it back and provide first aid.

"No! No! I'm fine, Tag, I'm fine," Ewing said. "I felt a bullet hit my pant leg, my boot—but I'm fine."

Tagliaferri locked the seat back in place and returned to his gun.

"Stand down, Greyhound Two," ordered Yurman. "We're gonna put in some more tac air. How's your fuel?"

"I'm good for one more go."

"Okay, Jerry. Repeat, stand by. I repeat, we have tac air incoming."

O'CONNOR WAS beyond tired; he was exhausted. Gone was the adrenaline that had coursed through his body and sustained him the past few hours. The fighting had been unrelenting. Any second, one of these bullets was going to make a hole he couldn't plug. Tuan was unconscious at his position.

The air strikes must have killed hundreds of the enemy—but still they came. They were everywhere.

"Hang on," Tornow said over the radio. "We've got more tac air coming in, and then we'll attempt another extraction. Where do you want it?"

Anywhere around the tree line to the south or west was good, O'Connor replied. He looked toward the other thicket and saw Mousseau leaning against two of the dead CIDG, which he had stacked like sandbags, the remaining three CIDG forming a triangular perimeter around him. He pointed up at the sky, holding his radio in his hand, and O'Connor signaled back. They tried to flatten themselves even farther into the earth they were sprawled on.

The first run hit the southern side of the PZ; then, instead of a second pass, the jets diverted to target a group of trucks coming down the Ho Chi Minh Trail to the west—hopefully clogging the road and killing the reinforcements that seemed limitless. O'Connor heard but didn't feel this set of explosions. Because they sounded farther away, he figured that the jets were out of ordnance and returning to base.

Mousseau and his split team remained vigilant. Not much was left of their thicket, its small trees splintered to pieces by the thousands of incoming rounds.

Despite his worsening condition and narcotic haze, O'Connor maintained his position at one side of the anthill, facing what he surmised was the enemy's most favorable approach. He was nearly out of ammunition: down to whatever was left in the clip of his carbine and a single spare clip, and his .22 "monkey" pistol with its silencer. Still unconscious and circling the drain, Tuan had a few grenades left in his webbing. If he had to, O'Connor could use those and the interpreter's AK-47, which might give an attacking NVA a moment of pause.

It was quiet again after that last bombing, and during this calm, O'Connor began to fade into unconsciousness, engulfed by the smoke, stagnant air, and smell of death.

"They're coming in!" Mousseau shouted, jolting O'Connor back to the living. Assuming the enemy was mounting a final assault to overrun the team, O'Connor "prepared for the worst," he later wrote. "I started to contact the FAC or C&C, but spreads of heavy auto, mortar, rockets, and grenades filled the PZ. I caught a burst of autofire in the abdomen, and the radio was shot out. I was put out of commission and just lay behind Wright's body, firing at the NVA in the open field until the ammo ran out.

"I was ready to die."

12

IF SOMEONE NEEDS HELP . . .

AT LOC NINH, Roy Benavidez gently set Michael Craig's body on a stretcher beside Greyhound Three. He said a prayer, then walked away, leaving Roger Waggie and David Hoffman kneeling beside their dead crew chief.

Within a few minutes, two more helicopters from the 240th returned from the border. The first was Mad Dog Two, the second gunship in the fire team for Greyhound Three and Four's extraction attempt. Pilot Michael Grant had been forced to abort his support run when Curry in Mad Dog One began trailing smoke and banked away from the PZ. Grant's aircraft had been shot up even more than Curry's, but somehow he'd stayed in the air long enough to help cover the downed crew until backup arrived. His control system was badly damaged, however, and Grant had been uncertain that he could make it back the extra miles to Quan Loi—the designated base for refueling, rearming, and maintenance on the mission.

Following close behind was Larry McKibben in Greyhound One, carrying Curry and his crew—all of whom had shrapnel and/or bullet wounds. They were immediately transferred to a medical transport helicopter and whisked away to the field hospital at Quan Loi.

Roy walked from helicopter to helicopter, overhearing conversations and collecting snippets of information from their crews: "Never saw ground fire like that before . . ." "If there's not at least a battalion of NVA down there . . ." From what he was witnessing—the radio transmittals, the firsthand reports from the extraction attempts, the shot-up aircraft, the death of Michael Craig—Roy held little hope for the team's survival.

He returned to Greyhound Three, where Waggie and Hoffman were going over their slick and counting bullet holes: fourteen in all, the worst of them a gaping, jagged gash on the panel that covered the tail rotor driveshaft. With closer inspection, they realized that it had been caused by a bullet ricocheting off a bearing; they weren't sure how much longer this aircraft could fly.

Roy, who still hadn't found out which Special Forces team members were involved, asked Waggie if *he* had any idea. Waggie didn't know their names, but he recalled seeing "that big black sergeant" among them when he'd flown backup during the insertion. That man, Roy suspected, was his friend Leroy Wright.

There was a hum of turbines, and Roy saw the rotors on Larry McKibben's slick begin to spin. Without a moment's pause, he grabbed a medical bag that had been left on the helicopter pad and ran to Greyhound One. In back, crew chief Dan Christensen and his gunner, Nelson Fournier, were behind their weapons.

"You going back in?" Roy asked.

"We're gonna try," said Christensen. "At least drop them some ammo." He held up an assault pack of ammunition.

"I'm in," Roy said. "You need a bellyman."

Christensen informed McKibben over his intercom, and McKibben looked back to see Roy, medical bag in hand, already halfway inside the slick. He gave Roy a thumbs-up, and Roy climbed all the way in and set the medical bag on the floor beside him.

Then they were airborne, flying low over the pancake-flat farmland of the Mekong Delta, leaving the ominous round hump of Nui Ba Den rising three thousand feet above the delta in their wake. The American radio relay station on the mountaintop—which Roy had used to keep tabs on a different Special Forces team the night before—was critical for missions into Cambodia.

Everyone on board was silent and stone faced—and Roy was just another passenger taking the bus to work. Christensen and Fournier were cordial strangers; they looked out their windows down the barrels of their M60s, keeping to themselves, leaving the driving to the guy on the stick up front.

Although they were all working on the same team and had the same objective, they had little to say and knew little to nothing about one another. Roy didn't know that Larry McKibben, the pilot, was a fellow Texan, with a sister whom he missed like crazy about to graduate from high school, or that he sent home tape-recorded letters every chance he got. Or that the copilot, Warrant Officer William Fernan, was, at twenty-six, the old man on the slick's crew, with a wife named Diane and a degree in biology from the University of Washington that allowed him to actually identify many of the plants and trees of the jungle they were flying over.

Nor did Roy know that Christensen was a twenty-four-year-old father of three from Wisconsin who spent his summers in the Dakotas baling and combining wheat and hay. Or that nineteen-year-old Fournier went by the nickname "Sonny Boy" back home and was a favorite human jungle gym for his nieces and nephews. One of Fournier's proudest moments, after getting his helicopter door gunner's wings, had been winning a radio in a raffle right before he'd deployed. It was the only thing he'd ever won.

As he watched the world rush by below, Roy pondered his spontaneous decision. Was it because he couldn't sit back and listen to his friends getting slaughtered and not do anything about it? Was it an involuntary response, like when he was a kid, jumping into a fight without considering the consequences? Was it his Yaqui blood, the ancestral warrior in him? Or was it rooted in the lesson he'd learned from Grandfather Salvador? *When someone needs help, you help them.*

He noted the aircraft commander and copilot's personal weapons: two M16s strapped on the back wall. In the event of a crash landing, the crew chief would hand these weapons to the pilots as they exited the helicopter. Both gunners also had holstered .38s strapped to their thighs, and Roy realized with a start that in his haste he had broken the cardinal rule of any Special Forces soldier; the most basic rule of a buck-private grunt. He was going into battle without his weapon.

Had this been a regular mission, he'd have brought along his carbine and revolver as unconsciously as he'd bring his arms and legs. But he was not on a regular mission, and he carried none of his normal survival gear: radio, a compass or two, pen flares, a map, signal mirror, two or three shots of morphine. He had no web gear, the load-bearing, vest-like carryall that accommodated the standard twenty-one magazines of ammunition, his pistol, water canteens, smoke canisters, and grenades. He had no rucksack, which carried extras of all the items above, plus a Claymore mine, explosives, medical supplies—including a blood expander and IV bags—and other mission-specific equipment. Strapped to the side of the rucksack was a short machete called a "banana knife," and, shoved around anything that might rattle, he kept his poncho and poncho liner, as well as food rations to sustain him for a day or two. Beyond all of this, and his personal weapon, he would carry an extra weapon—a grenade launcher or a sawed-off shotgun.

Today, as he sped to the massive firefight taking place within Cambodia, Roy had with him the medical bag, the small bottle of Tabasco sauce he'd intended to use for the breakfast he hadn't eaten, and his recon knife, eight inches of steel blade custom made without a serial number or identifying marks at the Counterinsurgency Support Office in Okinawa, Japan.

He was covered head to toe in tiger-striped camouflaged combat fatigues, but he might as well have been wearing one of the loincloths of the Montagnard tribesmen employed by SOG—something Green Berets had been known to do while training and bonding with the indigenous warriors who fought beside them. They called it "going native."

Not long after 3:00 p.m. Ewing in Greyhound Two was orbiting east of the PZ, waiting for the air strikes to stop so he could follow in as second extraction slick to whoever was inbound, when Yurman came over the radio and instructed him to come around and begin a descent for a low-level vector into the PZ. Taken aback, Ewing replied, "It's not my turn," then immediately thought, *What the fuck? Did I really just say that?*

"We've got an opening; I need you now," said Yurman, and Ewing rogered, circled, and set up for final approach.

"I'm here, Greyhound Two," McKibben announced over the radio. "I'll go in next."

"Negative, Greyhound One," Ewing said. "I'm already on my way in."

"Nope, my turn," said McKibben as he banked wide around Ewing and cut in front of him.

"Okay, Greyhound One," Ewing replied. "I'll go down with you to draw some fire."

Roy listened in over the radio while McKibben flipped to the ground frequency and announced that they were incoming. The only response was gunfire.

"It's going to be hot," McKibben told his crew. "If they can't get to us or we can't get to them, we'll drop ammo."

Both Christensen and Fournier checked their weapons and positioned themselves with their M60s down and forward, ready to provide suppressive fire. Looking forward through the cockpit, Roy saw nothing but treetops and smoke.

O'CONNOR WAS lying behind Wright's body, bleeding steadily, fading in and out of consciousness, waiting to be overrun, when through the din of gunfire he heard the faint but distinct *whop, whop, whop* of approaching helicopters.

The beating rotors coaxed him away from the descending darkness, allowing a sliver of hope. He envisioned a swarm of helicopters, brimming with weaponry and soldiers, a "strike force coming en masse to recover what was left [of us]," he would write in his statement, "but instead a lone slick flew into the middle of the PZ and hovered with door gunners blazing."

The enemy fire shifted from the team on the ground to Greyhound One. McKibben had dropped into the PZ a hundred yards east of the thickets and flared to a hover ten or fifteen feet off the ground. Faint streaks—NVA tracer rounds—crisscrossed from both sides of the clearing while the door gunners returned fire, blasting away at the tree line. To Christensen, there were so many barrel flashes it looked like the blinking lights on a Christmas tree.

"We're taking heavy fire," McKibben reported over his microphone. "I don't think we can get in close enough." He began to pull pitch.

"Wait!" Roy shouted back. He edged his way to the door of the slick. "Just get me as close as you can. I'll get to them." With one hand on the medical bag and his feet dangling, he watched the grass swirl about from the rotor wash, ten or fifteen feet below, while Fournier strafed the trees with his M60 on full automatic. Taking a deep breath, Roy crossed himself several times, pushed the medical bag out the door, and jumped.

PETE GAILIS was looking down on Greyhound One from Mad Dog Four as his pilot, Gary Whitaker, dove into the PZ and released two rockets. Warrant Officer Cook, the copilot, directed his miniguns on a group of NVA, and seventeen-year-old Specialist 4 Danny Clark, an infantryman turned door gunner, swung his gun methodically from target to target, dropping the enemy with short bursts from his M60. Having been outnumbered himself on a search-and-destroy mission just months prior, Clark knew that every NVA he killed from the air took some heat off the guys on the ground.

On the other side of the gunship, Gailis had swung his M60 on a smooth, steady arc to the left, providing suppressive fire into the southern tree line. The helicopter banked, and he could see Greyhound One drop down suddenly, flare, and hover off the ground in the northeast corner of the PZ, some distance east of the beleaguered team.

As tracers flew everywhere, several NVA soldiers ran into the open and sprayed the slick with bullets. A body went out its door and Gailis thought, *Oh my God, they're shooting 'em out of the aircraft!* It was inconceivable to him that anyone would "willingly jump into the battle when everybody on the ground wanted out."

O'Connor watched the Special Forces soldier in his jungle fatigues jump from the helicopter and disappear in the grass. Then he was up and running hard, following in the wake of the slick that had dropped its nose and raced toward the team's position, gaining altitude as it went. O'Connor provided cover fire for the lone soldier, pausing briefly to look up as the slick passed directly overhead. A crewman tossed out a web belt of ammo pouches, but its trajectory took the belt far beyond his position, landing to the west of the thickets.

HO CHI MINH TRAIL / ROAD

.5 miles
west

0   50

yards

Extraction / Rescue

tac air strikes

KIA
enemy

CART PATH

2

N

NVA group   machine gun .50   tree nest
(elevated machine gun)

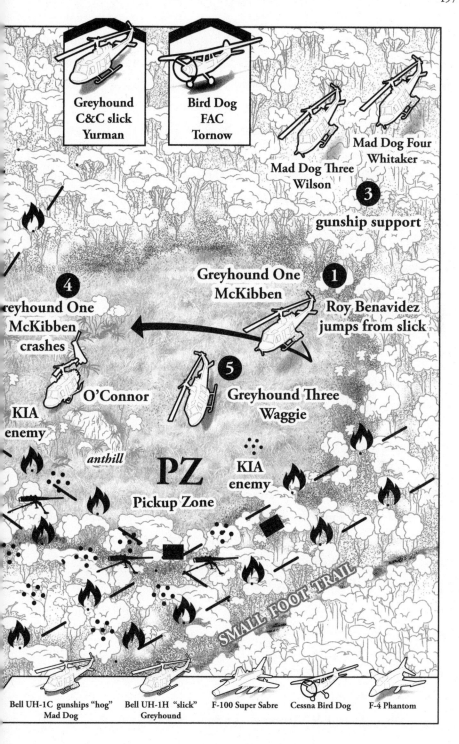

Greyhound
C&C slick
Yurman

Bird Dog
FAC
Tornow

Mad Dog Four
Whitaker

Mad Dog Three
Wilson

3

gunship support

4

1

Greyhound One
McKibben

Roy Benavidez
jumps from slick

Greyhound One
McKibben
crashes

5

O'Connor

Greyhound Three
Waggie

KIA
enemy

anthill

PZ

KIA
enemy

Pickup Zone

SMALL FOOT TRAIL

Bell UH-1C gunships "hog"
Mad Dog

Bell UH-1H "slick"
Greyhound

F-100 Super Sabre

Cessna Bird Dog

F-4 Phantom

Just a few strides into his mad dash, fifty yards from O'Connor, the soldier abruptly went down. He was back up and running a moment later, heading for the nearest cover: the northern thicket where Mousseau was also providing cover fire.

Bullets tore up the grass around the soldier as he ran, and at least two RPGs were fired at him. He went down a second time.

Mad Dog Four banked low and tight over the trees and came back around, with both Gailis and Clark firing on automatic, raining brass over the floor of the helicopter and out the doors into the PZ below. When the M60 ammo, mini-gun ammo, and rockets were gone, Whitaker made one more pass to draw fire, and both gunners took up their M16s and fired their remaining bullets as Gailis searched the grass for the soldier he thought had been shot from the slick.

In the northern thicket, Mousseau was scanning for the Special Forces soldier when he heard someone calling out softly yet urgently, "Leroy! Leroy!"

"Who is that?" Mousseau called back.

"It's Benavidez," Roy answered. "I'm coming in."

Roy crawled through the trampled grass into the blood-soaked perimeter, up to Mousseau who was propped between a CIDG body and the roots of a small tree; a few yards away, Bao and two more CIDG were prone at their weapons. Wiping blood from his eyes—his face had taken shrapnel from the RPG blast—Roy examined Mousseau's bandage then pulled up his own pant leg to find that a bullet had passed completely through his calf.

"Where's the rest of the team?" he asked, and Mousseau nodded toward the other thicket. "Okay," said Roy, "let me have your radio. We're getting out of here."

A moment later, FAC Tornow, Yurman, the Greyhounds, the Mad

Dogs, the fighter-bomber pilots—all the personnel who had been fight-ing to keep the team alive on the ground and everybody else who had been monitoring the deteriorating situation from afar—were surprised to hear a new voice on the ground. He identified himself with the call sign Tango Mike Mike and reported he was with the team.

"They're in bad shape down here," Roy said. "Multiple wounded. Request immediate medevac."

He looked over to the adjacent thicket and spotted O'Connor. "You okay?" he shouted.

"Ammo?!" O'Connor yelled.

"Who's alive?!"

Chien had been killed, leaving just O'Connor and Tuan. He raised two fingers. "We're going out!" Roy yelled back. "Try and get over here!"

Tuan was semiconscious when O'Connor told him they were get-ting out. "We gotta move," he urged, but Tuan was too weak from blood loss to do anything but lie there. "Don't leave me here," he pleaded.

"I won't," O'Connor assured him. "Let's go." O'Connor began to slide forward on his side, guarding his stomach wound, while physically pushing the interpreter in advance of him—a few painful inches at a time. A slick passed overhead—either McKibben or Ewing targeting the enemy with long bursts of fire that were lost in the steady reports of the AK-47 fire, larger-caliber machine-gun fire, and mortar rounds.

A few more inches and O'Connor faced the gap between the thick-ets where the first two CIDG had fallen hours earlier. Machine-gun fire raked across his path, and Roy waved him back.

As Roy threw a smoke grenade, O'Connor squirmed backward to the modest but effective cover of the anthill, pulling Tuan with him. "Don't leave me here," Tuan said again. "Don't leave me."

★

GREYHOUND ONE was providing cover fire over the PZ when McKibben heard Roy say, "Identify smoke."

"I see green smoke," McKibben replied. He came in fast over the treetops and flared to a hover a few yards west of the northern thicket—placing his slick between the team and the western tree line, where the heaviest concentrations of enemy fire were coming from.

The rotor wash turned the thick, billowing green smoke into a swirling haze. Gunfire erupted from the clearing's edge, and Fournier answered from the right side of the helicopter, steadily firing rounds from his M60 at knee- to chest-level—a horizontal line of protective lead into the tangle of charred, napalmed jungle. A second slick, Ewing's, came in a hundred feet off the deck, closer still to the trees, drawing some fire while his right-door gunner strafed even deeper into the vegetation.

Roy stayed crouched in the thin cover of the thicket beside Mousseau and his CIDG, all wounded. He picked up an AK-47, likely the one Mousseau had retrieved from one of the dead, and then—under the temporary cover offered by Greyhound One's door gunners, Roy said, "Let's go!" In a hunched-over run, he ushered Mousseau, Bao, and the other two CIDG toward the helicopter. They limped and dragged their way toward the open door of the slick as Roy stood beside the skids, covering them until the final man had heaved himself on board. Then Roy signaled to McKibben, directing him to the other thicket.

Holding Greyhound One steady, its skids a couple of feet off the ground, McKibben gently nosed down and crept forward while Roy jogged alongside, firing into the southern tree line. They got as close to the thicket as possible—some twenty feet away—and Christensen had a clear line of fire in the ten and eleven o'clock of the southern tree line. Anything that moved, he hit.

Roy darted the distance and dove down beside O'Connor, leaning up against the base of the anthill. Tuan was six feet farther down the berm-like hill, and a few feet farther still was Leroy Wright's body.

"Can you walk?" Roy asked O'Connor.

"I can crawl," O'Connor said, then gestured to Tuan, who had fallen unconscious again. "He can't."

"What does Leroy have on him?"

"The SOI [standard operating instructions] and some maps in a green plastic pouch tucked in his shirt."

Noticing that O'Connor carried only a .22 pistol, Roy handed him the AK-47. "Cover me," he said, and crawled through the grass to Wright's body.

Unbuttoning and reaching inside his friend's shirt, he pulled out the pouch of sensitive material. Wright's camera bulged in his chest pocket, and he took that as well. Hearing movement, Roy quickly crawled back to Tuan, grabbed two grenades from his web gear, pulled the pins, and tossed them into the tall grass just beyond Wright's body. Two NVA jumped up to run, but the grenades exploded and took both men down.

Slapping Tuan's face, Roy was able to revive him enough to get him to move over to O'Connor, with Roy pushing from behind. Roy retrieved his weapon from O'Connor and explained that the helicopter could not get any closer because of the trees. "You're going to have to crawl," he said, then crouched low, turned his back on O'Connor and Tuan, and returned to Wright's body, where he dropped to his knees. He was determined to bring Leroy back to his wife and his two boys, whose drawings he had seen taped to his locker at Ho Ngoc Tao, with the word *Daddy* scribbled in crayon at the top.

Tears were rolling down his cheeks, Roy realized, but there was no time to mourn—the pitch of Greyhound One's engine was already getting higher, screaming as it hovered impatiently. O'Connor and Tuan were almost to the slick's door, and a CIDG reached out to help them aboard. Roy worked his arms under Wright's body—prepared to drag Wright to the slick if he couldn't lift his 200-plus pounds up onto his shoulders—when something slammed into him so hard it pitched him forward, knocking the wind out of him. A bullet, the third he had taken in the half hour he'd been on the ground, had entered his back, exiting beneath his left armpit.

There was a heat that came with the impact, as though he'd been touched by fire, run through by a red-hot spear that ignited his insides. And then, the explosion.

ON GREYHOUND Two's second pass across the PZ, Ewing's door gunners expended the rest of their ammunition. Greyhound One was still hovering beside the thicket. The green uniforms of the enemy speckled the woods around the clearing, their numbers increasing by the minute.

"Mac, come on, man, you've been down too long!" Ewing said over the radio.

"Larry, get the hell out of there!" Yurman cut in.

As calmly as if he were picking up some buddies to go to a movie, McKibben replied, "Yeah, they're just getting them on board now. Be done in a minute . . ."

Tornow had dropped in altitude and was in a wide observation bank, putting his binoculars to his eyes periodically to monitor the extraction, when he saw an NVA soldier run out from the tree line and unload his AK-47 into Greyhound One's cockpit. He watched helplessly as Greyhound One "spun awkwardly . . . almost in slow motion . . . the blades slicing the trees, and in a moment it lay in a twisted shambles on the ground."

Greyhound Two had banked out over the jungle for another pass, and Ewing was contemplating whether he should hover directly on top of Greyhound One to draw fire when he heard McKibben key his mic and expel a soft groan, almost like an exhale.

"Mac! Mac! You okay?!" asked Ewing, streaking back over the clearing. He saw the wreckage at once, the dust still hanging in the air, and he knew that his friend and wingman, Larry McKibben, was dead.

Oh God Oh God Oh God, what happened? he thought. *Did my hesitation kill him? Oh, please no! I was going in! I swear I was going in! He cut me off. Oh, Larry, man, f—k! I'm sorry! I'm sorry! It should have been me!*

A MOMENT before, Tornow had been cautiously hopeful that his twelve men, dead and alive, were coming home. Now he was hit with the despair of having both the Special Forces team and a slick crew trapped in the PZ, with the enemy emerging from the trees all around. The main body of the slick was nosed over on its right side, the tail boom broken and separated from the fuselage, lying in the grass. Bodies were dumped out on the ground beside the wreckage, the wounded attempting to crawl away. Through his binoculars, Tornow could see McKibben was slumped in his seat, motionless.

Yurman watched Greyhound Two making a slow, low pass over the clearing and knew his door gunners were unloading on the NVA in the open. He would not allow another helicopter to be shot down.

"Do not attempt extraction, Greyhound Two," Yurman ordered Ewing. Greyhound Two's gunners reported they were out of ammo; the helicopter's fuel was nearly at bingo. Turning the slick's nose east, Ewing gained altitude and headed back to Quan Loi to rearm and refuel.

"Mac, you copying this?" Yurman continued to radio. "Anybody on Greyhound One, you copy?"

Tornow, too, was trying to reach anyone on the ground. He prepped his fast movers, even as he received only a long, deafening silence.

★

WHEN O'CONNOR came to, he heard "a steady hissing sound, like steam escaping." Then he felt someone going through the rucksack on his back.

"Radio, radio," said a CIDG from Mousseau's team. Confused, O'Connor rolled over and saw the slick about ten feet away, pitched over, nearly on its side.

Roy, his face bloody, the left side of his shirt soaked with blood, was at the right door, which was angled toward the ground, pulling the crew and team members out of the crumpled rear cabin. McKibben and Fournier were dead—McKibben from a bullet to the head and severe abdominal wounds, Fournier crushed by the transmission. Some survivors were dazed and lay sprawled motionless on the grass; others rallied around Mousseau, who sat low beneath the tail boom. Meanwhile, the slick was taking so many hits from enemy fire that it sounded like a tin can at a gun range—not a good sign, given the overwhelming stink of jet fuel and burning oil.

O'Connor called out to Roy, who turned to look at him. "You okay, O'Connor?" he asked.

"I think so," O'Connor replied.

Sending a slightly wounded CIDG in O'Connor's direction, Roy said, "Form a perimeter." He pointed at a slender, wispy tree beyond the front of the helicopter, growing beside a mound of earth—what was left of the anthill. Its top had been gouged off when Greyhound One's main rotor plowed into it during the crash. They were back where they started.

"I need ammo and a weapon," O'Connor said.

"The chopper's gonna blow," Roy said. "Move out! Get weapons and ammo from the dead."

Mousseau, along with Greyhound One's copilot, William Fernan, Bao, and another CIDG crawled away from the tail boom back to the northern thicket, while O'Connor, Tuan, and the remaining CIDG moved toward the anthill.

"O'Connor!" Roy yelled. "Do you have a radio?"

With the help of the CIDG, O'Connor was able to retrieve two emergency radios from his pack and another from Tuan's rucksack.

THE NVA were either terrible shots or they were focusing all their efforts on the slick, because somehow Roy, Fernan, Bao, and the two CIDG were able to scavenge the dead NVA close to their original perimeter, each yielding a weapon.

Ammunition, however, was scarce. "Single shots!" Roy told them. "No auto." He pointed out the designated field of fire each was responsible for. "Save your bullets," he said. He crawled over to O'Connor and retrieved a radio. "I'll come back in a few minutes. I'll call the tac air closer."

Taking in the scene around him, O'Connor saw that Roy had organized the remnants of a nearly destroyed recon team and slick crew "into a force to be reckoned with," he wrote in his statement years later. "Seriously wounded, he crawled around, constantly under fire, and gave tactical orders, took charge of air support, medical aid, ammunition and . . . saw to it that we positioned ourselves in a way that would increase our chances of survival, inflict maximum casualties on the enemy, and secure the PZ against almost impossible odds."

O'Connor felt the fight that had been lost in him coming back. It was Roy's "courage, actions, words, and coolness" that did it, he would write. "He boosted our morale, giving us the will to fight and live."

Still, they were a battered group, almost out of ammunition, and the downed helicopter was like blood in the water, emboldening the NVA to move in and finish them off.

13

LAST CHANCE

O'Connor lay on his side, watching his designated field of fire through the torn-up grass. Unable to scavenge a weapon from the dead, he was armed only with his suppressed .22 caliber pistol and an old World War II–era bayonet he'd picked up in Fayetteville, near Fort Bragg. The bayonet was the perfect commo tool—for cutting and spooling wire, as a screwdriver or hammer or even a crowbar—but that and a .22 pistol would do little against the numerous enemy he could make out thirty or forty yards distant, seemingly milling around in the tree line. Other NVA were slowly, but increasingly boldly, working their way toward them and the helicopter wreckage. His immediate thought was that these soldiers must consider them easy prey, that they'd move in and capture or kill the American and South Vietnamese puppet soldiers stunned from the crash.

Suddenly, a man appeared near O'Connor's position. In a single moment, he identified the soldier as NVA and made the decision to play dead, allowing the enemy to move closer and closer until he was just above O'Connor. The soldier looked down and O'Connor lifted his pistol and fired four or five shots into his chest.

Stripping the man of his AK-47, ammunition, and canteen, O'Connor then lugged the body onto its side to use as a sandbag.

Apparently aware that the survivors had left the downed slick, the NVA shifted the bulk of their fire from the wreckage to the area around it, including the two thickets. RPGs ripped across the PZ at grass height, and mortars whistled down toward their positions, with explosions that heaved up earth and sent burning shrapnel into their midst.

O'Connor rose up, just high enough to locate Roy, who was himself low in the grass and on the radio in the other thicket. There was a bullet hole through the emergency radio O'Connor took from his belt and held in his hand. He turned it on anyway and found that he could receive but not transmit. Holding the radio close to his ear, he monitored Roy's transmissions as he identified targets for Tornow and communicated directly with the gunship pilots.

It was just shy of 4:00 p.m., and the gunships, alternating their runs with F-100 Super Sabres, F4 Phantoms, and A-37 Cessnas, continued to pound both the clearing and the tree line surrounding it. But for every swath of decimated jungle, a different section would light up with barrel flashes and tracers, revealing another NVA rifle team, sniper, or platoon, all being skillfully maneuvered to maintain pressure on the Americans and CIDG in the PZ.

The foliage around the PZ was so thinned out by the devastation that the outlines of bunkers and defensive positions had become visible from the air, hinting at the true scope of the enemy's strength. "It was a shock," says Paul LaChance, crew chief on Mad Dog Three. "These weren't fighting positions they just threw together; there were permanent bunkers. I saw at least two bunkers—and if I could see two, there were more. Later, when we debriefed, I was thinking this had to have been the outer defenses for a regiment, maybe even a division. Not hundreds of troops, but thousands. If not right there, they were nearby and getting trucked in."

CREW CHIEF Dan Christensen came groggily to his senses in a world that was sideways and shaking so violently he couldn't see straight. He was lying in the grass, and the trees in the jungle around him were coming out of the ground, with exploding bark and branches and dirt flying everywhere as if a tornado were touching down. He saw the debris from the helicopter and smelled the smoke and burnt oil and remembered—McKibben was dead, and so was Fournier, but what about Fernan? Was he still in the wreckage? *They're going to blow it up. . . . I gotta move.*

He tried to open his mouth, but it was locked up, his jawbone cracked in half in the crash. His pant legs were dark, soaked with blood from where he'd been hit by bullets or shrapnel. He reached for the sidearm on his hip, but the holster was empty. *Where's my pistol?* he thought, trying to wriggle himself up. Then what looked like a "human ketchup bottle" moved toward him, a Special Forces soldier whose face, hands, chest, neck, arms, and legs were covered in coagulating, black, caked-on, and smeared blood: Roy Benavidez.

Roy motioned for Christensen to stay down. Pointing up with one hand, a radio in the other, Roy signaled that help was incoming. Christensen gave Roy a thumbs-up. Dropping his chest to the ground, Roy used his elbows to move through the grass toward O'Connor's group, staying as low as possible as O'Connor and the CIDG provided cover. Roy jerked suddenly to one side, but kept moving.

Roy's radio was still in his hand when he reached O'Connor. "How bad you hit?" O'Connor asked, and Roy replied, "I don't know. I think just a flesh wound. I'm fine. How are you guys holding up?"

"Me and Tuan, we're in bad shape." He motioned to the CIDG. "This guy is wounded but holding his own. We're all going easy on the ammo."

"Save it for anybody coming through there," Roy said, indicating the intersection where the cart trail entered the clearing to their west.

With the help of the CIDG, Roy and O'Connor rolled the bodies of dead NVA and CIDG, using them as sandbags to fortify their position. As they pulled another body back from the tall grass, intense fire and a fusillade of RPGs hit them. The CIDG clutched his stomach. Roy grabbed his own leg, dragged the wounded man back with him to the perimeter, and urgently asked O'Connor for the radio.

The heavy automatic-weapons fire picked up. O'Connor reached behind him and brought his hand back, covered in fresh blood—he had caught a large metal fragment above his left kidney. He was in so much pain, he couldn't talk and was on the verge of passing out; the CIDG beside him was moaning, his hands pushed against his stomach.

Spotting the radio beneath O'Connor's legs, Roy grabbed it and tried to make contact. Its batteries were very weak. He clutched it tightly against his ear, listening for a response, but could hear nothing above the explosions and automatic-weapons fire.

MAD DOG Four had barely touched down at Quan Loi when Pete Gailis and his gunner, Danny Clark, jumped out to refuel and rearm their gunship for the third time that day.

They took on only three-quarters of a tank; less weight in fuel meant they could carry more ammo. Each taking a side of the aircraft, they loaded seven rockets into both outrigger pods, and—careful to stay away from the downward-pointing miniguns (infamous for accidentally discharging)—they ripped off the closure lids of the trays and loaded them with ammo. Next, they replenished the ammo for their

M60 door guns. All in all, thousands of rounds of ammunition and rockets fully armed the gunship in ten minutes.

His side finished, Gailis walked away from Mad Dog Four. He could still hear the miniguns, his own M60, the rotors, the engine, the "goddamn noise," he says. "I'd been on the ground for ten minutes, and it was still ringing in my ears. It was just so loud, I needed some quiet, and as I walked, I was thinking to myself, *I do not want to go back there. There's no fucking way I'm going to get back on that helicopter.*"

He stopped and stood, his boots cemented to the tarmac. He took maybe a minute, then turned around and looked at the gunship.

Danny Clark glanced at Gailis and their eyes met, just for a moment. Clark knew Gailis didn't smoke, but he went over and patted his back and handed him a lighter and a cigarette and said, "I think you might need one of these."

Gailis held it up to his nose, smelled the tobacco, and started to light it. He stopped. Handing Clark his lighter and cigarette, he said, "Let's go. Let's get those guys home."

At 4:30 p.m., Roy finally reached a gunship on the weak radio and directed its pilot, Louis Wilson, to the section of the woods where the most fire was coming from. Mad Dog Three immediately swooped in, hitting the area with rockets first, followed by passes with miniguns. The enemy fire quieted, though sporadic gunfire continued to crackle through the air. Bullets thudded against the bodies that formed a low, crescent-shaped wall extending from the side of the anthill.

O'Connor asked Roy to search his pocket for the two remaining syrettes of morphine he knew were there. Injecting O'Connor in the shoulder, Roy looked him in the eye and said, "We're getting out of here, so don't sweat it. We're getting out." Roy administered the other morphine shot to the CIDG, then gave himself one from the medical bag.

"Batteries are going fast," O'Connor told Roy, referring to the radio. "Don't monitor. Save it for tac air only." Nodding, Roy bandaged O'Connor with some dressings off his harness and placed a tourniquet above O'Connor's ankle, which continued to bleed from the earlier gunshot wound. He put a pressure bandage on the CIDG's stomach and inspected the tourniquet around Tuan's arm.

The interpreter had his AK-47 propped up over the dead bodies stacked around him; his good hand held the rifle steady, finger poised by the trigger. Half dead and barely conscious, he said to Roy, "Don't leave me, please." He repeated his plea again while Roy tightened the tourniquet. He repeated it one more time as he passed out. The CIDG with the stomach wound was now unconscious as well. Roy felt for a pulse. Still alive.

Roy returned to O'Connor and told him to hang tight. "I'll be back," he said. "We're getting out of here. Stay down."

GREYHOUND PILOT Warrant Officer William Darling was not part of the mission package that day, but he had volunteered to assist by monitoring the Special Forces team and staying in contact with the radiomen in the TOC. When the team first reported they'd been compromised, he'd flown with the slicks to Loc Ninh along with Thomas Smith, Yurman's copilot on the C&C slick who had given up his seat to Major James.

For the past hour Darling and Smith had been helping Waggie patch up Greyhound Three while tuned in on the radio to Tornow, who was alternating the air support in waves—fast movers, then gunships; fast movers, then gunships. There were gaps of silence between runs, during which the status of the men on the ground was unknown. Those monitoring the radio held their breath, wondering if they were in the process of being overrun. Yet every ten or fifteen minutes, Roy's voice—always accompanied by gunfire—would announce that they were still there, to keep it coming.

A fresh wave of fast movers had just been ordered when Yurman came on the line to request a SITREP from Waggie.

They were short on aircraft. In addition to Curry's gunship, Mad Dog One, McKibben's Greyhound One, and Armstrong's Greyhound Four were down, leaving just two slicks. "Waggie's [Greyhound Three] was questionable, sitting at Loc Ninh," says Yurman, "and Jerry [Ewing, Greyhound Two] was refueling at Quan Loi. He'd been into the PZ twice now. His aircraft had taken rounds, but nothing critical had been hit as far as I could tell. Before I sent him in, I wanted to see if Waggie could fly, because I wasn't sure Ewing could get everybody on board. Nine guys on the ground, that's a lot of weight."

Waggie told Yurman that he was still concerned about the large hole on his tail boom, but that the slick had sounded fine when he'd powered up. "I'll fly," he said. "But I need a crew." Darling—who had flown as Waggie's copilot in the past—and Smith volunteered on the spot, as did Special Forces medic Ron Sammons, who had been on alert for this mission at Loc Ninh. He would be the bellyman.

"I've got a crew," Waggie reported back thirty seconds later. "We'll be there as fast as we can."

They took off immediately, with Darling and Smith wearing the standard protective equipment—a ballistic helmet and chest and back plates, the latter placed under their rears to reinforce the airy nylon-strapped seats of the door gunners. Darling had considered Michael Craig not only a good friend but also "the best crew chief in the country." When he took Craig's position, he knew he had big shoes to fill. He also couldn't help but notice where the nylon straps were stained dark from his friend's blood.

Like most pilots, Darling and Smith had basic training on the M60 and had sat in the back a few times for fun, blowing off rounds while returning to base or during ash-and-trash (non-assault supply or trans-port) missions. Neither ever expected to be sitting in those seats while flying into a hot PZ. As they cleared the rubber trees and headed west, they did final checks on the M60s, squeezing off a couple of rounds into the rice paddies to test the weapons.

A full crew of warrant officers flying an extraction just didn't hap-pen. It was the first and only time Yurman would experience this ar-rangement. "We've got tac air inbound," he informed Waggie and his new crew. "You're next."

WHEN O'CONNOR came to, he had no idea how long he'd been out. He instinctively scanned the area around him. Tuan was moaning and shifting about, as was the CIDG with the stomach wound. Mousseau was with Roy—who, seeing that O'Connor was awake, signaled for him to stay flat and cover his head.

A slick was coming in, and fast movers and gunships were going to "prep" the PZ. O'Connor, who had the metal fragment embedded in his back, asked the CIDG to help him take off his rucksack so he'd be ready to run. He pulled it up beside him as a shield, covered his face, and angled his head toward the embankment. Signaling to Tuan, he said, "Stay down. We're going to get out of here."

The first pair of jets streaked overhead and dropped their bombs. "Strike after strike after strike right onto the PZ and back onto the wood lines and the clearing in front of me that intersected with the small road," O'Connor later wrote. "Branches and slivers of wood, metal, dirt, et cetera, were stinging us; rolling my head from one side to the other I caught some of the hot debris in my left eye and arm. The heat from the jet's afterburners was unbearable, and I wondered how long it would last."

Next came the gunships—Mad Dogs Three and Four, plus a fifth gunship that had flown up from Bearcat with First Lieutenant Rick Adams and Chief Warrant Officer Don Brenner, who were well over their allotted flying hours but bringing all the "smoke" (firepower) the 240th could muster.

It was now or never, and the enemy seemed to sense this, for they returned fire in kind, launching RPGs straight up at the gunships, causing the rounds to come down like artillery.

Early in the war, the NVA and Vietcong learned that the safest place during an air strike was as close as they could get to the American position. That is probably what prompted the main force of roughly a platoon to rise—grass and branches stuffed into the meshing of their helmets and clothing—and reveal themselves as they moved forward from the trees and across the cart path, using the downed slick for cover.

From his gunner's seat on Mad Dog Four, Clark could see dead bodies scattered everywhere; the living NVA would drop down and play possum, making it difficult to ascertain targets. He looked for any enemy movement and pumped rounds into bodies, dead and alive.

Tornow coordinated with two Cessna A-37s to cover the gunships after two sets of fast movers—F-4 Phantoms—dropped ordnance, engulfing half of the PZ in black smoke. "It was a final try," says Warrant Officer Jesse Naul, Mad Dog Three's copilot, who looked out his window to see one of the A-37s just above the treetops with its landing gear and flaps down "in an attempt to fly slow enough to strafe alongside us as we went in."

"The air support was like a swarm of bees," O'Connor would later write, "and through the middle of it came a lone slick that touched down about twenty–thirty meters from us. I put the last magazine of ammo in my weapon, and I knew this was our last chance to get out."

★

THE SKIDS had not yet touched the ground when medic Sammons jumped out of Greyhound Three and sprinted to Roy. Between the whine of the slick's engine, the fast movers and gunships flying overhead, and the enemy ground fire, the white noise of battle was deafening.

Helping up a CIDG, Roy passed him forward to Sammons, who put the man's arm around his neck and ran toward the helicopter, where Smith and Darling stood behind their M60s putting out protective fire. The NVA were continuing to advance despite the massive firepower coming at them from Greyhound Three and the gunships making runs overhead.

For both O'Connor and Mousseau, the blood loss from their numerous wounds and the fatigue of the extended battle had finally caught up with them. O'Connor lifted his orange signal panel and Sammons acknowledged his position. Mousseau attempted to move toward the slick but was unable to even crawl, and Roy ran to his side, got down on his knees, and put him over his shoulder.

Covering their flank as best he could, O'Connor watched Roy try to get to his feet, Mousseau on his shoulder. Then, what O'Connor had thought was a dead CIDG rose up from the grass directly behind Roy. For a second, O'Connor wondered about the identity of this CIDG before he realized it was an NVA soldier.

The soldier must have been out of ammunition. Or else he was hoping to capture a live American, a valued prize. Raising his AK-47 like a baseball bat, he clubbed Roy on the back of the head.

Roy went down to his knees, dropping Mousseau. O'Connor took aim, but Roy was already on his feet again, spinning to face his attacker and blocking O'Connor's line of fire. The NVA butted him in the face with his weapon.

O'Connor was able to get off a few rounds, but missed and was afraid to try again for fear of hitting Roy, who pulled out the only weapon he still carried, a knife, as the NVA lunged at him with his bayonet. The bayonet blade caught Roy across his left forearm, cutting deeply, but he managed to squeeze the barrel of the rifle between his arm and his left side and trapped it. The NVA yanked his rifle free, slicing Roy on the side. Before he could strike again, Roy wrestled him to the ground and thrust his knife deep into the man's side. Yanking it out, he drove the knife down a second time into his chest. At last the soldier was still.

Staggering to his feet and visibly shaking, Roy turned to face O'Connor. "I'm okay," he shouted.

O'Connor lowered his AK-47 and yelled back, "My interpreter is still alive—make sure they get him!"

Roy leaned down and tried to retrieve his knife from the NVA's chest, but it would not come free. Hefting the barely conscious Mousseau back onto his shoulder, he used his free hand to help a wounded CIDG, who was crawling in the direction of the slick, up to his feet. He took the CIDG's AK-47 in hand, and they lumbered toward the helicopter together while O'Connor struggled to provide suppressive fire to the west, where the enemy was shooting from behind him toward Greyhound Three.

Sammons dove down beside him. "Can you walk?" he asked.

"I don't think so," O'Connor said.

From the right side of Greyhound Three, Darling on the M60 machine gun faced the incoming wounded. Behind them, a hundred or more uniformed NVA poured from the trees and charged across the PZ. Roy was nearly to the door with Mousseau and the CIDG when he swung the AK-47 toward the tail of the helicopter. Darling immediately snapped his head to the right and saw two NVA coming up from the rear, in a position his machine gun could not reach. Before Darling could move, Roy shot them both dead.

As Roy hoisted Mousseau up into the slick's cabin, Darling glimpsed a gruesome wound exposed through Roy's torn shirt: his intestines were spilling out around the forearm he had squeezed against his abdomen. Instead of climbing on board the helicopter, however, he turned around and staggered in the direction of the remaining men.

He won't make it back, Darling thought.

SAMMONS HELPED O'Connor and a CIDG to their feet, and with their arms around his neck, one on each side, he half-carried, half-dragged the two wounded men toward the helicopter.

Darling fired over the tops of their heads and to their sides to slow the enemy onslaught. Then he signaled urgently to Sammons with a flat hand down, and Sammons dropped to his knees, pulling O'Connor and the CIDG with him.

"You need to crawl the rest of the way," Sammons shouted. "Go!"

O'Connor glimpsed Sammons as the medic swung around, lifted his carbine, and sprayed fire into the advancing NVA. The pain from his abdominal wound was excruciating for O'Connor. Crawling was impossible, so "I picked up a weapon," he says, "and used it as a crutch and on my knees worked my way to the chopper with the CIDG behind me."

Clutching his side and hunched over, Roy ran to him. "We'll make it," O'Connor said. "But my interpreter is still back there."

"Okay, okay!" Roy said, passing O'Connor, passing the CIDG, passing Sammons, and heading for the thicket and into the teeth of the enemy.

O'CONNOR HAD almost reached Greyhound Three when Sammons grabbed the harness on top of his web gear and pulled him and the CIDG the remaining few yards to the skids. He pushed them into the helicopter and climbed in after.

Bullets slammed into the side of the slick and whizzed through the cabin. One found its mark, impacting Darling in the left shoulder and upper chest, spinning him around. He pulled himself back onto the gun and continued to squeeze off suppressive fire for the last man on the ground, who was running for the helicopter, a CIDG soldier in his arms.

In the back of the slick, O'Connor was slumped against a wall, the open door framing the smoldering Cambodian jungle. He saw Darling's back, his shoulders jolting from the kick of the M60 on full auto, laying out cover fire for the enigma that came into focus: Roy, carrying Tuan. Roy handed off the interpreter and turned again to face the enemy. He "was pulled aboard still firing his weapon," says O'Connor. "Then he gave a thumbs-up sign to the pilot, and the chopper lifted off."

14

DELIVERANCE

GREYHOUND THREE CLEARED the trees surrounding the PZ, dropped its nose, and raced east low and fast just above the jungle. In back, Sammons provided first aid, but it amounted to "little more than putting the live people on top of the dead," according to Darling. "We had so many seriously wounded that the blood flowed out of the helicopter." They crossed the border into South Vietnam at roughly 6:00 p.m., and Waggie headed straight for Loc Ninh, where medical "Dustoff" helicopters were on standby, poised to transport the wounded to field hospitals.

Of the original twelve-man B-56 team, only O'Connor, Mousseau, Bao, Tuan, and two other CIDG had made it into the slick alive—all were critically wounded. Fernan, the copilot, and Christensen, the crew chief, were the sole survivors from Greyhound One; Christensen, too, was critically wounded.

As they flew out of the PZ, Roy had climbed over the pile of bodies and found a place between the pilots' seats, where he leaned back against the console. That is where the medics discovered him after the helicopter landed at Loc Ninh, his body motionless, eyes crusted shut with blood, arms crossed over his gaping abdominal wound.

Roy was lifted off Greyhound Three and placed with the dead beside the tarmac a few yards from the artillery battery at the Special Forces camp where he had—only a few hours earlier—been on his way to grab some chow.

In his haste to leave no one behind, Roy had accidentally loaded three dead NVA soldiers onto the helicopter. Now the five-foot-six-inch American lay beside them as their bodies were placed one by one into body bags—a tragic finale for Roy Benavidez, who devoted his life to his country only to be mistaken for an enemy soldier.

But being mistaken for the enemy wasn't nearly as tragic as being mistaken for dead. Roy could hear what was going on around him, but he was frozen in shock—unable to move, unable to open his eyes, unable to speak—unable to do anything as he was stuffed unceremoniously into a suffocating black body bag. "The zipper was coming up," Roy recounted, "and I couldn't tell this guy, 'I'm still alive!'"

Then he heard the familiar voice of Green Beret master sergeant Jerry Cottingham exclaim, "That's no damn gook. That's Benavidez!"

Assuming that Roy was dead, Cottingham called a medic over to confirm. The medic knelt over the body bag, rested his hand on Roy's chest, and checked the pulse on his neck. "When I felt that doctor's hand on my chest," Roy later said, "with all the energy I could summon, I spit at him. Actually, I sprayed a mixture of blood, spit, and mucus."

"Stop!" the medic said to the soldier about to pull the zipper shut. And the body bag was replaced with a stretcher.

★

EN ROUTE to Loc Ninh, Waggie on Greyhound Three reported that he wasn't certain he'd gotten all the survivors. When Ewing on Greyhound Two heard this, he knew instantly what had to be done.

"Guys," he said to his crew over the intercom, "we're going to do a sweep, make sure we have everybody. Take a good look around; I'll get in real close."

As Ewing set up for final approach to the PZ, the waves of NVA he'd seen earlier seemed to have dispersed. U.S. forces would often destroy downed aircraft with a massive air strike once survivors had been extracted, and the enemy had most likely moved back into the tree line—or down into tunnels and bunkers if this was indeed a major command complex—in anticipation.

Crew Chief Paul Tagliaferri got on the intercom. "I'm gonna get out and take a quick look," he told Ewing. "If there's anybody left alive and I can't move them to the aircraft, I'm gonna stay with them till help comes."

"Tag," Ewing replied, "there's nobody else coming."

Tagliaferri did not respond.

They began to take fire as Greyhound Two came in fast and touched down. Tagliaferri jumped out with two M16s, first-aid kits, and extra ammo and ran directly to Greyhound One and crawled inside while Ewing hovered closer, drawing fire, and his gunner strafed the tree line to the west. Looking toward the downed slick, Ewing could see his friend Larry McKibben slumped over to the side.

In Greyhound One, Tagliaferri checked to confirm that Fournier and McKibben were dead and dashed around the wreckage and surrounding grass, calling out for survivors. After nearly a minute, he sprinted back to Greyhound Two and jumped on board.

With one last look at McKibben, Ewing ascended out of the PZ and headed east. Staving off tears, he asked his copilot, First Lieutenant Bob Portman, to take the controls.

Unbeknownst to Ewing, the 162nd Assault Helicopter Company, the Vultures, was on the way from Ho Ngoc Tao to bring home the dead. McKibben had many friends in the 162nd since the Vultures had been his first assignment in Vietnam, and five of their helicopters would retrieve his body—along with those of Fournier, Wright, and the remaining CIDG—from the PZ under heavy fire as truckloads of NVA reinforcements approached from the Ho Chi Minh Trail. Though the aircraft took multiple hits, there were no casualties.

At Loc Ninh, helicopters were rushing the survivors, many fighting for their lives, to various field hospitals. In and out of consciousness, Roy was in the back of one, on a stretcher beside Lloyd Mousseau, who had fought hard the entire battle, receiving his most severe wounds from enemy fire only as he climbed on board Greyhound Three.

Mousseau, who had sent his daughter, Kathy, a card for her third birthday a few days before the mission, died holding Roy's hand shortly before landing at the 93rd Evacuation Hospital at Long Binh. He was twenty-six years old.

THE FOLLOWING morning, May 3, 1968, Ewing and a contingent of 240th pilots and crewmen crammed into the back of a slick for the half-hour flight to Long Binh.

Dan Christensen, McKibben's crew chief, was in a long row of patients in the post-op ward. His face was bruised and swollen, his jaw wired shut, and his legs bandaged from the bullet and shrapnel he'd taken before they'd crashed.

When Ewing asked Christensen if he needed anything, he nodded. "Do you know what happened to my .38?" he managed to scribble on a piece of paper.

The disappearance of his sidearm had been haunting Christensen since he'd regained consciousness in the PZ, watching the world blow up around him. The impact of his helicopter slamming into the ground had cracked his helmet and broken his jaw, but as a crew chief, he'd been taught to protect the aircraft and pilots at all costs, and to *never* surrender his personal weapon. He wanted to be sure he hadn't let down McKibben or Fernan. No matter how deep he searched his memory, however, he could not figure out what had happened to his gun.

"Can you find it?" Christensen wrote to Ewing.

Ewing asked a nurse the procedure for recovering a patient's weapon and was directed to a locker but found no revolvers. A clerk told him it might have been tangled up in the clothing that was cut off and discarded in a dumpster behind the field hospital. Following the clerk's directions, Ewing stepped out of the hospital into the stagnant, hot, humid air and made his way to two metal dumpsters. He swung open the metal lid of one and was hit by a stench that made him retch.

"The dumpster was three-quarters full," says Ewing. "Bloody clothes, burnt boots, cracked flight helmets, old bandages, shit, puke, and rot baking in the sun." Repulsed but determined, he climbed inside and began poking through the gore. Only a few minutes into the task, he was nauseous to the verge of passing out.

Standing tall, trying to get some air, he saw the hospital door open. Another clerk lugged a thirty- or forty-gallon trash can to the other dumpster, swung open the lid, and strained to tip the can's contents in. That dumpster was also approaching full.

"How often do you empty these?" Ewing asked.

"Every other day, Sir. They'll get this stuff tomorrow."

So this was from one day, he thought.

In that moment, Ewing was "done." Not just from looking for the .38, but also from everything about the war. He was "empty."

He got out of the dumpster, closed the lid, and walked away down a dusty red-dirt road. A thunderstorm opened up, and Warrant Officer Jerry Ewing climbed up on the hood of a parked jeep, buried his face in his hands, and began to wail.

WHEN O'CONNOR woke up after surgery in intensive care, a nurse pointed out two of the other survivors to him: Tuan and Roy. All three had outgoing drainage tubes and incoming IVs and bandages virtually from head to toe. Tuan's arm had been amputated.

Roy lay in a bed across the hall, his jaw wired shut like Christensen's, and too far away to talk anyway, so the two men waved to each other by wiggling their toes. They remained in intensive care for several days, and one morning Roy awoke to find O'Connor's bed empty. He didn't want to ask, but he assumed that O'Connor had died in the night. That was how it was.

On May 20, 1968, Roy left the hospital at Long Binh; made the journey inside the hull of a medical transport C-130 to the hospital at Tachikawa Air Base, Japan; then to another medical transport to the United States and San Antonio, Texas, where he was wheeled on a gurney to Fort Sam Houston, Brooke Army Medical Center. Unlike 1965, he was awake and aware throughout the trip. Lala held his face in her hands and kissed him, refusing to let on how shocked she was by the extent of his wounds. She had received a Western Union telegram from the secretary of the Army on May 5 that stated, "Your husband, staff sergeant Roy P. Benavidez, was slightly wounded in Vietnam on 2 May 1968, as a result of hostile action. He received multiple fragment wounds to the face, the neck, and the abdomen. Since he is not, repeat, not seriously wounded, no further reports will be furnished."

The same day Lala received the telegram, seventeen-year-old Debbie McKibben was studying for her senior high school year final exams. Her mother, Maxine, was making dinner in the kitchen. Debbie heard a knock on the door, opened it, and when she saw the officer standing there, "It was as though an electrical shock had gone through my body," she says.

Maxine asked the officer if he would stay with them after he delivered the terrible news, until Cecil got home from work in a few hours. She offered the man coffee, then sat on the living room couch and held Debbie. A couple of hours later, Cecil opened the door with a smile. "Then his face, his whole body, just sagged under the weight of the news. I only remember him saying 'No,' the second he saw us and the officer. He knew," says Debbie.

Debbie retreated to her bedroom and buried her face in her pillow, remembering Larry sitting there beside her almost two years before—but it seemed like just yesterday—telling her, "I'm going to go fight communism there so you don't have to face it here. I'm not afraid—I want to go."

ROY HAD sustained more than thirty wounds and for the next year would continue to undergo extensive surgeries to repair his left arm and hand; remove half of his left lung; and extract shrapnel, bullet, and bone fragments from in and around his kidney, liver, intestines, colon, lungs, and heart.

As soon as he was able, he wrote a letter to Roger Waggie to thank him and the other pilots and crew who had extracted the men on May 2; he also requested the address for Larry McKibben's family. A couple weeks went by with no response, and he wrote Waggie again, concerned. More weeks passed with no response.

At the end of July 1968, a second lieutenant was walking the ward, handing out Purple Hearts to healing soldiers "like prizes at a carnival show," says Roy. "It was nothing like I would have expected for these men who had taken a bullet or worse for their country." When he reached Roy's bed, he read the clipboard and handed Roy four Purple Hearts and a small box containing a Distinguished Service Cross, the second-highest award a soldier can receive, second only to the Congressional Medal of Honor.

"Congratulations, Sergeant," the lieutenant said. "With all due respect, Sir," replied Roy, "it takes more than a second lieutenant to award this medal."

On September 10, 1968, almost four months into his stay at Brooke Army Medical Center, Roy stood at attention beside his bed and saluted General Westmoreland, who had been promoted to chief of staff of the U.S. Army, and had scheduled time to visit the wounded while on official business at Fort Sam Houston. While members of Roy's family and a small contingent of officers and reporters looked on, Westmoreland said, "Many years ago, I met [Staff Sergeant Benavidez] at Fort Gordon, Georgia. I was impressed with his appearance. I was impressed with the self-discipline that he displayed. I was impressed with him as a soldier. I said, 'Sergeant Benavidez, you should go Airborne.' He accepted my advice. He went Airborne, and he's still a paratrooper, I believe. Aren't you, Sergeant?"

"Yes, Sir," Roy said, astonished by the general's recall. "And I will be one, Sir, for a long time."

Westmoreland went on to read the citation that began "For extraordinary heroism in connection with military operations involving conflict with an armed hostile force in the Republic of Vietnam . . ." and ended with "Because of Sergeant Benavidez's indomitable spirit, the lives of eight men were saved."

Roy shook Westmoreland's hand and stood for a photo with Lala and his brother Roger, his forced smile betraying his sadness. He was proud of the medal, proud that he'd honored the Benavidez name, that he'd performed his duty for his country—but in his mind he was back in Cambodia with O'Connor, Wright, Mousseau, Christensen, Fernan,

Fournier, McKibben, and the CIDG who had fought alongside them and lost their lives. They were the real heroes. And what of Waggie? Roy wondered if he would ever hear from him or if he, too, had been killed in a subsequent operation.

At the end of September, Roy finally received a letter from Vietnam:

> Dear Sir,
>
> I know that you are disappointed in me but hope you understand. After your second letter, I left [to fly a mission at] the Cambodian border. We had 2 ships go down and lost the entire crew of one. Bill Fernan, who was flying with Larry McKibben when he was killed, was the ship that didn't come back. We did recover one crew. I left Bear Cat 10, July and have only been here once since. I went on R & R to Hawaii on 13 August. While I was there, we had 2 pilots killed and a crew chief. My roommate was killed June 24. We lost 6 pilots that day. It has really been bad. I am the only one left from the platoon that Larry knew. Hope you understand my situation and forgive me for not answering promptly. We are having a lot of action here. Seems like they are everywhere.
>
> > Take care.
> > Waggie

ON NUMEROUS occasions during his stay in the Fort Sam Houston hospital, Roy was advised to retire from the Army for medical reasons. He refused. A year and one week after he'd jumped on the helicopter at Loc Ninh, Roy checked out of the hospital on May 9, 1969. He had in hand orders for temporary duty with the 10th Special Forces Group at Fort Devens, Massachusetts, and a copy of the Winter 1968 edition of *Tour*

365, a magazine given to departing soldiers at the end of their tours in Vietnam.

An Army-prepared history of Vietnam and the U.S. involvement through 1968, *Tour 365* began with a letter from the new commanding general in Vietnam, Creighton W. Abrams: "Your tour of duty with the United States Army is ended. May your trip home and reunion with family and friends be the pleasant happy occasion you have anticipated. You go home with my best wishes. As Veterans of this war, you can now look back with perspective on your experiences and know the trying and difficult tasks inherent in fighting to protect the freedom of peace-loving people against Communist invaders. You know of the local Vietcong terrorists who kill and maim their own neighbors. . . . People at home will want to hear your story of the war. Tell it."

The magazine ended with a closing letter from Frank T. Mildren, the deputy commanding lieutenant general in Vietnam, who wrote: "You may leave this land of Vietnam—the jungles, mountains, and coastal plains—with that inner satisfaction of knowing you have served the cause of free men everywhere. The Republic of Vietnam and, indeed, our own nation, are greatly in your debt for your efforts. Now you are going home to rejoin your family and friends. They are proud of you and are anxiously awaiting your return."

In direct contradiction to those words, Roy's orders advised him not to wear his uniform at airports, train stations, bus depots, and essentially anywhere in public, because there had been a number of conflicts between returning veterans and those who opposed the war. They were taking their frustrations out on the soldiers, calling them "baby killers," spitting on their boots, and perpetrating other hostile acts.

But Roy continued to wear his uniform proudly. He wore it when he drove to Jacinto City outside Houston and knocked on the door of the house where Larry McKibben had grown up.

Inside, he embraced Cecil and Maxine and held the framed photo of their son they took off the wall to show him, as well as the Distinguished Service Cross they had been presented. He told them how sorry he was for their loss, showed them his own DSC, and said he would not have been able to do what he did—and eight men would not have survived—if it weren't for their son's bravery. He said to them what he couldn't say to Larry McKibben, what very few Vietnam veterans would hear upon their return: "Thank you."

AFTER ONE parachute jump—and one painful landing—at Fort Devens, Roy decided it was his last. His body couldn't take it. Six months into his temporary duty at Fort Devens, he moved to Fort Riley, Kansas, at the request of Major General Robert R. Linville, Commanding General, 1st Infantry Division—whom he had chauffeured in the past—to become the general's full-time driver. There, on November 20, 1969, Lala gave birth to their second daughter, Yvette Benavidez.

Roy reenlisted for another six years in 1971, the same year that, on April 24, two hundred thousand people marched on Washington, DC, to protest the war. In early 1972, Roy moved his family back to Fort Sam Houston, where General Patrick Cassidy was in need of an experienced chauffeur. Roy and Lala's son, Noel Benavidez, was born on August 26 of that same year.

General Cassidy retired in 1974 and gave Roy the opportunity to choose his next assignment. Roy had dreamed of bringing his career full circle by advising and training Special Forces and infantrymen. A new readiness group was being formed at Fort Sam Houston to do just that, and while it would be a physically demanding job, working in the field among young, fit soldiers, he was up for the challenge. General Cassidy made the recommendation, and Roy secured a position that kept him and his family at Fort Sam Houston, not far from home in El Campo.

Roy lived with a great deal of pain as he worked in the field, but his dedication and performance remained exemplary, as evidenced by the letters of recommendation for promotion that filled his personnel file, from high-ranking officers such as Major General Linville, who wrote: "As a true soldier of honest dedication, there is no one I would recommend more highly." That sentiment was echoed by Brigadier General John A. Seitz, Colonel Wilfrid K. G. Smith, and Colonel R. D. Tice, all of whom applauded Roy's character, dedication, and commitment to his fellow soldiers.

Perhaps most telling were the comments of Lieutenant Colonel Richard E. Cavazos, who wrote of Roy's duties as the assistant operations sergeant in the largest brigade in the 1st Infantry Division: "The constant requirements would have overwhelmed a lesser man. Despite the discomfort that SFC Benavidez suffered due to wounds received in two tours, he always gave his utmost in any task. SFC Benavidez has been a sterling example. He conducted himself at all times with a demeanor that elicited the admiration and respect of everyone. He is highly decorated and the courage that he displays at all times under the most trying of circumstances marks him as a true soldier's soldier. His initiative, professional knowledge, and readiness to assist his fellow soldiers more than qualifies him for [promotion]."

Roy had risen to the rank of master sergeant and was the senior enlisted adviser to the team readiness group. He was thirty-nine years old and, because of the numerous surgical and battle scars that covered his body, was known by his fellow NCOs as "the walking road map." He would become noticeably embarrassed when his service in Vietnam was brought up or the Distinguished Service Cross he'd wear on formal occasions was remarked upon. If he was referred to as a hero, he was quick to say, "I appreciate that, but the real heroes didn't come home."

Some of Roy's superiors, concerned by the noticeable suffering he put himself through to push the troops in their training regimen, agreed to take steps that might speed up his honorable discharge without dishonoring the man, according to a fellow NCO. A major who worked closely with Roy wrote: "[It] became apparent to the members of the team that Benavidez would not admit that he was physically unable to climb, run, carry heavy loads, or keep up with the rifle platoons and squads during rigorous field training exercises. . . . Although [he] made every effort to hold up his end of the log, he could not, and the team made adjustments to place him in situations which would spare him from physical efforts which would aggravate his extensive injuries."

Another major said of Roy: "[Though] Benavidez never once complained, his physical condition did not permit him to function satisfactorily. Any lesser man would not have even attempted to accomplish the mission. Due to this man's sincere devotion to his country and the U.S. Army, it is a disservice to have [him] on active duty and not be able to perform. He has all but paid the supreme price—life—through his heroism in Vietnam."

IN MARCH 1969, after the NVA launched a series of rocket attacks against Saigon, President Nixon authorized Operation Menu, a covert, massive bombing campaign that targeted NVA base areas in Cambodia and Laos, most of which had been identified by SOG recon teams. The area in the Fishhook where the May 2, 1968, mission took place was bombed repeatedly after being designated one of the most likely locations of COSVN (NVA headquarters).

Two years later, in 1971, the *New York Times* began publishing excerpts from the Pentagon Papers, making public the top-secret study compiled by the Department of Defense outlining U.S. military and political involvement in Vietnam from 1945 to 1967. Congress voted to withdraw troops by the end of the year, but the war raged into 1972, with the NVA launching the Easter Offensive against the South Vietnamese in March and President Nixon retaliating a few days later with a massive bombing in North Vietnam.

The majority of American ground forces left Vietnam in August 1972, though thousands of airmen, support personnel, and Special Forces "advisers" remained in-country. In November Nixon was re-elected president for a second term, and by January 1973 a cease-fire was signed by representatives of the United States and both North and South Vietnam, with the United States agreeing to withdraw remaining combat troops. North Vietnam released nearly six hundred American prisoners of war in March, and on the 29th, the U.S. involvement in Vietnam was officially declared over.

South Vietnam would continue to fight for two more years, conceding defeat only after the capital of Saigon was captured on April 30, 1975. Le Duan, the current leader of the reorganized Vietnamese Communist Party, unified Vietnam under a communist government, whose repressive social policies included "reeducation camps," hard labor, and executions.

In December 1986 new leadership enacted economic and political reforms; though the Communist Party continued to hold all political power, private ownership of farms and factories was encouraged, along with economic deregulation and foreign investment: a communist government with a capitalist economy, like China.

The impact of the Vietnam War was far-reaching. Total American deaths numbered 60,000; wounded, over 150,000; and more than 2,500 servicemen missing in action. At least 1,500 of them remain unaccounted for today. Though numbers vary greatly, casualties for South Vietnam are estimated to be at least 220,000 killed and over a million wounded, while NVA and VC forces purportedly suffered losses of over a million and an untold number of wounded. Hundreds of thousands of civilians also lost their lives across Vietnam, Laos, and Cambodia.

In Cambodia, the Khmer Rouge under the leadership of Pol Pot continued to gain strength and support during the Vietnam War, especially after Prince Sihanouk was deposed in March 1970 in a coup d'état led by General Lon Nol. Sihanouk set up a government-in-exile in China, aligning himself with China, North Vietnam, and the Khmer Rouge to resist the Lon Nol government, which was backed by the United States.

The resulting civil war lasted five years, until April 1975, when Pol Pot and the Khmer Rouge overthrew the Lon Nol government and initiated social engineering with the goal of a classless peasant society. Over the next four years, under the totalitarian dictatorship of Pol Pot, executions, forced labor, malnutrition, and poor medical care resulted in the deaths of an estimated one to three million Cambodians—as much as 25 percent of the Cambodian population—whose bodies were buried in mass graves that became known as "killing fields." The government of Pol Pot and the Khmer Rouge was overthrown by Vietnamese forces in April 1979 during the Cambodian–Vietnamese War.

From Fort Bragg to Fort Sam Houston, word about the events of May 2, 1968, had gotten around during the 1970s, and within the tight circles of the Special Forces community, Roy Benavidez was becoming a legend.

He brushed it off as war buddies telling stories over a beer at the NCO club, but a single subject always came up: Why had Roy not received the Congressional Medal of Honor? "Some thought I had," he said. "Others thought I should have, and a few had heard I had at least been recommended for it. But the discussions had almost always been over a drink, and I really never thought it was more than just talk."

Eventually Roy made an inquiry about the original documentation. The response he received from the Army Decorations Board was that they were unable to locate any documentation aside from the citation of the Distinguished Service Cross. Colonel Jim Dandridge, a former Special Forces intelligence officer who had been involved with the Daniel Boone mission with MACV-SOG and was based with Roy at Fort Sam Houston, told Roy he was certain that Lieutenant Colonel Drake had put him in for the Medal of Honor. Furthermore, he knew Drake was currently the director of plans, training, and security at the U.S. Army School/Training Center at Fort McClellan in Alabama.

Dandridge invited Roy to his office, and he rang Drake on the spot and handed the phone to Roy.

It was April 1, 1974. The last time Roy had seen Drake was at the 93rd Evac Hospital in Long Binh when he had visited with both O'Connor and Roy in the intensive care unit.

"Benavidez?" he said now. "I thought you died."

"No, Sir," Roy replied. "Not quite."

Drake clarified that he had put Roy in for the Distinguished Service Cross (DSC) knowing that the Medal of Honor required massive documentation he didn't have. Even the DSC had been no easy award to obtain. "All I was able to put together was some sketchy material from a few people," Drake told Roy, "including a couple of chopper pilots. You and O'Connor were gone—I didn't even know if you survived—and Mousseau and Wright were dead."

When they got off the phone, Dandridge apologized to Roy. He really thought that Roy's actions had warranted the Medal of Honor, and he was sorry for the misinformation. Once Roy had left, Dandridge called Drake back, and Drake put the wheels in motion by writing a recommendation to upgrade Roy's DSC to the Medal of Honor, citing new evidence not known at the time. The Army Decorations Board declined, stating insufficient evidence.

★

Roy CONTINUED to struggle while performing his job. After his annual physical on October 16, 1975, an army doctor wrote: "In my judgment, Master Sergeant Benavidez is not capable of performing the duty of MOS 11B5SLA in combat because of his physical limitations."

But Roy still wasn't ready to retire. Although his body was beaten down and he was in constant pain, walked with a limp, and dragged himself through exercises, he requested to be tested for the physical requirements of three military occupational specialties: military policeman, correctional specialist, and special services. The result: "There are no MOS's for which MSG Benavidez is both physically qualified and technically qualified through experience and/or training."

Off the record, a doctor told Roy that he not only qualified for, he *deserved*, disability benefits. "I'm not disabled," Roy replied. "I can walk. I can still get around."

"You're forty years old," the doctor said. "You've got a long life ahead of you, and like it or not, these injuries from your wounds are not going to go away. And it's all service related." Roy would likely have to stand before a board and answer questions about his service and medical situation, the doctor explained. "All you have to do is tell the truth. Let them decide."

And so Roy agreed to a formal hearing on August 4, 1976, relaying to the board his doctors' reports and injuries, more than thirty in all, each incurred during combat. Bullet, shrapnel, and bayonet wounds, to the joints, organs, and his left eye. The most concerning, chronic "issue" was a shortness of breath that resulted from all the shrapnel remaining in his body.

"I am an adviser," Roy said. "And this takes a lot of exertion, being out in the field or falling in with the troops in combat situations, setting an example before the enlisted men. It's embarrassing for a senior noncommissioned officer to fall out in front of his men." Roy paused for a long moment before continuing. "It's a bad example."

"At this time do you have any limited motion in your back?" the board asked him.

"Yes," Roy answered. "I can bend over with time, touch my toes. I've done it because I'm very active, I've been doing exercises or PT for twenty-some-odd years, as long as I've been in the Army. To me, it hurts my pride even to come before the board, a medical board . . . but I have to realize that I'm just incapable of doing it, and rather than letting my noncommissioned officers corps down, I might as well step down."

After an hour of questioning, the board closed for deliberation. Fourteen minutes later, they emerged and found Roy "unfit to perform his duties due to numerous injuries resulting from combat wounds." The resulting physical disabilities, they recounted, "are permanent and are rated at 80 percent. The board recommends that Master Sergeant Roy P. Benavidez be permanently retired."

"I guess I won't make thirty years," Roy said to Lala after receiving the decision. To which she replied, "Benavidez, I can't believe you made twenty. Let's go home to El Campo."

15

METTLE FOR MEDAL

MASTER SERGEANT ROY Benavidez officially retired on September 10, 1976. He'd served three years in the Texas National Guard, and twenty-one years and four months in the regular Army.

His daughter Denise was ten years old, Yvette six, and Noel four when Roy and Lala returned to El Campo for good. A lot had changed in Roy's hometown since his childhood. For one thing, the segregated neighborhoods were the exception, not the rule. Their plan had been to build a home on the lot next to Lala's parents', but they decided to look around, and Lala fell in love with a house in a neighborhood that wasn't Mexican, or white, or black, or Asian. It was diverse, or as Roy described it, "American"—exactly the type of street he wanted his kids to grow up on.

Just as Roy and Lala had dreamed, their three children each had their own room with a desk and a bed. Lala began planting bulbs and flowers in the ground outside the house instead of the pots they'd carted from base to base, and Roy enrolled himself in Wharton County Junior College, determined to get a degree. He would sit on the left-hand stool at their kitchen counter studying, and—a few months after their return—jotting down notes for a speech he had been invited to give at a Rotary Club luncheon being hosted by Jaro Netardus.

Netardus, who worked with the Wharton County Savings and Loan, where Roy did his banking, had been a local high school football star who went on to play for Texas A&M in college, and then served in the U.S. Air Force Reserve for twenty years. He was a big supporter of the military, and when he came across Roy's name, he remembered reading an article about him when he'd been presented with the Distinguished Service Cross.

In the easy, conversational tone he'd learned from years of Benavidez storytelling, Roy stood at the podium and talked about being taken in by his uncle, Nicholas Benavidez, picking sugar beets and cotton, growing up in El Campo, joining the Army, marrying his wife, and traveling around the world on deployments, ultimately ending up in Vietnam. He explained how, wherever he was in the world, his wife had sent him copies of the *El Campo Leader-News*. "I left copies of the *Leader-News* all over the world, and all over Vietnam," Roy said. "So the Vietcong, the ARVN, I bet even General Westmoreland, know who Ricky Ricebird is."

Ricky Ricebird was the El Campo High School mascot, and as the attendees of the luncheon chuckled, Fred Barbee—the publisher and editorial director of the *Leader-News*—leaned over to his son, Chris, and said, "We gotta meet this guy."

A short while later the Barbees were interviewing Roy, with plans to run an article about him in the paper. They learned that Roy's former commander had been attempting to upgrade his Distinguished Service Cross to the Medal of Honor, but Roy said he was happy enough to have the DSC. "I feel bad sometimes," he told the Barbees, "even wearing this. But I do it because it reminds me of the guys who didn't come home. They are the real heroes. If you write any stories, you need to be sure you make that real clear."

Fred Barbee was able to obtain a copy of Roy's DSC citation and was floored by Roy's actions and the events of May 2, 1968. At the luncheon, says Chris, "Roy had made it sound like he flew in and did what any other soldier would do, helped the wounded on board the helicopter, and they flew away. He said something along the lines of, 'If somebody needs help, it's your duty to help them.' I think that was when my dad made it his mission to help Roy—to see that Roy was properly recognized, or at least given a fair shot."

Most of the information available to the public about the mission had been compiled by Lieutenant Colonel Charles Kettles, who learned about Roy in April 1974 through Dandridge and Drake. Kettles had assigned Captain James Mason to locate witnesses and was able to obtain statements from Roger Waggie, Jerry Ewing, William Darling, Jesse Naul, James Fussell, Gary Land, Michael Grant, and Ron Radke of the 240th. None of it was deemed "sufficient evidence."

Fred Barbee passed the files along to an acquaintance, Texas congressman Joe Wyatt, who assigned one of his staff to work on it, according to Chris Barbee. "He started putting information together, and every time they felt they had enough to go to the Army Decorations Board, it kicked back, saying there was not enough new corroborative evidence or testimony."

Barbee requested copies of the paperwork Drake had submitted for Roy's Distinguished Service Cross, but "they could not find the file," says Chris. "So Dad really thought we were getting the runaround, and that just made him more determined. We received testimony from the pilots and crew who took part in the rescue; one fellow [William Darling] said in his statement that Roy's guts were hanging out, and [Roy] still refused to get back on the helicopter before all the survivors were on board. We started reading other Medal of Honor citations for comparison, and nobody could understand why Roy had not received the award the first time around. Even after his commander [Drake] wrote an official request to upgrade the award because he had learned new information about Roy's action that he did not know back in 1968, it was denied. Each time. Denied. Denied. Denied. It was as if they had the rubber stamp out before they even opened the envelope. None of it made sense; it was a terrible injustice."

But after a while it did start to make a certain type of sense to Fred Barbee, who had a theory. "Maybe it doesn't have anything to do with the facts," Barbee said to Roy one day in his office. "I think we're dealing with a matter of politics here."

When Roy told Barbee he didn't understand, Barbee—who knew the proximity of Loc Ninh to the Cambodian border—said, "Cambodia, Roy. You were in Cambodia that day. You know it, I know it, and the Army knows it. The trouble is, while you and your buddies were getting chopped to pieces, the government back here was saying that no American servicemen were in that country. They still say there were none of our soldiers there. If they recognize you any more than they already have, they just might have to tell the American people where you were."

Barbee's theory was not far-fetched. On February 19, 1968, a sergeant named Fred Zabitosky was on a Studies and Observation Group recon mission in Laos when his team had been attacked by the NVA. After fighting off the enemy, and in the process of being extracted, Zabitosky was thrown from a helicopter as it went down. Seriously wounded with crushed ribs and severe burns, he pulled the unconscious pilot from the flames and carried him through enemy fire to another helicopter before being extracted. President Nixon presented the Congressional Medal of Honor to him a year later, on March 7, 1969.

Soldier of Fortune magazine would run one of the first "illegal" articles about SOG thirteen years later in its June 1981 issue. "Zabitosky's superiors were uncertain whether he could be awarded the Medal of Honor," wrote Jim Graves. "Medals were hard to come by for SOG soldiers because it was assumed that it would be difficult to control the media: Dead heroes tell no tales. The only SOG recipient of the Medal of Honor before Zabitosky was 1st Lt. George K. Sisler, and his award was posthumous." The article went on to explain how, just a few days before the public ceremony in March of 1969, Zabitosky was invited to the White House for a private meeting with Nixon and Army chief of staff William Westmoreland, who told Zabitosky, "We never thought this would be approved." And, said Nixon, "In your citation we can't put Laos. I appreciate the project. I know what happened. I know where you were when you got it, but unfortunately we have to write your citation as being in Vietnam."

In the summer of 1978, SOG had, to the best of Roy's knowledge, never been exposed, nor had anybody exposed the missions conducted secretly in Laos and Cambodia in the 1960s. Roy was still under an oath of silence, and for that reason, Barbee's comment about telling the American people where the fight took place made Roy "very uncomfortable."

ROY CONTINUED to attend college classes, doing his studying in what everyone in the house knew was "his" seat: the stool at the end of the kitchen counter—everybody except the new family cat, Ozzy.

Roy would get down at eye level and berate the cat, nose to nose, what Roy and the Benavidez kids called "Mexican standoffs." After his years in the Army, Roy could speak basic Korean, German, Vietnamese, and Japanese, and he'd try them all out—including Spanish—in his attempt to talk the disrespectful "furball" out of his seat, all while entertaining the kids.

Then he would get in a martial arts stance and feign karate moves, the kids would laugh, and Ozzy would not budge. Eventually Roy would pick the cat up and move him.

One day Roy faced Ozzy and said, "You know, kitty cat tastes good with Tabasco." Ozzy jumped down, and Roy said to his children, "Figures that he speaks English."

"We knew he was in pain, though," says Denise. "He always had a limp when it was cold, or in the morning, and he'd walk it off, like he'd done in the Army for so many years."

"Mind over matter is what Dad would say," says Noel. "If you don't mind, it doesn't matter."

Every morning except Sunday, when the family went to church, Roy would walk "at Friendship Park," says Yvette. "Five or six laps around the park—he'd do about five miles every day. It was therapy."

DURING THE summer of 1977, Fred Barbee assigned reporter Steve Sucher to keep track of Roy's case—to compile evidence and conduct interviews—but as happened with anybody who spent time with Roy, Sucher quickly became a friend. He and Roy would have a beer or two, and, says Sucher, "I'd hear some of the details about that day that gave me a deep appreciation for what he went through—what all of those men went through."

Roy's story ultimately appeared in the February 22, 1978, issue of the *El Campo Leader-News* as a cover story with a photo of Roy in uniform, an op-ed written by Fred Barbee under the title "Has Washington Forgotten?" Taking up several full pages, the article both honored Roy by telling his story and questioned the motives and competency of the Senior Army Decorations Board.

"This board," wrote Barbee, "whose members are anonymous and whose actions are not subjected to any sort of public scrutiny, supposedly

Sergeant First Class Leroy Wright, team leader B-56 recon team. *Wright Family Archives*

Staff Sergeant Lloyd Mousseau, assistant team leader. *Benavidez Family Archives*

Brian O'Connor, team radioman, with CIDG, including point man Bao (top left); translator Tuan, wearing O'Connor's Green Beret; and grenadier Chien (far right). *O'Connor Family Archives*

Specialist 4
Bob Wessel,
door gunner on
Greyhound Four.
*Armstrong Family
Archives*

Specialist 4 Gary Land (left),
Greyhound Four crew chief.
Armstrong Family Archives

Warrant officers James
Fussell, Roger Waggie,
Larry McKibben,
and Jesse Naul (left
to right) standing
behind Warrant Officer
William Armstrong with
captured NVA weapons
(or gifts from Special
Forces). *Ewing Family
Archives*

Specialist 5 Paul LaChance,
Mad Dog Three crew chief,
in front of his gunship.
LaChance Family Archives

First Lieutenant Robin Tornow, FAC for the mission
(left) and Special Forces captain Jerry Ledzinski.
Ledzinski Family Archives

Chief Warrant Officer Louis Wilson,
Mad Dog Three aircraft commander.
Wilson Family Archives

Specialist 5 Pete Gailis, Mad
Dog Four crew chief, at Camp
Bearcat. *Gailis Family Archives*

Specialist 4 Nelson
Fournier, Greyhound
One door gunner.
U.S. Army Photo

Warrant Officer Jerry
Ewing, Greyhound Two
aircraft commander.
Ewing Family Archives

Specialist 4 Dan Christensen,
Greyhound One crew chief.
Christensen Family Archives

Specialist 4 Danny Clark, seventeen-year-old door gunner of Mad Dog Four.
Clark Family Archives

Warrant Officer William Darling, who volunteered as door gunner on Greyhound Three.
Armstrong Family Archives

Cecil and Maxine McKibben, with their daughter, Debbie, looking on, receive the Distinguished Service Cross for their son, Larry.
McKibben Family Archives

Roy's retirement photo, September 2, 1975. *U.S. Army Photo*

The photo used in the *El Campo Leader-News* cover story that originally ran on February 22, 1978. *Benavidez Family Archives*

Lala, Roy, and Roger Benavidez with General Westmoreland moments after Roy received the Distinguished Service Cross in 1968. *U.S. Army Photo*

The Benavidez children, Noel, Yvette, and Denise, dig into President Reagan's jelly beans, 1981.

Reunited, Brian O'Connor and Roy Benavidez, with President Reagan.

President Reagan drapes the long-awaited Medal of Honor on Roy Benavidez.

All: White House Photo

has reviewed a request submitted first in 1974 by Sgt. Benavidez's former commanding officer, Lt. Colonel Ralph Drake, to upgrade the Distinguished Service Cross to the Congressional Medal of Honor. The request was based on new and substantive evidence not available when the sergeant was first put up for the DSC.

"This faceless Senior Army Decorations Board reportedly (but, in the aura of official secrecy, who knows for sure) reviewed [the case] in June 1976 and again in April 1977. In both instances the board disapproved upgrading the DSC to the Medal of Honor with the same obtuse reason given, that 'no new substantive information' had been presented.

"One wonders what the distinguished Senior Army Decorations Board used for comparison, since by the Army's own admission, the original recommendation for the award for the DSC and accompanying supportive statements had been lost. . . . Nevertheless, a third attempt was made through Congressman John Young's office in October 1977."

Barbee reported how, two months later, Secretary of the Army Clifford Alexander sent Congressman Young a letter informing him that the request had been denied, and in response to Young's request for the reason why, Alexander wrote the congressman, "It is neither fair nor equitable to subject the members of the 'Board' to microscopic inquiry with respect to their votes of conscience. Therefore it is Department of the Army policy not to reveal exact reasons for or against any specific commendation."

"What, then, happened on that awful day in May ten years ago in the Republic of Vietnam?" continued Barbee in his article. "Or, perhaps this particular action on May 2, 1968, actually took place outside the boundaries of Vietnam, perhaps in an area where U.S. forces were not supposed to be. . . . Perhaps that is a contributing factor to the continuing 'runaround.'"

The *Victoria Advocate*, a daily newspaper in nearby Victoria, Texas, carried Barbee's story the following week. From there it was picked up by the Associated Press, which ran various edited versions across the country, and in some of the American news sections of international papers.

It was July of 1980 (more than two years after the original article had been published), and in Fiji, Brian O'Connor was reading the paper when he came across the all-too-familiar date of May 2, 1968. He was shocked and got "a little wet in the eyes" once he realized that Roy Benavidez—who he had assumed died in the hospital in Vietnam—was alive. As he read further and learned that Roy had not received the Medal of Honor because of insufficient eyewitness testimony, O'Connor was determined to do the right thing. But first he had a call to make.

Roy was watching television in his garage den when the Benavidez phone was answered by seven-year-old Noel. When he announced who was on the phone and handed it to Roy, tears began to roll down his father's face.

"I was speechless," remembered Roy, who couldn't say more than a word or two without getting choked up.

"I was convinced he was dead," says O'Connor. "He knew I was dead."

In fact, O'Connor had been moved from the 93rd Evac Hospital at Long Binh in the middle of the night and transported to Japan, where a team of doctors began a very long process of rebuilding him head to toe. O'Connor told Roy that he was still around because of the talents of the doctors who, over the course of two years of surgery and hospitalization, removed bullets and shrapnel, repaired him with bone grafts, and rearranged his insides and got them working about as good as new.

Now he was doing what he'd wanted before the war interrupted, and then nearly took, his life, and that was art. He had a well-stocked bookshelf and a little studio in back with a kiln where he made and fired pottery. In fact, he'd been a professional production potter since

1970. He had also become a member of the Special Forces Association, hidden in plain sight; if Roy had ever questioned whether O'Connor had died, one call to the association would have provided him with a phone number and address.

Now that O'Connor had been "found," he was awash in emotions and memories. "I'm writing a statement on what happened that day," he said to Roy. "When they read what I'm going to write . . . you're going to get the Medal of Honor, Roy. I'm going to see to that."

HE BEGAN with: "This statement, on the events that happened on 2 May 1968, is given as evidence to assist the decision made on awarding the Congressional Medal of Honor to Master Sergeant Roy Benavidez. Because of the classified nature of the mission, some important details will be left out which should not in any way affect the outcome of the award."

Like Roy, O'Connor was bound by the thirty-year oath of silence he had signed in 1967. He couldn't disclose, even a decade after the war, any information on SOG or the classified locations of its operations, so he simply put that his team had been inserted "west of Loc Ninh."

Then, for ten pages, O'Connor recounted a condensed and appropriately militaristic play-by-play. While he had witnessed numerous heroic acts that day, he focused solely on Roy, who he believed was the only person whose voluntary actions that day warranted the Congressional Medal of Honor.

He concluded with, "The above statement is to the best of my recollection, . . . but be advised that I was critically wounded myself and because of my condition I didn't see or can't recall other acts of heroism that Benavidez or other team members may have done. Please feel free to call me if you have any questions about the above statement."

In an additional statement, O'Connor added his own op-ed of sorts:

It is my sincere belief that MSG Benavidez deserved the CMH back in 1968 and still does this very day. I know that all battles are hell, but he on his own voluntarily came into a situation probably knowing the odds were vastly stacked against him. From the moment he jumped out of the chopper until his last recovery run to get my interpreter he was in complete control of us, the survivors, the support, as well as himself.

He organized the remnants of a recon team and chopper crew into a force to be reckoned with. Although wounded, he saw to it that we positioned ourselves in a way that would increase our chances of survival, inflict maximum casualties on the enemy, and secure the PZ against almost impossible odds. When seriously wounded he crawled around, constantly under fire, and gave tactical orders, took charge of air support, medical aid, ammunition and retrieved sensitive classified documents and equipment and boosted our morale, giving us the will to fight and live.

Whatever mechanism it is that clicks in certain people under special circumstances clicked in Benavidez that day. . . . [H]is defiant attitude and sense of duty to get us out of there alive surpassed above and beyond the call of duty [and] borders on the realm of the humanly impossible.

Writing very personally, I was ready to die, and I'm sure the other team members realized the futility of continuing on against such odds. It was Benavidez's indomitable spirit and courage that made us hold on for an extra five or ten minutes that then dragged into hours, and it paid for eight or nine of us because he knew exactly what he was doing. The problem is he never received just recognition for his actions. Perhaps this was because of the times and the classified status of the mission and the difficulty in locating me. I hope your review board can make use of the statement I provided and feel free to use this additional statement if necessary.

This new statement was submitted in summer of 1980 along with all the preceding documentation and statements that had been submitted yearly since Drake first resubmitted for the award upgrade on April 9, 1974. The package was also sent to then President Jimmy Carter for a second time, just as it had been sent to President Gerald Ford before him.

O'CONNOR HAD been awarded the Bronze Star with Valor for his actions on May 2, 1968. Those few who were privy to the details of the mission—especially O'Connor's steadfast devotion to the CIDG, and his calm resolve even as his body failed him due to massive wounds—believed that he, too, deserved at least the Silver Star or perhaps the Distinguished Service Cross (which had been awarded to Wright and Mousseau). They felt that O'Connor should have pursued the upgrade of his own medal; his actions certainly warranted it. But O'Connor's mission was to see Roy's award, not his own, upgraded. He was proud of his Bronze Star with V.

O'Connor was soon contacted by a member of the Decorations Board, the first of several interviews held to confirm and further question the validity of his statement.

Satisfied with O'Connor's statement and interviews, the Decorations Board bumped Roy's request for upgrade to the next tier in the process. They then presented yet another hoop for Roy to jump through before he could receive the Medal of Honor: the statute of limitations had expired and an Act of Congress would be required to allow an official decision. Still, O'Connor's statement had clearly made an impact, as Major Robert Roush, a former officer with the Army's Military

Awards Branch, agreed to testify, along with Texas congressman Joe Wyatt, before the House Military Personnel Subcommittee on November 1, 1980, requesting that Congress consider a bill to exempt Roy Benavidez from the time limit on awarding medals for heroism. "I must stress," testified Roush, "that Sergeant Benavidez voluntarily joined his comrades, who were in critical straits. He constantly exposed himself to withering fire, and his refusal to be stopped, despite numerous severe wounds, saved the lives of at least eight men."

The extension was granted, and a month and a half later, President Carter signed the bill. He was, however, unable to schedule the required presidential ceremony to award the medal before he left office, probably due to the Iran hostage crisis.

The new president, Ronald Reagan, made the ceremony a priority, arranging for Roy and thirty-nine members of his family to be transported to and hosted in Washington, DC, and on February 24, 1981, Noel, Yvette, and Denise helped themselves to the president's signature jelly beans, which he kept on his desk in the Oval Office. In fact, Reagan allowed Noel to take the entire jar, with a promise to share with his sisters.

Roy, Lala, and their children stood before a cadre of press for photos with Reagan, First Lady Nancy Reagan, and Secretary of Defense Caspar Weinberger. The ceremony would take place at the Pentagon, but the president gave the assembled press corps a preview when he said, "You are going to hear something you would not believe if it were a movie script. Wait until you hear the citation."

Later that afternoon, Roy and his family assembled in the inner courtyard at the Pentagon, and Reagan addressed the crowd of thousands that included Colonel Ralph Drake, Sergeant Jerry Cottingham (who had interceded when Roy was being zipped into the body bag), and Brian O'Connor, who had met with Roy the night before for a private, tear-filled reunion.

Men and women of the Armed Forces, ladies and gentlemen:

Several years ago, we brought home a group of American fighting men who had obeyed their country's call and who had fought as bravely and as well as any Americans in our history. They came home without a victory not because they'd been defeated, but because they'd been denied permission to win.

They were greeted by no parades, no bands, no waving of the flag they had so nobly served. There's been no "thank you" for their sacrifice. There's been no effort to honor and, thus, give pride to the families of more than 57,000 young men who gave their lives in that faraway war. . . . There's been little or no recognition of the gratitude we owe to the more than 300,000 men who suffered wounds in that war. John Stuart Mill said, "War is an ugly thing, but not the ugliest of things. A man who has nothing which he cares about more than his personal safety is a miserable creature and has no chance of being free unless made and kept so by the exertions of better men than himself."

Back in 1970 Kenneth Y. Tomlinson wrote of what he had seen our young men do beyond and above the call of military duty in Vietnam—a marine from Texas on his way in at dawn from an all-night patrol stopping to treat huge sores on the back of an old Vietnamese man, an artilleryman from New Jersey spending his free time stacking sandbags at an orphanage to protect the children from mortar attacks, an Army engineer from California distributing toys he'd bought in Hong Kong to the orphans his unit had adopted. . . . None of the recent movies about that war have found time to show those examples of humanitarianism.

The stories go on and on. Bob Hope, who visited our men there as he had in two previous wars, said of them, "The number of our GIs who devote their free time, energy, and money to aid the Vietnamese would surprise you." And then he added, "But maybe it wouldn't. I guess you know what kind of guys your sons and brothers and the kids next door are."

Well, yes, we do know. I think we just let it slip our minds for a time. It's time to show our pride in them and to thank them. . . .

I have one more Vietnam story, and the individual in this story was brought up on a farm outside of Cuero in De Witt County, Texas, and he is here today. . . . [His] story, which had been overlooked or buried for several years . . . has to do with the highest award our nation can give, the Congressional Medal of Honor, given only for service above and beyond the call of duty.

At this point, Weinberger escorted Roy to the podium to stand beside Reagan.

"Ladies and gentlemen, we are honored to have with us today Master Sergeant Roy P. Benavidez, U.S. Army, Retired." Almost without exception, citations for valor were read by an aide or member of a president's cabinet, but Reagan himself read the citation—the contents of which he said had been "lost for too long a time":

On May 2, 1968, Master Sergeant (then Staff Sergeant) Roy P. Benavidez distinguished himself by a series of daring and extremely valorous actions while assigned to Detachment B-56, 5th Special Forces Group (Airborne), 1st Special Forces, Republic of Vietnam.

On the morning of May 2, 1968, a 12-man Special Forces Reconnaissance Team was inserted by helicopters in a dense jungle area west of Loc Ninh, Vietnam, to gather intelligence information about confirmed large-scale enemy activity. This area was controlled and routinely patrolled by the North Vietnamese Army. After a short period of time on the ground, the team met heavy enemy resistance, and requested emergency extraction. Three helicopters attempted extraction, but were unable to land due to intense enemy small arms and anti-aircraft fire.

Sergeant Benavidez was at the Forward Operating Base in Loc Ninh monitoring the operation by radio when these helicopters returned to off-load wounded crew members and to assess aircraft damage. Sergeant Benavidez voluntarily boarded a returning aircraft to assist in another extraction attempt. Realizing that all the team members were either dead or wounded and unable to move to the pickup zone, he directed the aircraft to a nearby clearing where he jumped from the hovering helicopter, and ran approximately 75 meters under withering small arms fire to the crippled team. Prior to reaching the team's position, he was wounded in his right leg, face, and head.

Despite these painful injuries, he took charge, repositioning the team members and directing their fire to facilitate the landing of an extraction aircraft, and the loading of wounded and dead team members. He then threw smoke canisters to direct the aircraft to the team's position. Despite his severe wounds and under intense enemy fire, he carried and dragged half of the wounded team members to the awaiting aircraft. He then provided protective fire by running alongside the aircraft as it moved to pick up the remaining team members. As the enemy's fire intensified, he hurried to recover the body and the classified documents on the dead team leader. When he reached the team leader's body, Sergeant Benavidez was severely wounded by small arms fire in the abdomen and grenade fragments in his back. At nearly the same moment, the aircraft pilot was mortally wounded, and his helicopter crashed.

Although in extremely critical condition due to his multiple wounds, Sergeant Benavidez secured the classified documents and made his way back to the wreckage, where he aided the wounded out of the overturned aircraft, and gathered the stunned survivors into a defensive perimeter. Under increasing enemy automatic-weapons and grenade fire, he moved around the perimeter distributing water and ammunition to his weary men, re-instilling in them a will to live and fight. Facing a build-up of enemy opposition with a beleaguered team, Sergeant Benavidez mustered his strength, and began calling in tactical air strikes and directing the fire from supporting gunships, to suppress the enemy's fire and so permit another extraction attempt. He was wounded again in his thigh by small arms fire while administering first aid to a wounded team member just before another extraction helicopter was able to land.

His indomitable spirit kept him going as he began to ferry his comrades to the craft. On his second trip with the wounded, he was clubbed from behind by an enemy soldier. In the ensuing hand-to-hand combat, he sustained additional wounds to his head and arms before killing his adversary. He then continued under devastating fire to carry the wounded to the helicopter. Upon reaching the aircraft, he spotted and killed two enemy soldiers who were rushing the craft from an angle that prevented the aircraft door gunner from firing upon them. With little strength remaining, he made one last trip to the perimeter to ensure that all classified material had been collected or destroyed, and to bring in the remaining wounded.

Only then, in extremely serious condition from numerous wounds and loss of blood, did he allow himself to be pulled into the extraction aircraft. Sergeant Benavidez' gallant choice to join voluntarily his comrades who were in critical straits, to

expose himself constantly to withering enemy fire, and his refusal to be stopped despite numerous severe wounds, saved the
lives of at least eight men. His fearless personal leadership, tena-
cious devotion to duty, and extremely valorous actions in the
face of overwhelming odds were in keeping with the highest
traditions of the military service, and reflect the utmost credit
on him and the United States Army.

"Sergeant Benavidez," said President Reagan, turning to Roy, "a nation grateful to you, and to all your comrades living and dead, awards
you its highest symbol of gratitude for service above and beyond the call
of duty, the Congressional Medal of Honor."

EPILOGUE

EVEN BEFORE ROY and his family returned to El Campo the next day, the phone at the Benavidez home was ringing with requests for interviews and invitations to speak across the nation. Roy told his family what President Reagan had said to him in parting—that it was his duty to share his story, especially with the children. "They need to hear stories like yours," Reagan said. An Army public affairs officer informed Roy to be prepared for a flurry of media interest in him, that it "would probably last a few months, maybe a year," says Denise, "and then it would calm down, and everything would get back to normal."

The following day, Roy brought the Medal of Honor to the El Campo cemetery, where he stood by the graves of Grandfather Salvador and Uncle Nicholas and thanked them. Next he went to the home of Art Haddock—Roy's boss at the Firestone tire store and his mentor— and gave *him* a hug. The following week, he accepted his first speaking invitation at the El Campo junior high school and began to hone the message he would continue to deliver to any school that requested him to speak. "Like a fool," he would say to audiences, "I dropped out of school. I'm not proud of it. An education is the key to success." And then he told his story, from the streets of Cuero to the jungles of Vietnam—never mentioning Cambodia.

"He would always tell me that I should never forget who I am, never forget where I came from," says Noel, who was in the audience at his own elementary school a few weeks later. "And always give back to the community."

Shortly thereafter, Roy drove to Jacinto City to meet with Cecil, Maxine, and Debbie McKibben, thanking them again for the actions of their son and brother. In private, Roy said to Cecil that he felt Larry deserved the Medal of Honor—and he intended to put together the documentation necessary to upgrade the Distinguished Service Cross he had already been awarded.

Not long after her brother was killed, Debbie, who had been suffering excruciating headaches, underwent exploratory surgery that left her blind for a number of months. With the slow return of her eyesight came the diagnosis of obstructive hydrocephalus: the flow of cerebrospinal fluid to the brain was being obstructed. Three more surgeries eventually repaired the problem, but it had been a difficult time for the McKibben family. Their faith, as well as their memories of Larry, had given them strength. Although Cecil was grateful for Roy's offer to champion the upgrading of the DSC, he felt that going through the process to see his son's heroism and courage recognized officially would dredge up too many old memories and pain best left alone. They would rather hold on to the good ones and keep living life, grateful for the freedoms that Larry McKibben and so many others had paid for with their lives.

In the final tape that Larry sent home to his family, he had talked about the tail rotor blade with the bullet hole that he'd placed above his bunk. Cecil had requested it through Larry's roommate, Ronn

Rosemark, and now it sat in the corner of the McKibbens' living room as a tribute to Larry's bravery and service. But it was Larry's own words from a tape he'd sent from Vietnam that remained indelible in the hearts and minds of the McKibben family:

"The one good thing about this place, you sure learn not to take anything for granted. Not anything."

IN OCTOBER 1981, Roy was invited to address the cadets at West Point, where he spoke about the importance of the relationships between officers and enlisted men. He shared the story of warrant officers William Darling and Thomas Smith, who volunteered to jump on board Greyhound Three, piloted by Roger Waggie and David Hoffman, to man the door gunner positions, generally held by enlisted men, and go into the fire to pull the men on the ground out. It was an example of "officers and NCOs working together," Roy said. He then talked about seeing the West Point motto for the first time on the plaque behind the desk of the officer he'd had to answer to for striking the drunk lieutenant in Berlin. He had adopted the motto as his own, he said, and it had changed his life.

Roy had recounted this story to audiences so many times over the previous eight months that it had already made its way to West Point. After his talk the cadets presented him with a coveted West Point saber—the first and only enlisted man ever to receive one—inscribed with the words "MSG Benavidez, we will not only remember you as a great American soldier, but also as the epitome of our motto: Duty, Honor, Country."

ON FEBRUARY 22, 1983, Roy received a "Termination of Benefits" letter from the Social Security Administration. He, along with more than three hundred thousand other veterans who had been found permanently disabled, now had to prove their disability for a second time in order to continue to receive benefits.

Four months later, Roy stood at a hearing before the House of Representatives Select Committee on Aging to testify for all the veterans who had been deprived of their benefits. He explained that he had volunteered to go to Vietnam to serve his country, and that "those men that went along with me, my comrades, their widows, their sons, their daughters right now are being deprived of their disability benefits. People call me a hero. Mr. Chairman, members of the committee, ladies, and gentlemen, I am not a hero. I appreciate the title, but the real heroes are the ones that gave their lives for this country, the ones that are lying disabled for life without limbs, and the ones that are blind, the ones that can't move at all, in those beds. I'm here to testify because there has been a gross injustice. . . . We didn't ask to go and fight a war for this country and we didn't . . . fight for luxury, we didn't . . . fight for money, we didn't . . . fight for popularity. We went in the defense of this country, to live free . . . and enjoy the freedom that we have right now, all of us."

The committee applauded Roy at the conclusion of his testimony, and the following week he was informed personally by committee chairman Edward R. Roybal that all Social Security benefits would be reinstated for him and the three hundred thousand other veterans.

Roy continued to juggle his time between his family in El Campo and speaking engagements across the country for years to come, to corporations, military schools and bases, and to his favorite audience—children. He also wrote and published two memoirs over the next decade, *Medal of Honor* and *The Three Wars of Roy Benavidez,* dedicating the latter to "Our nation's young people, tomorrow's leaders."

In 1986, he hand-delivered a copy of his first memoir to Art Haddock, who had recently suffered a massive heart attack and was convalescing at home. Mr. Haddock, whose faith had been his compass in life, had told his daughter as he was being rushed into the operating room the same thing he'd told Roy thirty years before at the Firestone shop: "God makes no mistakes." With Roy's book in hand, he said it again.

On May 26, 1988, Mr. Haddock passed away. Roy walked him to his grave as an honoree pallbearer.

Fred Barbee passed away on October 2, 2007, at age seventy-eight, and his son, Chris, took over as publisher of the *El Campo Leader-News*. Barbee—who began his career as a newspaper printer during his teens—considered his journalistic efforts to help Roy earn his Medal of Honor one of his most important achievements in sixty-plus years as a newspaperman.

IN MAY of 1997, Mad Dog Three crew chief Paul LaChance's fourteen-year-old son, Mike, joined his parents at the 240th Assault Helicopter Company's first reunion in Washington, DC. His son didn't know a lot about the war in Vietnam—there was only a short paragraph in his U.S. history textbook and his father wouldn't talk about it. Mike knew he was never supposed to wake his dad up without making some noise first, but he didn't know what PTSD, post-traumatic stress disorder, was or that his father's frequent nightmares were rooted in his memories from the war. He didn't know that Paul LaChance would curse the Bronze Star with Valor he'd received for running through enemy fire to tackle crew chief James Warr and put out the flames that had engulfed him. He didn't know his father had said he would give the medal back in a second if he could only erase Warr's screams from his memory.

Though LaChance wouldn't talk about the war, he wanted his son to meet some of the men who had been his brothers in arms. In the

Sheraton Hotel ballroom, Mike watched his dad shake Pete Gailis's hand, tears in his eyes. He learned that his father had been a crew chief and door gunner on a gunship, that he was the "line chief" for all the gunships in the 240th, and that he was an "old Mad Dog."

Gailis and LaChance stood facing each other, shaking their heads and smiling, as if they couldn't believe it had been almost thirty years since their tours in Vietnam. They could still feel the grip of their M60s, the pendulum weight of the gun supported by the strap in the doorway; they could still smell the metallic oil and the jet fuel and see the earth rushing beneath them and pick out the blinking lights from the tree line. They could still lead their "targets" in their minds and pull the trigger in memories they both loved and hated and ultimately forgave themselves for. "Leveling the playing field" is how LaChance described going in and providing close air support for teams in contact. "Go in, get them out, and come home alive."

And here he was, alive, with his family and his buddies.

Gailis, after returning from his tour, had joined the U.S. Army Reserve as a helicopter mechanic, got married, divorced, and then met the love of his life, Susan. With five children from both marriages, dogs from the second, and a home with a picket fence, he considers himself "fortunate now and I was lucky then." His tour ended "just in time," he says. After hundreds of combat missions, he had become deadly consistent with his M60. He could, 90 percent of the time, judge the airspeed, lead his targets, and squeeze off just a few rounds to knock an enemy runner down, open up his chest or head, and watch the blood spray.

"There was payback involved," he says, "after losing so many good friends and seeing so many bodies loaded up. There'd be a farmer on a dike in a rice paddy, and we'd just taken fire, but this guy has no weapon. It was common for them to take a few shots and then toss their AK into the water so it's a fifty-fifty chance that he's a VC or a farmer. We'd come around, and he's just looking up at me, and giving me a terrified 'Don't shoot I'm innocent' look, or is it a 'Fuck you, I'm not armed, you can't shoot me' look? The right thing to do is not shoot.

"So I played this game where I opened up and walked rounds all the way down the dike, kicking up dust, and he'd stand there, nowhere to go. Right before the bullets got to him, I eased off the trigger . . . and then started up on the other side of him, and walked the rounds away. I played God. I didn't kill him, but I wanted to. I *really* wanted to. And that's when I knew it was time to go home."

Around the banquet room filled with tables and chairs, none of the hundred or so people present sat. Like LaChance and Gailis, there were smiles, tears, handshakes, and hugs among the servicemen in their fifties. Some looked at each other like ghosts. Most had never counted on their buddies surviving their tours, much less seeing them again in the real world. Some had been desperate to put the horrific memories behind them, while others had pined for the brotherhood of war, which they couldn't find at home. Most had just moved on to the next stage of their lives.

Very few had kept in touch with each other, so now they shared family photographs and gathered around photo albums—the black-and-white yearbooks commemorating their war. Often their eyes and fingers would stop on the forever-young face of one of the thirty-eight members of the 240th Assault Helicopter Company who were killed in action.

Two men from the May 2 mission—David Hoffman, who had been Roger Waggie's copilot on Greyhound Three, and Thomas Smith, who had volunteered to man the door gunner position on Greyhound Three on the final, successful extraction—were among twelve pilots and crew killed in a three-ship midair collision caused by poor visibility less than two months later, on June 25, 1968. Three more men from the May 2 mission—William Fernan, who had been Larry McKibben's copilot on Greyhound One, and Steven Hastings and Donald Fowler, who had been crew chief and door gunner on Michael Grant's Mad

Dog Two—were in a helicopter crash later that summer, on August 1, while supporting a mission on the Cambodian border. Despite search-and-rescue attempts, none of the crew, including aircraft commander Peter Russell, were recovered. Three years later, the wreckage was discovered; Fernan's remains were identified and returned to his family, while clues at the site—helmets with undone straps, unbuckled pilot's restraint straps, and opened C ration tins—suggested the other three Americans had survived the crash. They remain missing in action to this day.

Dan Christensen, the only man who had been on Greyhound One to survive the war, never did find his .38. Though he attempted to return to the 240th—with his jaw wired shut and on crutches from the bullet wounds to his leg—he couldn't talk his way out of the hospital and back to Bearcat. He was sent home and medically retired. Forty years later, his grown children learned about a 240th reunion online. "Seeing those guys was one of the best days of my life," Christensen says. "We spent the whole weekend just hammering out a lot of things that needed hammering."

The aircraft commander of Mad Dog Three, Louis Wilson, was wounded on July 31, 1968, while supporting B-56 in another mission, but he survived the war and returned to duty at Fort Benning, Georgia. After leaving the Army in 1970, he earned a degree in nuclear engineering, then joined the Army National Guard in 1980 as a helicopter pilot, retiring as a Chief Warrant Officer 5 in 2006 and from his full-time job as a nuclear engineer in 2013.

Al Yurman returned home to the United States after having attended the memorial services for each of the thirty-five of his fellow 240th brethren KIA during his one-year tour. He was asked by the Army to go back to Vietnam because of his experience in the Fishhook area, but he turned down the request and finished his military career toward the end of 1970. (A few months later, American forces under the directive of President Nixon invaded Cambodia to take out North Vietnamese bases, matériel, and troop concentrations.) Yurman went on to work for the National Transportation Safety Board, investigating major airline and private aircraft crashes for more than sixteen years. He remains an expert witness and aviation accident investigator in the private sector.

There wasn't a man in the room who hadn't been affected by the war or the May 2, 1968, mission. For Jerry Ewing it was those four words he'd uttered that continued to haunt him, even more than the memory of McKibben's hunched-over body in the wreckage of his slick.

"It's not my turn," he had said when Yurman told him to take a run into the PZ to extract the team. That night after the mission, he had admitted to Yurman how devastated he was by McKibben's death, that he was so sorry for what he'd said. Yurman had replied, "Jerry, you were just confirming. I had said it wasn't your turn; you didn't hesitate. Once I told you I needed you, you were going in. You were doing your job. Larry cut you off." Yurman's words did little to console Ewing, who couldn't shake the fact that he had not just said, "Yes, Sir."

Ewing returned home from the war a month and a half after the mission and became an instructor pilot for a couple of years at Fort Rucker before getting out of the military and landing a job at Ross Perot's Electronic Data Systems. He got divorced, then met and married the love of his life, had kids, and life was once again pretty good. Except for those four words. After three decades, he still felt like a coward. If it hadn't been for that momentary hesitation, he thought, it could very well be Larry McKibben at this reunion rather than Jerry Ewing.

And he might have made it out alive the way William Armstrong, Greyhound Four's pilot, did after being shot in the head. He'd managed to hold the controls steady and get his slick above the trees before handing them off to his copilot, James Fussell. As it turned out, the bullet had entered at the base of his head as he'd leaned forward and traveled upward between the curve of his skull and helmet lining, fracturing but not shattering his skull. His crew chief and door gunner Gary Land and Robert Wessel, who had kept their M60s running despite their own wounds, had kept the enemy from overrunning the aircraft. As far as Armstrong was concerned, they had saved his life, as he told them when he saw them at the reunion.

As a result of the traumatic brain injury he sustained, Armstrong could no longer fly. After being medically retired from the military, he earned a degree in electronics engineering, worked in the nuclear power industry for twenty-five years, earned another degree in education, and taught until his retirement in 2014. Fussell joined the Air Force and eventually retired as a major after flying line fighters and ground attack aircraft. Land spent nine months in the hospital, finished his enlistment, and was eventually discharged from the Army; he went on to work as an IRS agent and receive a degree in accounting. Wessel finished his enlistment before going to work for the Ohio State Veterans Affairs as a councilor. The Special Forces bellyman who had also been on Greyhound Four, James Calvey, became a custom display designer for high-end trade show vendors.

Those at the gathering began to seat themselves for dinner, and Roy Benavidez, whom the 240th had invited as the guest of honor, approached the LaChance table and asked Mike if he could take the chair next to his. They introduced themselves, and then Mike noticed the medal around Roy's neck and asked what it meant. When Roy explained that it was the Medal of Honor, Mike innocently asked why Roy had one and his father did not.

Putting his hand on Mike's shoulder, Roy said, "You know what, son? I'm alive today because of your father and other men in this room. He should have one just like this. He earned it."

Mike's face lit up, and he leaned toward his father as he took his seat and said, "You never told me you were a hero, Dad."

Had it been anybody but his son, LaChance says he would have denied the comment. But this one time he let it hang in the air, like smoke from a rocket strike.

WHEN THE United States finished its involvement in Vietnam, its soldiers returned home but their Vietnamese counterparts would continue the war for two more years. The fate of most—including Bao and the other two CIDG who survived the mission—is not known. The CIDG interpreter, Tuan, however, had been flown to the United States for surgical procedures, where he remained, reportedly living somewhere on the West Coast.

After writing his letter to the Army Decorations Board, Brian O'Connor moved his family to the East Coast, continued his artistic pursuits—both academically and professionally—and earned various awards and degrees, including a master of fine letters and master of fine arts in Shakespeare.

Others veterans continued their military service. First Lieutenant Fred Jones rose to the rank of colonel, having served five years on active duty and twenty-seven years in the U.S. Army Reserve. He retired in 2001, but after the terrorist attacks of 9/11, Jones was recalled to active duty, serving five more years in support of the Global War on Terrorism. Currently, at the age of sixty-nine, he serves as a government civilian at the U.S. Africa Command in Stuttgart, Germany, supporting counterterrorism efforts on the African continent.

Robin Tornow, the forward air controller who risked his career by calling the Daniel Boone tactical emergency, was never reprimanded for doing so. In 1989, then Colonel Tornow wrote a letter to Roy, saying, "My 6 months as a FAC with B-56 were probably the most fulfilling in my career. I'll always reflect proudly on having served with such a great group of individuals." He retired in 1993 after thirty years of service as a brigadier general in the U.S. Air Force and passed away on August 22, 2010.

A few months after the 240th reunion, Roger Waggie succumbed to cancer; he was awarded the Silver Star posthumously for his actions on May 2, 1968. Most recently, Paul LaChance lost his own battle with cancer in the fall of 2014 after a full life of working various jobs—from trucking to catering—that allowed him to support and spend time with his wife, three children, and his boat, *The Other Woman*.

Some veterans dropped off the map, becoming difficult or impossible to reach, having moved on completely or continuing to fight private battles more than four decades after the end of the Vietnam War.

On November 29, 1998, sixty-three-year-old Roy Benavidez passed away at Brooke Army Medical Center in San Antonio from complications of diabetes. Moments before his death, his family circled his bed, held hands, and prayed over him. Noel kissed his father good-bye and said, "No regrets, Dad." Yvette and Denise did the same.

A soldier in battle dress fatigues entered the room, stood at attention, and saluted Roy's body, which was then escorted to St. Robert Bellarmine Catholic Church in El Campo, where he and Lala had been married, where his children were married, and where he attended Mass every Sunday he was home. He was buried with full military honors at Fort Sam Houston, not far from the Drop Zone bar and café, Roy's old hangout where his Army buddies from the Alamo Silver Wings Airborne Association continue to tell his stories at Special Forces Association meetings. They often refer to him as Tango Mike Mike, his almost mythical call sign that they'll tell you is known throughout the Special Operations community as a phrase spoken when courage needs to be summoned and quitting is not an option: "Tango Mike Mike."

Roy is survived by his wife, Lala, his three children—all of whom have college degrees framed and on the walls of their respective homes in El Campo—and eight grandchildren, who are either in college or heading in that direction. In addition to his family and his legacy among the Special Operations community, Roy's name lives on through the Roy P. Benavidez National Guard Armory in El Campo; a conference room at West Point; a U.S. Navy troop and cargo ship (the first U.S. Navy ship to be named after an Army enlisted man); a U.S. Army training center; a community park; two elementary schools (in Houston and San Antonio); and several sculptures.

THE CLASSIFIED after-action reports and briefings that documented Roy's and other SOG warriors' actions during the Vietnam War had been teletyped and sent from forward operating bases (including, but not limited to, Kontum, Ban Me Thuot, Song Be, and Ho Ngoc Tao) to the Military Assistance Command Vietnam, Studies and Observation Group headquarters in Saigon. They were then forwarded to the Office of the Joint Chiefs of Staff, Special Assistant for Counterinsurgency and Special Activities.

Copies were stored temporarily at each base in locked file cabinets and archived at the headquarters until April of 1972, when all of the records were burned. Though nobody seems to know exactly who ordered the destruction, "it's not a stretch to say that the order came from Washington," says SOG unit historian John Plaster. "Then-Chief SOG John Sadler would not have destroyed the records unless directed to do so by higher authority, and he told me face-to-face that they had been burned."

At the end of April 1972, MACV-SOG was officially deactivated and the headquarters was closed. The copies of the after-action reports that had been sent to Washington during the war are also apparently gone. Says Plaster, "Several scholars, writers, and SOG veterans have spent years trying to find them. For all we know, they were destroyed, too. When, where, and how, is unknown."

MACV-SOG WAS officially honored for the first time in April 2001, when President George W. Bush authorized the unit to receive the Presidential Unit Citation (Army) during a ceremony at Fort Bragg, North Carolina. The citation reads, in part:

> The Studies and Observations Group is cited for extraordinary heroism, great combat achievement and unwavering fidelity while executing unheralded top secret missions deep behind enemy lines across Southeast Asia. Incorporating volunteers from all branches of the Armed Forces, and especially, U.S. Army Special Forces, SOG's ground, air and sea units fought officially denied actions which contributed immeasurably to the American war effort in Vietnam.
>
> MACV-SOG reconnaissance teams composed of Special Forces soldiers and indigenous personnel penetrated the enemy's most dangerous redoubts in the jungled Laotian wilderness and the sanctuaries of eastern Cambodia. Pursued by human trackers and even bloodhounds, these small teams out-maneuvered, outfought and outran their numerically superior foe, to uncover key enemy facilities, rescue downed pilots, plant wiretaps, mines and electronic sensors, capture valuable enemy prisoners, ambush convoys, discover and assess targets for B-52 strikes, and inflict casualties all out of proportion to their own losses. . . . SOG's cross-border operations proved an effective economy-of-force, compelling the North Vietnamese Army to divert 50,000 soldiers to rear area security duties, far from the battlefields of South Vietnam. . . .

Despite casualties that sometimes became universal, SOG's operators never wavered, but fought throughout the war with the same flair, fidelity and intrepidity that distinguished SOG from its beginning. The Studies and Observations Group's combat prowess, martial skills and unacknowledged sacrifices saved many American lives, and provide a paragon for America's future special operations forces.

Close to three hundred Special Forces Green Berets assigned to the MACV-SOG were killed in action. Over fifty more remain missing in action—their last known whereabouts being either Laos, Cambodia, or North Vietnam.

IN 1991, during the surge of patriotism that resulted from the onset of Desert Storm—the First Gulf War—Pete Gailis went to the public library near his home in Salem, Massachusetts, wearing for the first time in public a sweatshirt he'd ordered years before. On his front was an American flag with the words: "Vietnam Veteran, Proud of my Service."

As he headed into the library, he held the door for a woman around his age. "How can you be proud of that?" she asked him.

She walked past, and Gailis replied to her back, "I *am* proud of my *service,* Ma'am."

Reflecting on the Vietnam War in the years since 9/11, Gailis says, "Things have sure changed. People finally realized that politics and service are two separate things. They shouldn't be, but they are. There were a lot of victories in Vietnam, there should have been a big one, but I think one thing the Vietnam veterans did for all the future generations: we took the bullet when we came home and eventually people realized it wasn't right. I think one reason people are so supportive of the military today is because of how poorly we were treated after the war. There was a GI who got a cup of blood dumped on him at the airport by a peace protestor when I returned home to Oakland. I was in uniform too and was told by an MP to go to the USO and either stay there until my connecting flight or change into civilian clothes.

"Today I go to the airport and see strangers shaking the hands of men and women in uniform, and it makes me smile. I don't think those people necessarily believe in the politics of our current wars, they just know this young man or woman is serving his country. That was all we did in Vietnam. I'll say it again: I'm proud of my service."

RESEARCH AND ACKNOWLEDGMENTS

To tell the complete story of any mission on the ground in Vietnam, you must also tell the story from the air. And so, I felt it was appropriate to combine my research and acknowledgments into one section—you cannot have one without the other.

During my research for this book, I was honored to speak to dozens of veterans of the Vietnam War—all of whom were either in the Special Forces or the aviation units that supported them. Thank you for your service, your trust, and your willingness to reach into the sometimes dark corners of the past. I simply could not have told the story of this covert mission in such depth without the candid and forthright interviews granted to me by those who were directly involved in the actions on the ground and in the air on May 2, 1968.

Thank you, Roy Benavidez, for your service and for sharing your inspiring story.

Thank you, Brian O'Connor, for spending hundreds of hours to clarify for me your part in the events leading up to and after, the mission, and for sharing with me details that had, until now, never been told.

Thank you to the men of the 240th Assault Helicopter Company for your interviews, writings, notes, documents, and photographs: Rick Adams, William Armstrong, Dan Christensen, Danny Clark, Jerry Ewing, James Fussell, Pete Gailis, Pete Jones, Gary Land, Morris Miller, Bob Portman, Louis Wilson, and Al Yurman. Thank you to Paul "Frenchy" LaChance, who spent hours with me in his home, on the telephone, and answering my e-mails, right up until a few weeks before he passed away after his long battle with cancer. He told me that his goal in finally sharing his story was to honor his buddies.

Thank you to the men who served at Camp Ho Ngoc Tao, Project

Sigma, Detachment B-56, who spoke with me and shared their mementos, writings, notes, documents, and photographs: Manny Beck, Ed Gammons, Nick Godano, Fred Jones, Jerry Ledzinski, Fred Lindsey, and Leonard Moreau. An additional thank-you to Nick and Jerry for the many, many hours they took to field my questions and answer my e-mail messages so that this story was "told right."

Thank you also to SOG veterans Mike Ash, Ben Baker, Dennis Cummings, Merle Eckles, Troy Gilley, Jim Harrison, John Meyer, Steve Spoelly, Carl Vencill, and Art Wilbur.

Thank you, retired Chief SOG General Jack Singlaub, for your multiple interviews. Thank you, James Reid and the Explorers Club in NYC, for bringing to light the details of Operation Vesuvius.

Thank you to the family members of the men in the story who spoke with me and invited me into their homes: Lala Benavidez, Denise (Benavidez) Prochazka, Yvette (Benavidez) Garcia, and Noel Benavidez. Noel also coordinated my time in El Campo, Cuero, and San Antonio, Texas, and put me in contact with the members of the 240th, informing me that his father had always hoped the air component of the mission would be fully told in a future book. Thank you also, Gene Sr. (Roy's older brother), Gene Jr. and David (Roy's nephews), Marjorie Armstrong, Alice Christensen, Jeff and Debbie (McKibben) Connor, Cheryl (Craig) Granna, Donna (Fournier) Johns, Joan LaChance and her son, Mike, Nancy (Haddock) Meissner, Kathy (Mousseau) Mueller, and Joan Singlaub.

Thank you, Terry Perkins, Curtis Thiele, and all at H.I.S. Tapes, Duplicating and Recording in Houston, Texas, for taking such care in transferring Larry McKibben's reel-to-reel tapes onto a CD for the family.

Thank you to Roy's Special Forces buddies from the Alamo Silver Wings Airborne Association, who put aside an afternoon to meet with me at the Drop Zone Café in San Antonio, Texas, including Fred Balderrama, Ed Fernandez, Val Martinez, Joe Rodriguez, and Rudy Villarreal.

While I received much of my information regarding the operations and history of MACV-SOG from personal interviews conducted during the Special Operations Association Reunion in the summer of 2014, virtually everything I learned there and from subsequent interviews was cross-checked with the work of former recon men and SOG historians John Plaster and Steve Sherman, whose electronic databases, CD-ROM compilations, and published books can be located online by searching their names. Thank you, John and Steve. Thanks also to Lieutenant Colonel Fred Lindsey, whose book *Secret Green Beret Commandos in Cambodia* provided great context and insights into the Project Sigma and B-56 missions. I also recommend *Across the Fence: The Secret War in Vietnam,* written by former recon man John Stryker Meyer.

All quotations and actions depicted in this book were drawn from eyewitness interviews; however, I also used quotations and paraphrased information from official operational orders, after-action reports, officer evaluation reports, and other documents. These historical papers were provided to me directly by the men involved.

Between these personal eyewitness interviews and documents, I was able to get a feel for what went on in each and every Greyhound slick and Mad Dog gunship involved in the mission on May 2, 1968. Over the passage of time, memories vary and I did my absolute best to put the events in the right chronological order so that those remembered from the air coincided with those occurring on the ground. All events that are depicted, and the locations where they occurred, are accurate to the best of the memories recounted and supporting documentation; recollections of the timing sometimes varied, however, and in the end I used the democratic approach, choosing the majority opinion where there was a discrepancy. I also weighed heavily the testimony written by eyewitnesses in the seventies and eighties—since it was closer to the time being depicted.

The Vietnam War was called "the living room war" because the media brought the war, for the first time, into the living rooms of America via newspapers, magazines, radio, and especially television. I have included quotations from the media that I hope will give readers a sense of what the American public and world were receiving at the time.

I was given permission from the Benavidez family to excerpt Roy's two memoirs, *Medal of Honor* and *The Three Wars of Roy Benavidez*. All of his descriptions, inner thoughts, quotations, and recounted dialogue are from these two books, the personal letters Roy wrote to family and friends throughout his lifetime, radio and television interviews, as well as his speeches. I was also provided with a copy of Roy's personal military personnel file, which includes the full and detailed history of the process to upgrade Roy's Distinguished Service Cross to the Congressional Medal of Honor. This included the written testimonies of military personnel who either witnessed the action or were directly involved in it, or were present and listened to events on the radio: William Darling, Ralph Drake, Michael Grant, Jesse Naul, Ronald Radke, Robin Tornow, and Roger Waggie. Thank you to Chris Barbee and Steve Sucher for your candid interviews, as well as Leonel Garza for insights into Roy's quest for the Medal of Honor.

Thank you also to Doreen Agard, Troy Anderson, Michael Hennessy, Maxine Keene, and Dean Shumate for your contextual research and help organizing the mountains of information. Thank you, Herbert Friedman, for your help and your archives in psywarrior.com regarding the psychological operations during the Vietnam War. Thank you, Joe "Ragman" Tarnovsky, for sharing with me your time with the 240th and for always making it clear that though you weren't there on the May 2 mission, you wanted to be sure those who were there were honored. Thank you, Mark Byrd, for recounting your conversations with Robin Tornow, and Molly Young for the transcripts and DVDs of Roy's television appearances.

Thank you, Chris Adams, for your detailed maps of the LZ, and Joe LeMonnier for the map of Vietnam and surrounding countries.

Thank you, David Adams, Jason Amerine, Matt Baglio, Don Bendell, Brian Berry, Linda Bubela, Carol Cepregi, Shannon Crabtree, Jackie Erickson, Chuck Fisher, Matt Golsteyn, Don Kirk, Chris Kyle, Melanie Luttrel, Pete and Marcelle McAfee, Diana Moreno, Michael Palgon, Jay Redman, George Schlatter, Bob Schoultz, Scott Schwarte, Joy Sheppard, Tommy Spaulding, Rick Stewart, Janet Wendle, and Seymour Topping.

Thank you to the hardworking, flexible team at Penguin Random House, including my editor, Roger Scholl, deputy publisher David Drake, Crown publisher Molly Stern, art director Chris Brand, production editor Robert Siek, interior designer Barbara Sturman, head of Design Elizabeth Rendfleisch, marketing director Jessica Miele, and senior publicist Penny Simon. Thank you to my talented longtime personal researcher and editor Rita Samols, who stays on call around the clock.

To my family and friends: Thank you as always for your help, incredible patience, and understanding.

To my children: Stories like this make me appreciate what a gift it is to be a father. Thank you for being you.

Only the spouse of a writer with young children could possibly understand how much I owe to my wife, Lorien, who isn't just a casual reader, but a down-in-the trenches editor of all my books. She is the secret to my success in so many aspects of my life.

The idea for this book came from an e-mail sent to me by Anita Fussell, the mother of my incredible, insightful agent, Christy Fletcher, of Fletcher and Co. I consider myself well read in the genre of Special Forces history, but somehow I had missed the story of Roy Benavidez and the May 2 mission. Anita suggested I make it my next book, bringing the story to light for the current generation of military readers.

On September 11, 2012, not long after I began my research for this book, I did a live video chat with Chris Kyle. Chris told me that he didn't feel comfortable with the nickname "The Legend," which had been bestowed upon him as the most lethal American sniper in history. I asked him if he'd heard of Roy Benavidez, and Chris said, "Now, *that* guy is a legend."

I had originally considered titling this book *Hero,* but Roy's children discouraged me; their father always said the real heroes didn't come home. Chris Kyle's words kept coming back to me, and I asked others in the Special Operations community, including Jay Redman, retired Navy SEAL and author, and Special Forces Lieutenant Colonel Jason Amerine, if they recognized the name Roy Benavidez. Every one of them did—and they universally described him with the same word:

"Legend."

INDEX

can visualize your new health-style as involving not the breaking of old habits but the making of *new* ones, you will feel very positive and excited about what the future holds for you.

Although change sometimes hurts, it is an important phenomenon. The only thing constant in this world is change. As Benjamin Franklin once said, "When you're finished changing, you're finished." Can you imagine how horrendously monotonous your life would be without it?

There is only one thing that can bring about fresh change, and that is new information. We don't claim to have the only answer or the best answer. What we have is a philosophy of health care, an approach to living that has been working for a great number of people.

There was a time when we were in pain and searching for relief, and we were fortunate enough to come into contact with a field of study that, although totally new and foreign to us, brought us the healing and well-being that we so desperately needed. As we began to share our work in this field with others, we saw them achieve their health goals as well. We personally have witnessed thousands of people improve their health using only a small part of this information. With the publication of our first book, millions have begun to improve their health!

What we are presenting here is a health life-style that, put into practice, can vastly improve your well-being. This is a life-style designed for those who wish to feel more certain about their health and more in control of what the present and future will bring them in that all-important area of existence. None of us wants to be sick. None of us relishes the idea that we may become a medical statistic. This is a simple, easy-to-follow health-style that can enable you to stack the cards very much in your favor.

Our experience is that a health-producing life-style brings us the health we all cherish. A disease-producing life-style brings the diseases we all dread. The main premise here is that **LIVING HEALTHFULLY IS NOT AN ART THAT WE MUST LEARN, IT IS AN INSTINCTIVE WAY OF LIFE TO WHICH WE MUST RETURN.** The pages of this book will, in commonsense, layman's terms, make that premise apparent!

Yes, what we have to say *is* different! Yes, it is a new approach. Yes, it contradicts many of the doctrines of the day, but it reaps a multitude of benefits for people, of that there is no doubt. It may not be the answer for everyone, but it is already affecting millions in a positive way, so there is certainly the chance it can benefit you also. It is something that you should at least be aware of, so that you recognize the option that is open to you. And that is precisely what it is, an *option*. We hope you have not put up a wall against change because of too many past disappointments, because the same wall that keeps out disappointment also keeps out that which can genuinely help you and is worthy of your consideration.

No one has *all* the answers. Not us. Not anyone. **What we are offering you is AN OPPORTUNITY FOR A NEW WAY OF LIVING.** This then is our vital message: **EVERYTHING WE NEED TO BE HEALTHY OR TO RESTORE OUR HEALTH HAS BEEN PROVIDED FOR US BY NATURE.** We offer you no program of treatment, but rather an intelligent plan of living that conforms to the laws and normal conditions of life and will not only preserve health but will also enable the sick to restore themselves to health. We present you an option of understanding, indeed, an *outrageous probability:* that **YOU CAN BE IN COMPLETE CONTROL OF YOUR HEALTH!** It will always be up to *you* whether or not you wish to embrace it.

Explore that option and see for yourself if it can benefit you the way it is benefiting so many others. What a shame it would be if you were to miss out on something that could dramatically increase the length and quality of your life simply because you did not investigate it and give it the opportunity to prove its worthiness to you.

We all wish to be happy and healthy. We all wish happiness and health for those we love. That is our common truth. We lovingly and respectfully offer you this blueprint for living as our contribution to your effort to become a shining, joyous, real-life example of living health!